TRIES THE LIMIT

TRIES THE LIMIT

GARRY SCHOFIELD
WITH PAUL CHALLENOR

MAINSTREAM
PUBLISHING

EDINBURGH AND LONDON

First published in Great Britain in 2000 by
MAINSTREAM PUBLISHING COMPANY (EDINBURGH) LTD
7 Albany Street
Edinburgh EH1 3UG

ISBN 1 84018 364 0

A catalogue record for this book is available from the British Library

Typeset in Berkeley Book and Stone Sans
Printed and bound in Great Britain by
Creative Print and Design Wales

CONTENTS

ACKNOWLEDGEMENTS

My thanks go to all rugby followers who have gained pleasure from any game I have played in, whether you supported my team or the opposition.

For their help in the completion of this autobiography, I offer my sincere gratitude to Paul Challenor, Raymond Fletcher, David Howes, Phil Caplan, Chris Oliver and Paul D. Kelly.

I dedicate this book to my two children, Danielle and Jonathan.

FOREWORD BY RAYMOND FLETCHER

I HAVE SAID IT many times and I'll say it again: Garry Schofield is the greatest British player I have seen in over a quarter of a century reporting international rugby league at both ends of the world. There are a few – Ellery Hanley and Martin Offiah come readily to mind – who were at least equal at club level, but in the Test arena Schofield stands supreme. The bare facts of his record-equalling 46 Test and World Cup appearances merely hint at his high ranking. To see him in action wearing the red, white and blue was to have it confirmed that he was an extra special talent. While many outstanding club players seemed to be overawed when faced with the might of Australia and New Zealand, Schofield relished the opportunity to take on the world's best. He repeatedly carried his top-class club form into Test matches and occasionally even exceeded it.

I first had the opportunity to write glowing reports of Schofield's magnificent international form on Great Britain's 1984 tour of Australia. The highlight was his major role in a wonderful second Test try, handling three times in the dazzling 80-metre movement. At the end of the 1980s I was one of the *Rothmans Rugby League Yearbook*'s panellists who adjudged it the try of the decade, and it remains high on the list of tries scored in any era.

It was on Great Britain's 1990 tour of New Zealand that Schofield confirmed my growing belief that he was the outstanding British international of the last 20 years or more. Although Mike Gregory set a fine example as the tour captain, it was Schofield who dictated on the field, particularly in the three Tests against New Zealand. Coach Malcolm Reilly had switched him to stand-off at the beginning of the tour, and it was to be a key factor in Britain winning a Test series Down Under for the first time in 11 years. He played a big part in all five of Britain's tries in the first two Tests to clinch the series, and it was his drop-goal that snatched an 11–10 victory in the first. Although Britain lost the final Test, Schofield was still the dominant figure as he had a hand in the first two of their three tries.

It was about this time that I first claimed that Schofield was the most influential international player of his generation. I stand by that to this day, even though the great Wally Lewis is generally accepted as the No. 1. While recognising Lewis as a truly great leader, he had around him an Australian team of near invincibility. In contrast, Schofield often had to inspire an internationally inexperienced team in battles against the odds.

Perhaps his greatest international achievement was in leading Great Britain to a shock 33–10 defeat of Australia in the second Test at Melbourne in 1992. Schofield had taken over the tour captaincy from the injured Ellery Hanley and proved a great ambassador for the game and his country both on and off the field. Britain had lost the first Test 22–6 and were badly hit by injuries. But Schofield inspired them to a memorable victory on that rain-lashed night, scoring one try and kicking a drop-goal that gave Britain a record-equalling 23-point margin of victory over Australia.

It was not only Schofield's performances on the field, but his demeanour off it that made him such a wonderful personality for rugby league. He realised the importance of the game's stars being readily available to the media – and therefore also to the public. I recall on the 1992 tour of Australia when he took over the captaincy from the unco-operative Hanley: suddenly the trip came alive. Even when his colleagues were celebrating immediately after Britain's shock second Test victory, he did not break away from the media gang until every question had been answered. He was even asked to slow down by one journalist, who had been used to jotting down the monosyllabic replies of Hanley.

There was also an occasion, after a Test match in France, when Schofield gave another inspiring performance despite a heavy cold and then sniffled his way through all the interviews whilst slumped on the dressing-room floor.

I was on the panel who elected Schofield as the Man of Steel in 1991 and have given him numerous Man of the Match awards, but I was once accused of deliberately ignoring him for another major prize. That was in 1984 when I went along with the remainder of the Man of Steel panel in selecting Joe Lydon as the Young Player of the Year. There was not a lot in it, but we

FOREWORD

thought Lydon clinched it with his Lance Todd trophy-winning performance in the Challenge Cup final at Wembley. Schofield had certainly had an outstanding first season with Hull, and a club official immediately assaulted me with a torrent of abuse after the award ceremony. Yet Schofield never questioned the choice and has never held it against me. Indeed, in asking me to write this foreword, I feel he has bestowed his own honour on me, for it has been a great privilege to do so.

Raymond Fletcher

1.

WHAT AM I DOING HERE?

THE WHISTLE BLOWS, and I kick off deep into Pocklington territory. It's Sunday, 30 April 2000, and several hundred spectators are watching the Yorkshire Rugby Union Shield final between the club I coach, Redcar RUFC, and Pocklington RUFC at York rugby ground. In their 79-year history Redcar had never reached a cup final, and I am thrilled to be involved in giving the club and, indeed, the whole seaside town, a day to remember.

Quite why I am here is hard to understand, as I have until recently known only one code of rugby: rugby league. Twenty-six years ago I set out playing league for Clapgate Primary School in Leeds, and now I am in the twilight of my career coaching and playing rugby union for Redcar in the north-east. The club, players and officials alike, have all made me very welcome, and their ambition and love for the game have made life easy for me. I have a fair financial package with great job satisfaction, and that counts for so much.

The approach came from Redcar shortly after I announced my retirement from rugby league. A member of the club based in Wakefield asked me if I would be interested in playing for them, as their last coach had very recently left for West Hartlepool to take up the post of player–coach there. I agreed to have a meeting with the Redcar officials at their ground. I had a look around the place and outlined my ambitions for the club. It appeared to be very well managed with good, modern facilities, and the team itself seemed quite capable, on a brief assessment of their strengths and weaknesses. I attended a second meeting before agreeing to take up a two-year contract running from September 1999. Yet I still yearn to be involved in rugby league – although you will come to appreciate the background to my current circumstances as this story unfolds.

One supreme irony also strikes me today. My opposing stand-off half is none other than my former Hull FC colleague, Gary Pearce. My professional career changed direction quite radically and acrimoniously as a direct result of Hull signing Gary from Llanelli RUFC way back in 1987. No player before or since has had such a profound effect upon my playing days as he had. Not that he is aware of that, and we will share a pint and a laugh about old times after I have seen his team off this afternoon!

This weekend I was part of the Leeds Rhinos hospitality team in Edinburgh for the Rugby League Challenge Cup final. At one stage in the week leading up to the game we didn't think the final had a chance of taking place, following the flooding of the burn adjacent to the Murrayfield stadium, which left the pitch under ten feet of water. The Scottish Rugby Union, the fire service and the military did a sterling job in draining the ground and clearing away the debris. We even heard that a salmon had been caught inside the stadium before the water level fell!

Apart from a couple of pints of Guinness on the Friday evening, I was unable to enjoy too much of the Edinburgh hospitality. With today's final in mind, my dad had arranged to meet me this morning at seven o'clock prompt to bring me back home to play for Redcar. Perhaps I might otherwise have predicted the result more accurately, for I had told my party of Rhinos supporters at the pre-match briefing the night before that Bradford Bulls were just too strong in all departments. Although the teams were closely matched, I forecast that the Bulls were the in-form team and would win 34–12. As it turned out there was just one score between the sides, Bradford winning 24–18. The Rhinos finished the stronger, more confident side, and would have won in hindsight but for the inability of Leroy Rivett, the Leeds winger, to cope with the high ball. Hull had nearly won the semi-final by using similar tactics, putting high kicks up into Leeds' right-hand corner and finding Leroy with little cover for the 'bomb'. What a difference a year makes. In 1999 Leroy Rivett had won the Lance Todd Trophy in the last Challenge Cup final to take place at Wembley, scoring four outstanding tries against London Broncos. Now some people cynically suggest that he was once again the most influential player in the final – but for all the wrong reasons.

I was quite envious of my co-writer, Paul, as I retired to my room on Saturday evening. Paul and his wife joined up with the actor Duncan Preston and his brother after the game to enjoy refreshments in a local hotel before discussing the fortunes of both Leeds and Bradford over a Japanese meal into the early hours.

The day was the finest of occasions as the majority of the population of the North of England descended on the Scottish capital, and young and old provided the most colourful and trouble-free gathering seen north of the border for many a year. I am certain the Scottish rugby authorities will be keen to repeat the experiment of hosting the Rugby League Challenge Cup final again in the near future.

In addition to coaching and playing with Redcar I am a broadcasting summariser for BBC Radio Leeds, covering Super League matches in West Yorkshire. This gives me the chance to keep up to date on the players and teams in the competition. I would love the opportunity to return to coaching and management in rugby league in a year or so, when certain outstanding matters have been resolved and I have achieved the requisite coaching qualifications. As I go round the grounds I do worry for the game as the period of News Corporation's mammoth investment draws to a close. Sadly, the money seems to have been used as a short-term fix by some clubs, and many missed the opportunity to merge and secure their future when it presented itself five years ago. Castleford's stadium, for example, the Jungle, is still largely a collection of old wooden stands and seats. Surely with the aid of grants and the guidance of Super League (Europe) Ltd, money could be raised to provide the fans with more modern facilities. Association football seems to have taken better advantage of the finance available, with new stadia cropping up to support their sport all over the country.

Sadly, we lose in the dying minutes of the Yorkshire Shield final to Pocklington. Our winger misses a one-on-one tackle, and they go over in the corner to win the trophy 20–16 – this in spite of my one try and four goals. Still, my ambitions for the club in my first year have been fulfilled: Redcar have reached the first cup final in their 79-year history, and we have also gained promotion by finishing third in the North II division. While I have never taken success for granted, it has never been far from my side – but always as the reward for hard work and dedication.

2.

SOWING THE SEEDS FOR LEAGUE

I WAS BORN on 1 July 1965 and throughout my childhood I lived in Southcroft Green, Belle Isle, Leeds 10 – not too far from Elland Road. I attended Clapgate County Primary School, which was where the seed of rugby was planted. The school's deputy head was none other than Mr Harry Jepson, a member of the board of Leeds rugby league club at the time, and so influential as I made my way in the sport. Harry is a legend in the administration of rugby league. From the age of eight I was brought up with the oval ball, as the round leather ball, both winter and summer versions, was banned from Clapgate. Harry saw to it that all young boys under his tutelage developed their rugby skills from the earliest age. It certainly paid off, for a number of former pupils made the grade in rugby league: myself, David Creasser, Neil Rayner and the Macintosh brothers Andy and Ian.

While I was there we must have broken every Leeds schools rugby record, and I look back with great pride over those times. Our rugby master was Roy Dougall, and so successful were we that Roy taught us for four consecutive years, rather than for just one winter as a single age group. In those four years, to the age of 13, we amassed 4,037 points for with just three points against! We conceded just one try in four seasons of schools rugby, and I can remember it to this day! It came as quite a shock to all of us. As Under-10s we made the local paper, and I was mentioned as being 4ft 4ins tall and five stone, playing stand-off. My try-scoring tally was listed as five against John Blenkinsop School, four against Seacroft Park and three against Belle Isle, our local rivals.

Not surprisingly, it was my speed that gave me an edge. My team-mates simply made sure they passed me the ball and then left me to finish it off with a touchdown! So much so that on one occasion Roy Dougall suggested that I should be left out of the team to enable all the other players to develop more of a feel for the game in their own right. I went home most upset and told my mother. Mum was always one to take up a cause, and she stormed down to the school to take up the cudgels on my behalf. Roy put her mind at rest, assuring her that I had jumped to a conclusion and would not in fact be left out. Instead, I was moved out to centre, with Dave Creasser switching from full-back to take over at stand-off. This move worked as Roy had hoped it would: more players were brought into the action and we all improved, sharing the tries between us.

We had a good, mobile pack including Richard Quarmby, Mark Bramley and Andie Mann feeding half-back Jason Moore, myself, Neil Rayner and Paul Simpson and a speedy winger in Mark Whitehead. We won all the schools trophies going, and we all moved on together to Parkside High School and Hunslet Parkside amateur club. My idol was the Leeds and Great Britain centre Les Dyl, and I was single-minded in my desire to emulate him. Back in 1977, when Leeds won the Challenge Cup at Wembley, Harry Jepson brought star players Alan Smith, John Atkinson, John Holmes and a young Kevin Dick to Clapgate to talk to us and show us the cup itself. This made a big impression on me, and I set my heart on playing at the highest level and joining Leeds when I was old enough.

Dad had been a keen footballer in his day, having trials with Leeds United in the 1950s, and my exceptional speed and balance at this early age must surely have been passed down from him. He and mum gave me nothing but encouragement from the start. Dad was a bus driver, and both he and mum worked for Leeds City Transport. They supported me in everything I did as a youngster, and were instrumental in my decision over which professional club I should join in 1983.

My two brothers also attended Clapgate Middle School. They also had no option but to play rugby, and my middle brother, Brian, was a very good player. Always a wholehearted soul, he wasn't the fastest and he wouldn't have said he was the classiest; but if you wanted somebody who'd give you 100 per cent then he was the sort of guy that you'd have in your side. He started out as a front rower, although if you saw him now you'd never believe that he played there at school. Today he weighs in at twelve stone wet through. As he grew up he moved into the hooking role and developed an outstanding tackling technique. As a junior you were always told to make sure that you tackled low, and when I used to go and watch him play I couldn't see a finer defender; he would tackle around the bootlaces, as they used to say. He should give me a fiver for saying this – I've never said it to his face! As he developed he was good enough to be picked for the Hunslet Schoolboys side, and he almost made the Yorkshire team. He continued to progress in the amateur game with Hunslet Parkside, and he was asked to go for professional trials by Featherstone Rovers. Like my younger brother, Colin, Brian had already turned out occasionally for Leeds when the club was short of Alliance team players. Norman Smith, the coach, would call on him from time to time. Then he went for trials at Featherstone Rovers. With trials both the player and the club give themselves a certain period of time to consider whether to commit themselves to signing or not. After some three or four games Brian began to ask Featherstone the question, although my advice was – another couple of games, and then they'll sign you. But, for Brian, it went on too long: he ventured the question again, the club asked him to play one more trial game, and he walked away. And that's the way he left the game. He never played another match, either for a professional club or back at the amateur level.

My younger brother Colin was an excellent rugby league player, built for the game, very fast, agile and mobile. I believe that if he'd made all the sacrifices and dedicated himself at a young enough age, he could have gone on to be a better player than I was. I know a lot of people would say that's a big call, but I believe that potentially he was that good. Unfortunately, as with some players I played with at Hunslet Parkside, from the age of 15 he started making excuses for missing training: the beer element would come into it; the girls would come into it, and Colin ended up not making the sacrifices he should have done. He represented Hunslet Schoolboys and Yorkshire Schools and had a bright career in front of him: then it came to that time of life when a lot of gifted youngsters fall down – at the middle hurdle, not the final one. The only professional games he played in the end were when Leeds were short of numbers for the Alliance team. We have a laugh and joke about it now, but deep down in some respects both Brian and Colin wish they had made those sacrifices and tried to make a career out of being a professional rugby league player, as I did.

I recall being picked for Yorkshire Schools Under-13s – as a full-back, for some unknown reason – to play Lancashire Schools at Warrington. Dad suggested that this would be my chance to show that I could tackle, and he was proved right. Schools trials were always an ordeal, and dad never attended them as a rule – although most other fathers would be there, making themselves heard on the touch-line and putting the teachers under undue pressure. As I moved up from primary to secondary school, the nucleus of Clapgate old boys who came with me gave Parkside High School such strength that our year fielded a first XIII and a B team. Not only that, but the two teams were contesting finals with each other! Again, we won all the trophies that were up for grabs in secondary schools rugby, much to the delight of headmaster Ken Bond and rugby teacher John Ball. Most of the other members of staff used to tell me that I was wasting my time and would have no real future, unless I stopped playing rugby and began to knuckle down and make something of myself careerwise! I thought of them all as I travelled down on the train to collect my OBE in 1994.

The schools' representative selection policy was in sharp contrast to that of BARLA, the British Amateur Rugby League Association. At Under-16 level I was unable to get into the county schools team, being on the subs' bench when Yorkshire played Lancashire. I was called on with 20 minutes left and had no real opportunity to shine. Shortly afterwards, much to my surprise, I was selected for the England Schools as a substitute! My old school chum, Dave Creasser, also made the team, which played France at Widnes. The coach, schoolteacher Denis McHugh, told us we were the best-prepared England Schools XIII he'd ever known. I made my début, coming on as a replacement on the wing. I had never played the position before, and we lost to the French 12–8 – thanks to a late try down my flank! This proved to be England's first defeat by France at this level, and the first of several début disasters for me! At the same time I was captain of BARLA's Yorkshire Under-16 side, playing in a more familiar position at centre.

The rugby-playing pupils of Parkside High School had all been encouraged to join Hunslet Parkside amateur rugby league. Here we came under the guidance of Ron Tinker, who looked after us all like a father. We played from Under-12s to Under-18s together, with Ron coaching us intensely and then making sure we all got home safely afterwards.The club was one of the most successful in the county, although we had no clubhouse and used to play our home matches at Belle Isle School playing fields. At Hunslet Parkside I began to work on all the aspects of my game that I felt were weak, tackling in particular. I never missed training, being the first to arrive and the last to leave. Don't get me wrong, I never did extra training: it was simply that I lived to play rugby, and my sole ambition was to turn professional.

Once we reached the age of 16 we were allowed to meet at the Grey Goose pub, courtesy of the landlord, Peter Jarvis, the Bramley and Halifax prop! I guess this is where the Parkside players tasted alcohol for the first time, drinking a few bitters or lagers and even meeting girls. That's when some of the players started missing training, and falling away from the standards of dedication and discipline required to go on and be outstanding players. Don't get me wrong, both David Creasser and I enjoyed a few pints; but we realised that sacrifices needed to be made, unlike some of our equally talented contemporaries. If they had had the desire to match their ability they would have made it as professional players – but once you start making excuses for bunking off training, it is the beginning of the end. I remember one lad saying that he couldn't come because he had to go and see the dentist at eight o'clock at night! How many dentists do you know who work at that time of night?

The Hunslet Parkside Under-17 team I captained was named Team of the Year by the monthly rugby league magazine *Open Rugby*. We won the Yorkshire Under-17 League and Premiership trophies, in addition to the knockout cup in that 1981–2 season. The previous season we had won all the five trophies we were entered for, which was all the more outstanding considering that we were then in our first year of Under-17 rugby, giving away two years in some cases to our opponents. No team had ever won the Under-17 cup twice with the same age group until we achieved it. Meanwhile, Leeds won the BARLA Under-17s Inter-District Cup with 14 of the 19-man squad coming from Hunslet Parkside! BARLA also selected eight of us for the Yorkshire county Under-17 squad, which was another record.

Our team in those days was Mark Reagan, Geoff Boyes, Richard Quarmby, Dave Gunney (son of legendary Hunslet and Great Britain forward Geoff), Andrew Bateman, Lawrence Kitchen, Wayne Baldwinson, David Creasser, Neil Rayner, Mark Whitehead, myself, Mark Bramley, Jason Moore and Tony Staniforth. Ron Tinker and his assistant Les McIver must have been very proud to receive that *Open Rugby* award on behalf of the club.

At Under-18 level we went on to win the BARLA National Cup, beating

Kells from Cumbria by 28–2 in the final at Blackpool Borough's ground, of all places. Dave Creasser was chosen as Man of the Match, and I scored two tries. Several of that team were then selected to tour New Zealand with BARLA's Great Britain Under-18s party in 1983, and I was proud to be appointed captain.

The touring party was written off before we even left home. We had recently been beaten by France Under-18s at Barley Mow, Bramley, a setback which saw my first introduction to Phil Larder, the future Great Britain coach. After the French game he took me on one side and made it clear to me that I would not make it as a professional rugby league player as I was not prepared to take advice from people! I was staggered: I never found out who those people were I was supposed to have ignored. Subsequently I believe I proved him to be way off beam.

None of us Parksiders had ever been abroad before, let alone travelled round the world to play rugby league, and we couldn't wait. It came as quite a shock when we landed and found out that the tour party's officials were booked into a local Auckland hotel, while the players were billeted out at various homes dispersed over some fifty square miles! You can imagine how we had been looking forward to several weeks away from home together, and how disappointed we were when the living arrangements became known! We only met as a squad when training sessions took place. Perhaps this was carefully planned, and it certainly paid dividends, for it proved to be the most successful BARLA Under-18s tour ever as we won seven out of eight games, drawing the Test series 1–1. A number of tourists went on to play rugby league professionally, including three Parkside lads in David Creasser, Mark Reagan and me, together with Deryck Fox, Mike Ford, Seamus McCallion and Gary Divorty.

3.

WHY I SIGNED FOR HULL FC

AS AFOREMENTIONED, dad was a keen footballer and my love of rugby league and the Leeds club in particular grew from his friendship with Syd Hynes, the Leeds centre, captain and coach. Dad took me to my first game at Headingley one Saturday afternoon: I can recall Leeds soundly beating Widnes 30–3, and the atmosphere was magical. It may have been ironic, though, for I realise now that my future coach, Dougie Laughton, could well have been in the Widnes ranks that day!

My ambitions were now firmly set on turning pro and playing for Leeds, although I wanted to achieve success with Hunslet Parkside and the Yorkshire and BARLA international representative sides before I moved into league full time. The Leeds club had been assured by Harry Jepson that I would sign for them over a year before my 18th birthday, and I was invited to visit Headingley. Sadly, however, I found the officials and players there were none too concerned about my visit, and they failed to make me welcome or take any interest in me. Perhaps Harry Jepson had been too complacent.

Shortly before the BARLA Under-18 tour to New Zealand, my family and I received a visit at home from Arthur Bunting, the coach of Hull FC, and one of the club's directors, Mike Page. In outlining their interest in my joining Hull after the tour they could not have been more positive towards me, and at the tender age of 18 I wanted to be made welcome and valued. Arthur invited me to attend first-team training at the Boulevard, and I immediately felt part of a great set-up. The players, internationals and all, saw to it that I was part of the social scene in the local pub afterwards too, which was an important part of team bonding in the 1980s. It was impossible not to be impressed by the likes of the New Zealand trio, Gary Kemble, James Leuluai and Dane O'Hara, and by great British names such as Knocker Norton, Trevor Skerrett, Kevin Harkin, Dave Topliss and Paul Rose.

Upon my return from New Zealand I signed for Hull in August 1983 for £22,000. That sum comprised a £5,000 signing-on fee and the remainder by way of incentive payments, as was the norm in those days for young players. These incentives covered appearances for the A team, first team, Great Britain Under-24s and the senior Great Britain side – and in my first season Hull had to pay me in full! In addition I was to receive match payments of £150 for a win and £50 for a loss.

Pre-season work was short and we usually trained on Tuesday and Thursday evenings, with Saturday mornings set aside for ball work and game plans in preparation for the Sunday game. How well I recall my début for the club in a pre-season friendly against Carlisle, who were coached by the former Leeds and Great Britain winger John Atkinson. I managed to sneak over for two tries and, after the game, £25 cash was thrust into my hands – my first pay-day. I joined up with another youngster at Hull with a promising career ahead of him, a goalkicking prop forward by the name of Lee Crooks. We were to form a lasting friendship and share many public and private ups and downs as our respective careers unfolded.

I used to travel over to Hull in the company of their West Yorkshire contingent of Trevor Skerrett, Kevin Harkin, Ronnie Wileman and Dave Topliss. What a carload! To begin with I made my own way to training, but I soon got fed up with it. I asked Trevor one evening at training if I could travel with the guys who lived over our way, and he told me that would be no problem. I felt very much part of a top club at that time. All the players in those days were part-time professionals. I had just finished my apprenticeship with Jack Lunn's building firm as a bricklayer. Trevor Skerrett was also a bricklayer, David Topliss had his own business and Crooksy was a painter and decorator. Most of the Hull lads did some sort of manual work. On training nights, I'd leave work around 4.30 p.m. to go to Trevor's house in Rothwell, about four miles away from my Belle Isle home. We'd meet up with Toppo, Kevin Harkin and Ronnie Wileman at Simpson's garage in Castleford at around 5.30 p.m. in order to make sure that we weren't late for training at seven o'clock.

The first occasion I travelled across to training with the Hull stars was quite an experience. I didn't arrive home until after midnight, as some of the lads were used to having six or seven pints after training and a fish and chip supper! As I needed a lift back I had to join them, though I was careful not to overdo it – not in those days, anyway! When I look at the fitness regimes and training schedules that the players observe in Super League in 2000 I find them hard to compare with anything that we did in 1983 – except that the balls we used were still the same shape and size as today's.

When I first started playing with the pros–and even with the amateurs, for that matter – I always made sure that the night before a game I was very early to bed. I would spend a very lazy day on the Saturday, not even going out food shopping or driving into Leeds to have a look around the clothes shops. Just a nice, relaxed, lazy day. While I was in my amateur days I would have been in bed for about eight or nine o'clock in the evening, but when I turned pro with Hull the preparation had to change somewhat. I would be in bed after watching the omnibus edition of *Brookside*, my favourite television programme, which would finish at 6.30 p.m. Not that I went straight to sleep: the portable TV would be switched on in the spare room, and whatever programmes were on that took my liking I would be watching. It wouldn't be the last time I was in the spare room, mind you, but at least on these occasions it was because I was making sure of a good night's sleep! I would wake early the next morning, but I would only get up out of bed after reading the Sunday papers. About ten o'clock I would have my pre-match meal, which for many years was beans on toast. The night before, a very orderly kit bag would have been packed and all the preparation done. My wife Adele and I would leave home at around 12.30 p.m. to get to the ground in time for the pre-match preparation, and in those days we would normally be kicking off at three o'clock. Sometimes my father would come over to watch me as well if it was a home fixture at the Boulevard.

After the game we would mix with the opposition players and a number of our spectators in the bar before moving on to the pub we used after training, the Norland. We'd go there for a couple of drinks, and then we would return to Leeds around eight o'clock at night. Very often Adele and I used to meet up with Dave Creasser, my very good friend from Parkside days, who had signed for Leeds. We would exchange stories over the opposition we'd played against that afternoon, how many cracks we'd received, how many tries we'd scored, how many goals we'd kicked, in the manner that only sportsmen know! On the way home we'd pick up a Chinese or Indian meal, and that was the week complete. We would usually have Monday off as far as Hull FC were concerned, before we reported back for training again on the Tuesday evening.

When you signed for a professional club in the 1980s you were not allowed into the first-team dressing-room on training nights until you'd earned the right to enter and the coach invited you in. Only on match-days did you share that dressing-room with the senior first-team players. In my first season, even though I played and scored for Hull on many occasions, I was not invited into the first-team dressing-room at training until the following February. I didn't mind, though: Arthur Bunting, the Hull coach, was merely carrying on a tradition that all clubs respected in those days, and he was right to do so.

4.

SCORING TRIES FOR FUN

MY FIRST SEASON with Hull FC, 1983–84, saw me finish as the league's leading try-scorer with 38. The season seemed to pass so quickly and, looking back, I think how fortunate I was to have chosen to join Hull at that particular time. The Airlie Birds had won the Slalom Lager Championship in the previous season, 1982–83, and finished second two seasons earlier, so I was joining a successful and confident outfit. The fans were certainly proud and loyal, and in Arthur Bunting the team had a top coach who showed me the importance of man-management. Arthur had brought together a number of top overseas international players to blend with some outstanding local prospects. In mixing youth and experience, his secret was that he got the best out of all of us for the good of the whole team. Team spirit was brilliant, and really we should have won more honours than we did.

Arthur Bunting showed his faith in me after that Carlisle friendly and picked me ahead of the Great Britain centre, Steve Evans, to make my first-team début against Warrington. It finished in a 22–22 draw, and I was playing against another Great Britain centre, Ronnie Duane. This proved to be a real introduction to the professional ranks, as Ronnie knew of my amateur reputation and gave me a very hard time. I did not play that well and felt I would be brought along in the A team for a few weeks after that. But to his credit Arthur persevered with me, and I am grateful to him for that and so much else. The Hull senior players also gave me sound advice at the time. Although I had gone straight into the first team they told me not to believe that I had made it: keep the right attitude at all times and work hard at your game, because nothing comes easily in rugby league.

In every dressing-room there is a comedian, one player above all others with the ability to make people laugh in the most serious of circumstances.

When I joined Hull they had a scrum-half from the Castleford area, Tony Dean, who could always be relied upon when needed to break the ice with his strange sense of humour. But even though I was the youngest player in the Hull first team when I arrived that year, nobody really took the mickey out of me. The other players simply encouraged me and treated me as if I was one of them – which of course I was.

Lee Crooks was our goalkicker that season, and although I had no inclination to kick goals, for some reason Arthur felt I should be designated the stand-in kicker in the event of Lee being dismissed or injured. So I had to practise the art, and while I still don't profess to be too accurate some would say that the coach was shrewd in his judgement: I ended up kicking over 50 goals in the last two months of my first season, in addition to all those tries.

My first senior try was scored in my second game, against Keighley at Lawkholme Lane in the Yorkshire Cup. To this day Kevin Harkin tells everyone that he put me in under the posts, and that in fact is what happened. On 9 October 1983, I scored my first hat-trick in the Slalom Lager Championship game against Leeds at Headingley. Later in this book I have chosen the ten most memorable games I ever played in, and this ranks as one of those ten: I had helped Hull FC to hammer the club I had always followed, by 40 points to 12, with my school pal Dave Creasser playing opposite me. Stand-off David Topliss set me up for my first try, while the second and third touchdowns were both down to my centre partner James Leuluai. The Leeds crowd was gracious in defeat, and my team-mates kept my feet on the ground by claiming a round of drinks from me in the bar afterwards!

As my try-scoring reputation grew, one home game later in the season caused some amusement at the club. From the back of the Threepenny Stand at the Boulevard a lone female voice repeatedly shouted, 'Give the ball to Garry!' Arthur Bunting is reputed to have told Hull director Mike Page, 'I'll deal with Schoey's dad, you go and sort out his mother over there!'

After only eight weeks in the professional ranks I was selected to travel to Villeneuve as a substitute for Great Britain Under-24s. We beat France 28–23, and I came on for St Helens scrum-half Neil Holding with seven minutes remaining. Ronnie Duane was one of our centres that day, while the hooker was to become one of my closest friends, Colin Maskill of Wakefield Trinity. I must have impressed for I was chosen again as sub for the return match at the Watersheddings, Oldham, on 4 December. On this occasion I had to come on after 38 minutes to replace none other than Ellery Hanley in the centre. I managed to score one try, and we won 48–1 in front of 4,287 loyal fans.

In the New Year I was back in France, leading the Great Britain Colts to victory over our French counterparts by 24–10 in Arles. I picked up two tries and teamed up with old pals Dave Creasser (Leeds), Gary Divorty (Hull) and winger Norman Francis (Leeds). The latter failed to make the impact he really should have done in the professional game, although he was to become something of a folk-hero in Leeds A team under coaches John Holmes and Paul Gill.

On 17 February 1984 my first season was made complete when I ran out with the senior Great Britain XIII in the second Dominion Insurance Test at Headingley against the French international side. I was selected to play at right centre, and my winger was John Basnett of Widnes, who was also making his début. We were both scoring tries regularly in the league and had a modest wager as to which of us would score that day. In the event neither of us received much opportunity, and my form was disappointing. We won 10–0 thanks to five penalty goals from second row David Hobbs of Featherstone Rovers. While this was not my first experience of French tactics of intimidation, it was a challenge for some of our forwards to keep their self-control under extreme provocation, kicking, biting, spitting and what have you.

The Great Britain coach Frank Myler restored my confidence following the game. He saw that I was very quiet in the dressing-room afterwards and made a point of telling me to put the match down to experience and to look forward to further international appearances if I continued to impress and improve at club level. These few words were very uplifting to me at the time.

Five days earlier I had flown down with Hull FC to take on Cardiff City at Ninian Park in the Challenge Cup first round. We won through 34–6 and I managed to touch down twice. Facing me was Steve Fenwick, the outstanding Welsh international centre in both rugby union and rugby league, and we became firm friends in later years. Cardiff also lined up with former Welsh union caps in Paul Ringer and Tom David, and were coached by an all-time Welsh great in David Watkins.

Although our cup run didn't survive the next round, we won nine of our last ten championship games to finish runners-up to our deadly rivals Hull

Kingston Rovers by one point. One of those victories saw us defeat the Robins at Craven Park on Good Friday by 36 points to 16, and I recall kicking eight goals in front of over 16,000 Humberside fanatics. The game ended in the most controversial of manners when Widnes referee Ron Campbell sent off Len Casey, the Hull KR captain, for allegedly kicking a Hull player and then punching our scrum-half, Fred Ah Kuoi. As Len left the field he pushed a touch judge and was subsequently banned for six months and missed the Great Britain tour to Australia in the summer. I scored in each of our last 12 fixtures and topped the league's try-scoring table, my 38 touchdowns being ten more than the next highest scorer, in addition to 57 goals.

I have left the Phillips Video Yorkshire Cup final till last. The Airlie Birds, as Hull were known, had won through to the final by beating Featherstone Rovers by 24–8 at home, Keighley by 30–8, and then Leeds in the semi-final by 20–16 at Headingley. We faced Castleford at Elland Road on 15 October 1983 in front of a great crowd of 14,049 despite continual pouring rain. Hull FC incidentally topped the attendances table that year, with an average crowd of 10,679 over the season. There was a strike by television technicians which blacked out the screening of the highlights of the final, which meant that armchair viewers missed the action from our 13–2 win. Our chain-smoking loose forward, Mick Crane, was voted Man of the Match with a try and drop-goal, and my other outstanding memory is of Cas coach Mal Reilly having to turn out at prop forward owing to injuries.

That night the Hull players, officials, wives and girlfriends all celebrated at the Waterloo pub in East Street, Leeds, near the bus station. Players from most West Yorkshire clubs would meet up on Sunday evenings at the Waterloo or the nearby Smiths Arms to talk rugby league, although both pubs have since been pulled down. That night was my first serious drinking session, and I remember how rough I felt the following morning! Castleford gained their revenge in the Premiership Trophy semi-final, beating us 12–22 at the Boulevard only to lose to Hull KR in the final by 18–10.

My club coach, Arthur Bunting, stormed out of the end-of-season awards dinner at the Willows Variety Club in Salford as young Joe Lydon of Widnes swept all before him, winning the Greenalls Man of Steel title, First Division Player of the Season and Young Player of the Season. Joe was the youngest ever Man of Steel at 20, and the first player to pick up all three awards in the same season. Arthur firmly believed that I should have been awarded the

Young Player of the Season, although I had voted for Joe as First Division Player of the Year. Joe and I were to be firm friends after touring Down Under together later that summer, and I held no grudge against him. I was just glad to have made such an impact in my first season.

5.

MY FIRST TASTE OF KANGAROO

DESPITE THE IMPACT I had made in my first season I was still shocked to hear of my selection to tour Australia, New Zealand and Papua New Guinea with the British Lions in the summer of 1984. I never believed I would be selected so early, although I was very hopeful that I might be considered in the future. I heard the news while I was working as a bricklayer with the building company run by Jack Lunn, who was also a director of Hunslet rugby league club. One of my workmates had gone for some dinner and dropped into the bookies on the way where he found out the names of the party. He ran back to tell me and forgot to collect the sandwiches! The following day I received confirmation by letter from the Rugby Football League that I had indeed been selected to tour, although I did not receive the customary telephone call from coach Frank Myler – probably because he would not have been able to call so many of us!

My selection was especially surprising to me because my Test début against France at Headingley in February had been pretty poor. The tourists selected were for the most part inexperienced, not merely myself but players such as Joe Lydon, Ray Ashton, Des Foy, Wayne Proctor and Mick Worrall, and the average age of our squad was just 23.

The press thought that it was too soon for some of us to go there and compete with the Australians just a couple of years after they had whitewashed Great Britain back home in 1982. Those 'Invincibles', as they had become known, were expected now to repeat their awesome destruction of Great Britain's youngsters.

We were written off not just by our own media, but also by many pundits in Australia. What added to the prophecies of doom was the number of more experienced guys, such as Trevor Skerrett, who had to pull out of the trip through injury. Brian 'Nobby' Noble of Bradford Northern was the youngest-ever Great Britain tour captain at 23. Many felt that Nobby did not have the experience to handle the responsibility, and that the captaincy really should have gone to Mick Adams of Widnes, who was named as a vice-captain. That said, Nobby did a creditable job, although by the end of the tour his form was struggling and there was a belief that Castleford's Kevin Beardmore should have been the Test hooker in his place. It was rumoured that one of the reasons Beardmore did not get picked was his was a name that was too long to fit on the back of Frank Myler's cigarette packet when he wrote down the team!

Throughout the tour I roomed with Joe Lydon, and we kept an eye on one another in more ways than one – particularly as I was due to be married. Before the tour party was announced, my girlfriend Adele had told me she was afraid that if I happened to be selected for the tour, it would finish our relationship. We had planned to marry in July, and that would have to be cancelled. In the event I was picked, and the wedding was postponed until 1 December 1984. I had to have two best men for that memorable Saturday, as Dave Creasser had to leave shortly after the ceremony to play for Leeds in a cup tie. The evening best man was Trevor Skerrett, who stood up in the Roundhay Mansion in Leeds and told everyone that this was the first and only time he'd play second fiddle to a Leeds player! Other players who attended included my tour pal Joe Lydon, Dave Topliss, and Hull's Australian imports Peter Sterling and his brother-in-law, John Muggleton. Leeds beat Wigan that day in the John Player Trophy second round by 10–4, and Dave Creasser made it worth his while by kicking a goal.

It was to prove an eventful weekend, as Hull played their John Player Trophy second-round tie at home to Oldham. We won 26–14, and I kicked three goals. My pal Lee Crooks had been less careful than Trevor and the other Hull lads with regard to his alcohol intake at my wedding, and yet he went on to claim the Man of the Match award! Both Leeds and Hull won through to the John Player Trophy semi-final on 5 January 1985, and although Dave Creasser scored a try and a goal, Hull won the day 18–6.

So I set off on the long haul Down Under for the second time as a rugby league player representing my country. My first trip had been with the BARLA Under-18 squad, but I knew this tour would be far more challenging. Our first stop-off was in Darwin, a striking city in Australia's Northern Territory. We arrived there about four o'clock in the morning and being a representative side it was compulsory for us to get changed out of the tracksuits we had been travelling in and into our official British Lions suits and ties. Not a comfortable experience, because even at that time of the morning the temperature was 25 degrees. We eventually cleared customs, and some two hours later we reached our hotel. After just three hours' sleep we were awoken in order to acclimatise to the conditions because none of us had experienced heat such as there was in Darwin.

We trained that morning, and Joe Lydon and I were left out of the side to play in the first fixture against the Northern Territory. The backs were Bradford's Keith Mumby at full-back, the two Des's, Drummond and Foy, on the wings, Duane and Hanley the centres, with Leigh's Steve Donlan partnering Ashton at half-back. I did not know it at the time, but this match was going to be a turning point in my tour. The most experienced centre in our party was Ronnie Duane, and unfortunately for Ronnie he suffered a serious knee ligament injury after just eight minutes. He was held up in a tackle before one of the Australian forwards came in and fell, kamikaze style, on to his knee. That was the end of Ronnie's tour, and the injury was responsible for shortening a very promising career. Ronnie played on for a further 12 or 18 months before having to retire. He was an excellent centre – big, robust and strong, and I am sure he would have made his mark as an international player had he not been so unlucky in Darwin.

But somebody's bad luck is somebody else's good fortune: while Castleford's John Joyner came off the bench to replace Ronnie in Darwin, I was to take one of the centre positions in the first Test just 22 days later. Frank Myler had wanted us to start the tour positively against the Northern Territory, and we managed to put up a decent performance, winning 40–13. Taking the heat into account, we had come through well, although the penalties we conceded were a concern and we needed to learn from this. The first try of the tour came from Steve Donlan, and both Nobby Noble and Andy Goodway touched down twice. Lee Crooks kicked three goals after coming on as a second-half substitute, and lost a few pounds in weight. The last impression I had of Darwin was of the aborigines who populated the Northern Territory: seven or eight of them could be seen from my hotel room enjoying a heavy drinking session under an old tree at five in the morning, the annoying part of which was the noise they made constantly blowing didgeridoos!

We then moved on to Wagga Wagga to play Riverina, and I made my tour début on the wing. Lydon, in at centre, scored as did Widnes full-back Mick Burke and Neil Holding. We had been trailing 18–14 with just 12 minutes left, and we were rescued when Holding shot over from 40 yards out. He had come on at scrum-half for Andy Gregory, who had been carried from the pitch with blood pouring from a gash above his eye following a vicious butt from his opposite number Ward, who was only sin-binned for the offence. Lee Crooks won the Man of the Match award for making an amazing total of 41 tackles.

Only two days later a big win followed over North Coast in Wauchope by 56–6, and two more days after that we won a close encounter with Western Division by 36–30, with Lee Crooks again claiming Man of the Match honours, while I came on for Tony Myler at stand-off in the second half. Our first big test was to follow three days later on the Sydney Cricket Ground. Frank Myler chose what many felt would be the nucleus of his Test team to take on North Sydney in the heart of Australian rugby league country, and I was grateful to be selected at centre for the first time on tour. Andy Goodway produced outstanding power, damaging runs and well-timed tackles in the second row, and with our other forwards following his lead we won 14–8 – with North Sydney's only try coming two minutes from time. Keith Mumby played in the centre with me and showed his excellent defensive qualities, while Des Drummond followed my kick to touch down early in the game.

We maintained our unbeaten record with a 28–18 win over Australia's Country champions Newcastle, and this time I played stand-off. It was a tough encounter: Worrall played on with a suspected broken hand, Holding damaged a finger, and Noble was grateful to have his jaw diagnosed as badly bruised rather than broken. Hobbs finished with a gashed forehead requiring stitches, and Lee Crooks retired with a thigh injury that needed a week's treatment and threatened to put him out of contention for the first Test. With the big game just one week away, the high penalty count against was still haunting Great Britain, on top of the growing injury list.

Frank had mentioned to us all how he wished to try players in different positions in the matches before the Tests in order to find out his best team. He lifted the younger players in Newcastle by telling us that we were putting several more experienced players under pressure for Test places, and that was how he wanted it to be. The one young player who was finding it difficult to reproduce his winter form was Joe Lydon. On our arrival in Sydney the Aussie media had made a great deal of the young, good-looking British Man of Steel, even comparing him to the great Kangaroo centre Reg Gasnier, and Joe's two tries in the Challenge Cup final at Wembley earlier in the year were replayed over and over. We could not understand all the hype: while back home rugby league remains something of a minority sport, in Sydney the game receives a very high media profile thanks to the numerous TV and radio channels which are all anxious to cover it. I think the fuss did get to Joe, and Frank had no choice but to leave him out of the team.

When the first Test side was revealed, I was delighted to be selected at no. 3 alongside Keith Mumby. Joe was a more talented centre than Keith, but Frank had no doubt been of the opinion before we left home that he had a young squad, and we could be in for a hammering. In reality, he was picking a team that would do no more than compete defensively, rather than going out there and trying to win the Test match. Although I was chosen as a centre with Ellery Hanley on one wing, it wasn't a very attack-minded side. Still, I did not think of this at the time. At scrum-half Neil Holding kept out Andy Gregory, and Greg wasn't too happy about that; he had already got the nickname of 'Mr Grumpy' and this situation meant that you could see why. But in team meetings held before the first Test side was announced, we had been told that people would be picked on form, and Frank had kept his word.

This was my first meeting with the Kangaroos at Test level, and their team was packed with class internationals. I was opposed by Gene Miles and Brett Kenny in the centres, while their half-back pairing was made up of the great Wally Lewis and Mark Murray, and I was to play with full-back Garry Jack and back-rower Wayne Pearce at Balmain later in my career. The match was no classic, for the Aussies played below the form we had expected of them, and with Great Britain defending doggedly for long periods we kept the margin of defeat down. The Sydney Cricket Ground was full, and yet the atmosphere was muted. The crowd was some way away from the playing area and therefore the noise was less audible – reminiscent of Don Valley Stadium in Sheffield from that point of view.

Neil Holding went off injured after 20 minutes, and I moved to scrum-half to accommodate Joe Lydon at centre. Having been 8–2 down at half-time we scored the try of the match on the hour mark. Des Drummond took the ball wide out and used his speed and swerve to power past five green-and-gold-shirted tacklers. I had anticipated Des's run, and was at his shoulder down the middle as he looked for support. One pass, and I was in the clear to dive over under the sticks for my first Test try. You had to be there to see the elation on my face, and I guess I overdid the celebrations – but it was my first international touchdown, and against the Aussies to boot. And remember: back in 1982 Great Britain had scored only one try in the entire series against the 'Invincibles'. I recall speaking with mum and dad after the match and finding out how delighted they both were for me. They were less happy that we had lost to the Kangaroos again, though, as the Australians scored two more tries and ran out winners by 25–8.

FIRST TEST AT SYDNEY CRICKET GROUND, 9 JUNE 1984

	AUSTRALIA 25	**GREAT BRITAIN 8**
1.	Garry Jack	Mick Burke
2.	Kerry Boustead	Des Drummond
3.	Gene Miles	Garry Schofield
4.	Brett Kenny	Keith Mumby
5.	Ross Conlon	Ellery Hanley
6.	Wally Lewis (captain)	Des Foy
7.	Mark Murray	Neil Holding
8.	Dave Brown	Lee Crooks
9.	Greg Conescu	Brian Noble (captain)
10.	Greg Dowling	Andy Goodway
11.	Brian Niebling	Chris Burton
12.	Wayne Pearce	Mick Worrall
13.	Ray Price	Mick Adams
14.	Chris Close	Joe Lydon
15.	Craig Young	David Hobbs
T:	Lewis, Price, Boustead, Murray	Schofield
G:	Conlan 4, Lewis dg	Burke 2

SUBSTITUTION:
Young for Brown (69 min)

SUBSTITUTIONS:
Lydon for Holding (22 min)
Hobbs for Crooks (73 min)

Referee: R. Shrimpton (New Zealand)
Attendance: 30,190

Wally Lewis was named Man of the Match but I thought that Australia's loose forward, Ray Price, made the greatest contribution to their win. I felt my second Test performance was sound, and the try was the icing on the cake. I wanted more, and I was to be lucky enough to get it.

There was one unfortunate incident in the last minute from a short kick-off I took following Murray's try. Aussie hooker Greg Conescu caught the ball in his hands, while in his mouth he caught both elbows belonging to David Hobbs. The TV cameras also caught the moment of impact perfectly, including a flying tooth. Hobbsy was immediately dismissed after being on the field for just seven minutes. He wasn't the first or the last international to be sent off on tour – as Les Boyd, the Australian prop forward who made a habit of it, will tell you. Usually the player avoids a suspension, is fined a few hundred quid and warned over his future conduct. In David's case, he received a three-match ban and a £650 fine. Still, as a member of the Test team, he would have been selected for only one of the next three games anyway.

The 'ham-and-eggers', as touring parties' midweek sides are generally nicknamed, swept aside Wide Bay 28–18 two days later, but not without fun and games involving the referee, Mick Hourigan. One of our officials had overheard the ref in conversation with a Wide Bay fan, telling him how determined he was to penalise the Lions as often as he could. The ref then turned out in a red shirt, as had Wide Bay, and it took a quarter of an hour before he changed jerseys. The penalties against us mounted, and perhaps it might have been better if Mr Hourigan had kept the red shirt on – it might have enabled someone like Brian Case of Wigan to pull off a big hit, claiming mistaken identity as his excuse! Afterwards Frank Myler felt the touring party should make a stand, and we boycotted the post-match function in protest.

Central Queensland were the next to fall to the ever-improving Great Britain XIII, by 44–12. With four tries and five goals in this game, I was making it very difficult for our coach to leave me out of the team for the second Test. We would be playing at Lang Park in Brisbane, a very intimidating atmosphere, and the talk among the players was that Frank might bring in more experienced players to handle this Test. I had never previously crossed four times in one game, and I went in from various distances ranging from 15 to 45 yards. The Hull KR second row Chris Burton was sin-binned near the end as the Aussies tried to play a more violent form of rugby in response to our big lead. As was my habit, I kept well out of all the physical stuff.

The midweekers won again in North Queensland with Ellery Hanley making his presence felt most impressively, before we suffered our first loss outside the Tests. On 20 June we visited Toowoomba, and a lethargic display saw us go down 16–18. By now the identity of the 'ham-and-eggers' within the touring party was clearly established, a situation which the management had allowed to develop. It is an understandable and natural phenomenon on major tours, and man-management skills are crucial in minimising the impact that it can have upon a squad. We needed competition amongst ourselves in events such as golf, go-karting and pool to give the midweekers the opportunity to feel that they were a valuable part of the tour – but nothing was arranged. Now it was apparent that some players who felt that they should have been picked in the Test team and weren't, began to take liberties with training and discipline. As the tour progressed, the number of training sessions dropped from three per day to two, and then just one. Granted, we were finding the hard grounds a problem with skin burns and infection, but the squad needed to be pulled together more than it was.

This was the first tour Great Britain had undertaken with a fitness conditioner on board. Rod McKenzie from Carnegie College in Leeds took full responsibility for improving and maintaining our physical fitness, and there was no doubt that we were the fittest squad to tour Down Under to date. At the start of the tour we would train three times a day, at 7 a.m., 10 a.m. and 3 p.m. Our diet and weight were as regularly monitored, and I found this gave me a sharper edge. Confident in my fitness levels, I felt I was peaking in time for the second Test, as were most of the Test probables.

We suffered complaints on tour in Sydney when we stayed at the posh Sheraton Wentworth Hotel. This hotel had been used by the England cricketers, and was really too smart for us. Rugby players are boisterous from time to time, particularly when little is organised for them to do, and some elderly guests complained about us to the hotel management. We had already been warned over the way we hung our washing, including our jockstraps and training gear, over our balconies to dry!

The management imposed no curfews, and the players soon found a number of bars for a relaxing drink. I remember Andy Goodway receiving plenty of stick from a couple of Australians in Sheila's nightclub in North Sydney one evening. Andy had been one of the outstanding players of the tour, and was not in the mood to take the verbal pommie-bashing. Eventually, one of the two Australians went to the gents and Andy followed him in, returning a few minutes later. No one knows what really happened, but he had a very peaceful evening thereafter!

What came as a big surprise was when we were told that only the cost of our breakfast was covered by the RFL. We were left to fend for ourselves at other mealtimes, and a number of us would head for the New South Wales Leagues Club where we could have a starter and a nice piece of steak for five dollars! My touring fee was £1,800, and most of the players left a large part of this at home with wives and girlfriends to cover bills, with the balance spread over the full 12 weeks on tour.

With the tour party now starting to fragment, we travelled on to Brisbane for the second Test. For the most part Frank Myler stuck with the first Test team, replacing Des Foy at stand-off with Tony Myler, while Keith Rayne came in at prop allowing Andy Goodway to move into the second row. Mick Adams and Andy Gregory were on the bench. The Australians also made a couple of changes, amongst which was the introduction of Mal Meninga at centre alongside Gene Miles.

The game was a great learning experience for me. Just 18 years old and 12 stone wet through, up against Aussie centres who were both over 6ft 2in and 16 stone – they threw me around like a rag doll all game. I soon realised that you can be as fit and confident as you like, but without upper body strength you will be slaughtered. With those hard lessons on board I had many good battles with Mal Meninga in future series.

The 27,000 crowd gave the game real atmosphere. We matched the Kangaroos up front for most of the match, but we just found their backs too hot to handle. Eric Grothe scored a first-half try, and we came in 6–0 down. Loose forward Wayne Pearce then drove through several tackles after 57 minutes to extend the lead, and shortly afterwards we hit back with what was subsequently voted the 'Try of the Decade'. I was lucky enough to be on the end of a move that began on our 22-metre line with Tony Myler breaking quickly from a play-the-ball. He passed on to Mick Adams, and I joined the action to interchange with winger Des Drummond as we cut through their midfield. Andy Goodway, the man in form, took Drummond's pass with the line 20 metres ahead, and I linked on Andy's outside to take the pass and dive over in the corner. The try was rated as one of Great Britain's finest at international level, and while I did not fully appreciate the impact it would have at the time, now I do.

Mal Meninga went over for the last score of the game, and we had lost the second Test 18–6 and with it the Ashes. The dressing-room was full of dejection. Great Britain had not won the Ashes since 1970, and before we left home people weren't giving us a cat in hell's chance of doing it on this tour – so I guess the consolation in the team's performances so far was that we weren't being hammered in the way that many people had expected.

Australia's star and captain Wally Lewis had come in for some special attention from one or two of our forwards in this match, not least when Mick Adams flattened him – although it was Keith Rayne who was sin-binned for it, by way of mistaken identity. Perhaps Keith felt aggrieved, because when he returned he tried himself to knock Lewis's head off. He missed, but was sin-binned again for a further five minutes. Nobby Noble finished with a broken nose courtesy of a Lewis elbow, one of several X-rays that were needed that night. It was a level of ferocity I had not witnessed before, and the emotions of the game I found draining – another new experience.

SECOND TEST AT LANG PARK, BRISBANE, 26 JUNE 1984

	AUSTRALIA 18	**GREAT BRITAIN 6**
1.	Garry Jack	Mick Burke
2.	Kerry Boustead	Des Drummond
3.	Mal Meninga	Garry Schofield
4.	Gene Miles	Keith Mumby
5.	Eric Grothe	Ellery Hanley
6.	Wally Lewis (captain)	Tony Myler
7.	Mark Murray	Neil Holding
8.	Dave Brown	Keith Rayne
9.	Greg Conescu	Brian Noble (captain)
10.	Greg Dowling	Lee Crooks
11.	Brian Niebling	Chris Burton
12.	Paul Vautin	Andy Goodway
13.	Wayne Pearce	Mick Worrall

14.	Steve Mortimer	Andy Gregory
15.	Wally Fullerton-Smith	Mick Adams
T:	Grothe, Pearce, Meninga	Schofield
G:	Meninga 3	Burke

SUBSTITUTIONS:	SUBSTITUTIONS:
Fullerton-Smith for Brown (68 min)	Adams for Crooks (18 min)
Mortimer for Murray (78 min)	Gregory for Burton (68 min)

Referee: R. Shrimpton (New Zealand)

Attendance: 26,534

We picked up two more wins on our way back to Sydney, but my room-mate Joe Lydon – 'Mr Eligible', as we called him – was now very frustrated as the high hopes he had entertained before the tour were now no longer achievable. Still unable to find the true form we had seen in the British winter, he was now involved in skirmishes on the field, leading to his dismissal against Northern Rivers at Tweed Heads. We had become firm friends on this tour, and I felt that it could have been me just as easily as it was Joe who endured this disappointment. Looking after me off the field must have taken more out of him than I ever imagined!

In the same Northern Rivers game I went off with a hip injury, and the hard grounds were taking their toll now, with half a dozen players invalided out of the remainder of the tour. Most of us had badly blistered feet, and I tried to look after myself as the third Test approached. Sadly, the tour management were losing the plot now, and the players' attitude to training had fallen away. Many drinking sessions were taking place, which for me was something new on the tour. The advice my father gave me now came to mind: 'When you find yourself in the company of experienced professionals, just sit back and take it all in.' Players such as Mick Adams gave me the benefit of their time and advice at this stage of the tour. Mick wanted to win the next Test and took care not to overdo the socialising, and I tagged along with him. 'If you really want to beat the Aussies you certainly can't afford to be out drinking and partying to excess.'

In the event we lost the third Test by 20–7, suffering a record tenth successive defeat by Australia in the process. They did not play that well, but we gave our poorest display of the series – this in spite of an Ellery Hanley try which put us ahead for most of the first period. Ellery had been selected as a winger in all three Tests, though Frank Myler encouraged him to move infield at every opportunity and this ruse paid off well. The Aussies found Ellery's upper body strength very hard to deal with, and their media recognised that they were in the presence of greatness. Down by 8–7 at half-time, we then dropped the ball too often and they ran away with the game, scoring two more tries. Thankfully, there was no repetition of the violent encounters which had marred the first two Tests. We scored one try in each of the three Tests, an improvement over the last Ashes series, but if we were seriously to challenge the Australians we needed to have more creative ambition. We showed by the quality of our tries that we were a talented young side, and we all looked forward to meeting the Kangaroos again soon.

THIRD TEST AT SYDNEY CRICKET GROUND, 7 JULY 1984

	AUSTRALIA 20	**GREAT BRITAIN 7**
1.	Garry Jack	Mick Burke
2.	Kerry Boustead	Des Drummond
3.	Mal Meninga	Garry Schofield
4.	Gene Miles	Keith Mumby
5.	Eric Grothe	Ellery Hanley
6.	Wally Lewis (captain)	Tony Myler
7.	Steve Mortimer	Neil Holding
8.	Brian Niebling	David Hobbs
9.	Greg Conescu	Brian Noble (captain)
10.	Greg Dowling	Brian Case
11.	Wally Fullerton-Smith	Chris Burton
12.	Wayne Pearce	Andy Goodway
13.	Ray Price	Mick Adams
14.	Brett Kenny	Mike Smith
15.	Ray Brown	Keith Rayne

T:	Grothe, Conescu, Jack	Hanley
G:	Meninga 4	Burke
		Holding 1dg

SUBSTITUTIONS:
Brown for Fullerton-Smith (62 min)
Kenny for Miles (69 min)

Referee: A. Drake (New Zealand)
Attendance: 18,756

Tony Myler, our first choice, played stand-off and performed well in spite of having cortisone injections to reduce inflammation in a knee. The injections were administered by our tour physiotherapist, Ronnie Barritt from Bradford Northern. The physio had a new piece of equipment with him on tour. The old means of treating dead legs and bruising by ultrasound machine took some time to work fully, and this time Ronnie had a new machine which delivered laser treatment. This equipment cut down on treatment time and was probably fine for bruising, but, unfortunately, Ronnie used it on Neil Holding's ear – almost perforating his eardrum!

Three days later we were sending out the midweek side against the Northern District in Whangarei, New Zealand, on the second leg of our tour. Eight more games lay ahead of us, before the final Test against Papua New Guinea. We won 42–8, and hooker Kevin Beardmore had an outstanding match, pushing for Nobby Noble's Test spot, while I came on as sub for a concussed Keith Mumby. Then it was on to the first Test against the Kiwis on 14 July at Carlaw Park in Auckland, where the pitch was ankle deep in mud. Needless to say, we did not relish the prospect of playing such an important game in such difficult conditions, particularly after the hard grounds we were used to in Australia.

The only change in the backs was at stand-off, with Hull KR's Mike Smith replacing Tony Myler shortly before kick-off, owing to food poisoning. Andy Goodway has good reason to remember the game – or at least to try to – as first he suffered mild concussion following a head-high shot from Kiwi centre Dean Bell that went unpunished, and then blurred vision from a similar challenge in the second half. All New Zealand's points came in the first period, with tries from Hull's Kiwis, Leuluai and Ah Kuoi, as they ran out winners by 12–0.

After that first Test I was found to have a stress fracture of the shin, which signalled the end of my tour. I flew home a fortnight later in the company of Lee Crooks, Ray Ashton and Harry Pinner, who were other late casualties. Our conditioner Rod McKenzie had returned home after the Australian leg of the tour, and levels of fitness, training, discipline and team spirit had continued to spiral downwards. Thankfully, on the field, Ellery Hanley was continuing to put in a big effort. Only Des Drummond and Keith Mumby played as many times, and Ellery was eventually top try-scorer on the tour with 12 in 16 appearances. The day after the first Test Ellery was in action again as we overcame the New Zealand Maoris 19–8, and Ellery kicked three goals! Joe Lydon was assaulted off the ball at the start of that game and was helped away after 20 minutes, unable to remember much at all.

The second Test took place just eight days after the first Test – and we had two matches in between! A scratch side turned out in Wellington to face Central Districts three days after the encounter with the Maoris, winning 38–6 thanks to a five-star, two-try display by Andy Gregory at scrum-half which forced him into the Test side. I could only watch as the second Test saw us suffer another defeat, this time by 28–12. Our changed pack was unable to hold the Kiwi forwards as the Tamatis and Sorensens, Owen Wright and loose forward Hugh McGahan ran amok. The following week, the day after my departure, the Lions lost the third Test 32–16, bringing the curtain down on Great Britain's first-ever whitewash by the Kiwis. I was sorry to miss the end of the tour but I hate losing, so I was determined to make the most of my break back home before the 1984–85 domestic season began. The tour had been an incredible experience for me, and I desperately wanted more.

There were one or two characters on the tour, with the young scrum-half Neil Holding standing out as the most entertaining through his impersonations of showbiz celebrities as well as his fellow-players and management! The two players who made an impression of a different kind on us throughout the tour were Ray Ashton and Des Foy. This was because they never opened their wage packets for the whole trip, and soon won the labels of tightest tourists. They never spent a penny, but were always the first in the queue for freebies. As it happened, Ray was injured and flew home on the same flight as Lee Crooks and I. Now Lee and I had spent all our money and were penniless, but good old Ray could not even bring himself to pay for cups of coffee for the three of us in the airport lounge! When Ray joined

Leeds a year or two later, I made sure that the dressing-room was fully in the picture as regards Ray's generous financial outlook!

The tourists eventually moved on to Papua New Guinea for the first and only Test. The players told me on their return that the sunshine and tranquillity there were very welcome. Some of the squad had been away from home for a full 12 weeks, and they were looking forward to unwinding back in England with their families and friends. At least they were able to finish on a high note, leading the Kumuls by 22–4 at half-time before going on to claim their only Test win of the tour by 38–20. The tour had been quite unsuccessful in the end, but many of the young players would be stronger for the experience.

On my return home I was approached by Dave Topliss at Hull to explore the possibility of my joining Balmain Down Under the following summer. Dave had himself played with the Balmain club, and Keith Barnes, their chief executive, had asked him to sound me out on this matter. At the same time I received a similar approach from Parramatta, who were also interested in signing me on the recommendation of Peter Sterling. Hull were keen for me to sign for Parramatta to strengthen the relationship between the two clubs, but Dave Topliss gave the Tigers a glowing reference, and when the financial offers were put side by side I had no real choice but to plump for Balmain. My first season with them was a short one, but their coach, Frank Stanton, was none the less impressed and wanted to offer me a long-term deal of up to five years. I was quite tempted, but my wife Adele felt uncertain over such a long commitment, and in the end I settled for just two further years with the Tigers.

6.

CUP-FINAL HEARTACHE

THE SECOND SEASON was always going to be hard for me. Having made such an impression in my first season, I had also returned from my first British Lions tour to Australia and New Zealand a couple of months earlier, where I had earned a few more plusses and made a few headlines. With a reputation, you know you are there to be shot at. A number of senior players had told me that my sophomore year was going to be a big test of character. While we were on tour one of the lads, Mick Adams, the Widnes captain and loose forward, sat me down and said, 'Well, your second season is going to be tough. You have got to make sure that you show the same sort of attitude you had before you started your first season, because the old pros know what you are capable of doing. They will make sure that it is not as easy for you as you made it look in that first season.'

It turned out to be a very up and down year. I was not playing as well as I knew I could for whatever reason – maybe through lack of confidence, maybe through thinking that I had already made the big time. I kept working hard, and believed in myself: I was not going to be a one-season wonder, and I wanted to play a lot more Test football. What helped me through was the sound advice I had taken in from the senior pros who had toured with the British Lions, and also from the elder statesmen at Hull such as Dave Topliss, Gary Kemble, Dane O'Hara – and even Lee Crooks. They told me that it was still there in my head, and I just had to get back out there and recover the confidence I had shown in my first season.

I had to expect some response from opposing players, though. John Joyner was never a dirty player, but he stood all over my hands during the Castleford fixture – the first time that had happened to me. In no uncertain terms I told him what I felt, and he came back with the quote, 'You were told it wasn't going to be easy, and now you know that you have to start cutting the grade.' Chris Arkwright, the St Helens loose forward, was another to reveal the darker side of rugby league football at this level, when I managed to tackle him and, for whatever reason, I gave him a bit of a dig to the side of the head. His immediate response was, 'If you do that again, you little bastard, I'll make sure that I pull both your legs off!' That taught me not to think that I was the be-all and end-all, because I wasn't. If I wanted to be cocky, there would be a price.

During that 1984–85 season I kicked just over a hundred goals, standing in for Lee Crooks who had lost his form. Despite bagging 23 tries, which made me the game's fifth top point-scorer for the year, I wasn't happy with the way I had performed. In October 1984 Maurice Bamford was appointed the new Great Britain coach in succession to Frank Myler following the defeats over in Australia and New Zealand. Maurice wanted to have a look at other players with an eye to the forthcoming series against the Kiwis in autumn 1985, and so I didn't feature in either of the springtime Tests against France. That merely added to my struggles, but my determination to regain my Test place was the greatest incentive I had that season to recover my form.

Hull finished sixth in the Slalom Lager Championship, with city rivals Hull KR again coming out on top. It is fair to say that our heavy involvement in all three cup competitions adversely affected our league form. The season started well enough for us, as we knocked out Halifax and York in the Phillips Video Yorkshire Cup competition before a resounding home win against Leeds in the semi-final by 24–1. I scored a hat-trick of tries and goals that day, one of my tries being a long-distance interception – something that was to become a trademark of mine. Captained by the 21-year-old Lee Crooks, we met Hull KR in the final at Hull City's Boothferry Park football ground, and in a classic encounter we recovered from 12–0 down to win 29–12. Steve 'Knocker' Norton was inspired, and he pulled us round after a shaky start. The class of our Australian Test scrum-half Peter Sterling also shone through, as we won the cup in fine style before over 25,000 Humbersiders. The only blemish on our day was the rapid dismissal of our substitute forward Paul Rose for an attempted high tackle after less than a minute on the field.

We then began our John Player Special Trophy involvement by disposing of Fulham in the first round 36–14, Oldham in the second round 26–14, and Dewsbury in the third round 22–8. This left us with a semi-final date on 5

January 1985 at Boothferry Park, when once again we were indebted to Peter Sterling and Steve Norton in overcoming Leeds 18–6 to earn a place in the final on 26 January. Our opposition was once again our close neighbours Hull KR, once again at Boothferry Park, but this time they gained their revenge for their Yorkshire Cup reverse by defeating us 12–0 in front of another crowd in excess of 25,000.

Our coach Arthur Bunting was keen for us to do well in all the knockout cup competitions, as it meant extra revenue for the club and a tremendous season for the fans. So, after these two excellent runs to consecutive finals, our Silk Cut Challenge Cup campaign began with a comfortable win at home to Carlisle by 52–6. That was rewarded with a difficult draw away at Halifax, but Arthur made sure we hit the ground running and we emerged as winners by 22–6. That result in turn earned us a difficult third-round tie at home to Widnes, where we were on top for most of the game but had to settle for a 6–6 draw. Gary Divorty went over to give us the lead, but we could not keep Joe Lydon quiet and he created an Andy Currier touchdown to set up a replay. We won a cracking game at Naughton Park 19–12 and marched on into the semi-finals.

We were matched against Castleford in the semi-final at Headingley, and it took us two attempts to get past them and book a place at Wembley. In the first semi-final we drew 10–10 and were let off the hook: shortly before the end of the game Castleford refused the opportunity to go for a drop-goal under the posts, and we scraped a replay. That match four days later was a tense affair in front of another 20,000 crowd. There was plenty of incident, with Peter Sterling suffering in particular when Malcolm Reilly put up a high bomb just before the hooter. Peter, who was in the full-back position anticipating what Malcolm might do, caught the ball under the posts, but Malcolm came straight through and clattered him, and all hell broke loose. There was a massive brawl, and I can remember David Plange and another Castleford player grabbing me and having a right go. Peter reckoned his eye had been gouged in the fracas, and he came out in the second half with his head bandaged. One Hull player, an international, was so incensed by what he believed Malcolm to have done that he walked past him at the end of the game and punched him in such a way that he could not be seen before running straight into the dressing-room. To this day Malcolm denies causing Peter Sterling's injury.

Peter Sterling was not the most enthusiastic of trainers and was never to be seen lifting weights in the gym: the only items he lifted were gambling chips in the casino at the Dragonara Hotel in Leeds. He often turned up bleary-eyed for training and once even fell asleep at the wheel of his car on the way home from the casino on the M62 – not the first Australian, and probably not the last, to accomplish this feat. Having said all that, the guy was pure genius. I have never seen a better player in my time, one who put everything into his game from kick off to final whistle. There was no edge to him at all, and he was forever passing on advice and discussing how to handle different situations with his team-mates. It remains one of my greatest joys to have played in the same team as Peter Sterling for a season or so.

In that replayed semi-final we also lost our full-back Gary Kemble to a late, high tackle by Castleford scrum-half Ian Orum. The game was highly charged and emotional throughout, but in the end we ran out winners by 22–16 with Lee Crooks kicking three goals and laying on three of our four tries to claim yet another Man of the Match award.

I was very much looking forward to playing in the final at Wembley, and the Hull team were confident they could take Wigan and lift the Challenge Cup. Unfortunately for us, James Leuluai had injured his shoulder and was struggling to be fit in time. I had been fortunate enough to play in every round of the cup, including the semi-final replay, and was hopeful of making the starting line-up. We reached our London hotel on the Thursday evening, and Arthur Bunting gave James a fitness test. We heard on the Friday morning that he had passed the test, at which stage I just had it in the back of my mind that I might be the unlucky one. Sure enough, when Arthur announced the team later on that day, I was disappointed to find that I was on the subs' bench and James Leuluai was selected to start, even though he hadn't played for three weeks. Gary Divorty, who had played pretty well at loose forward that season, was also left out and joined me on the bench. Still, we had a good team spirit at Hull, and several of the team commiserated with me at missing out.

The game itself was a classic and is talked about as being one of the best cup finals ever. Wigan began like a house on fire, with Australian stand-off Brett Kenny pulling all the strings. It was 20 years since the Riversiders had last won the trophy, and tries by Ferguson and Kenny followed by a long-range touchdown from winger Henderson Gill meant Hull went in at half-time 16–8 down. The try-scoring feast continued in the second half, and at one point Wigan led 28–12. With just over 20 minutes to go, Arthur Bunting made a double substitution, bringing myself and Gary Divorty off the bench. He could see that Wigan were tiring, and with Peter Sterling producing a never-say-die effort we managed to score the final three tries before running out of time and finishing runners-up by 28–24. Almost 98,000 spectators had witnessed a wonderful game of rugby league but, looking back, Hull could have won that cup had we been able to kick our goals. Between us Lee Crooks and I missed five out of seven attempts, and that made all the difference in the end.

After the final 'Sterlo' very graciously consoled me and suggested that Arthur Bunting might be wishing that he could go back a few hours and play me from the start, as I might have provided that little bit of extra edge for Hull in such a memorable match. It is always so much easier in hindsight to consider how the destiny of a game could have been changed. Although I was bitterly disappointed, the Hull side at that time had such a genuine team spirit that we all put the game behind us and aimed to be back at Wembley the following season to win the cup. It is also worth remembering that I came on with Gary Divorty in the second half, when the Wigan players were tiring. The pitch has always had a spongy surface, and its width combined with the adrenalin pumped by such a big occasion as the Challenge Cup final always takes its toll. To be fair to James Leuluai, he had an outstanding game. Notwithstanding the might-have-beens, I was grateful just to make an appearance in the final. I had never been to Wembley Stadium before – I had watched FA Cup finals and rugby league Challenge Cup finals on television year after year, but never visited the place. To walk out in front of 40,000 Hull fans wearing black and white and 40,000 Wigan fans wearing red and white was an unbelievable experience. I vowed to return to the place as soon as I could, for this was the stage on which I wanted to play my rugby, in front of so many passionate fans.

Wembley is not a place for losers, though. Apart from the consolatory round of applause when you do your lap of honour, it's back to the dressing-room for quiet reflection. The media make no fuss of the losing side, and we just wanted to get back on the coach and return to our hotel for the usual post-final dinner, disco and a few beers. The last players went to bed around four in the morning, and early the following week I made my way to Australia to fulfil my contract with Balmain. It had been a very up and down season for me; I was still learning and beginning to experience the highs and lows of winning and losing major finals.

A different challenge awaited me Down Under, as Adele and I landed in Australia. After the long flight we were met at the airport by Keith Barnes from the Balmain club, who took us to our hotel and then told me I had to be at training in half an hour's time! As you can imagine, as soon as we reached our room I was putting together my playing gear, leaving Adele to do all the unpacking. The emotion of flying halfway round the world and then being left to fend for herself was too much, and she burst into tears. She wanted to go straight back home on the next plane, and I had to persuade her that we couldn't do it: I was contracted to play for Balmain, and I had to give it my best shot. We were both close to our parents and families, and in Adele's case it was the first time she'd been away on a trip like this. I told her not to make her mind up immediately but to give it a few days, and I felt sure she would change her mind.

Off I went to my first training session, returning a couple of hours later. The Balmain team accepted me straight away, and contained a number of outstanding Australian players – Wayne Pearce, Garry Jack, Kerry Hemsley, Paul Sironen, Steve Roach, Benny Elias and Neil Whitaker – and we were coached by the great Frank Stanton. The following day in Sydney we were playing in a league match, and Adele had the opportunity to meet all the other players' wives and girlfriends together with representatives of the club. We were both made to feel so very welcome; since we were a long way from home, the Balmain club knew how important it was for us both to settle in. We were also fortunate enough in the fact that Lee Crooks and Des Drummond were playing for Western Suburbs down the road in Sydney, so we had plenty of company. Adele and Lee's wife were able to go out shopping together and support one another during the day so life worked out pretty well in the end.

An unhappy relationship thousands of miles from home just puts pressure on a player and interferes with his performance. We were both very young: I was 19 at the time, and while I would have liked to sign for four or five summers if I could, in the end Adele agreed to give it a couple of seasons – although we returned for a third later in my career. Balmain were very keen for me to to commit myself to them full time, but I could understand Adele wanting to return home to Leeds. We were living in Sydney, one of the largest cities in Australia, almost as big as London, and four months there was long enough for Adele. We had just got married, and I did not want to put her under more pressure than was necessary.

My first season Down Under was a great success. I finished up top try-scorer for Balmain with 13 tries, and we made the cup final of the midweek cup competition, the National Panasonic Cup. Wayne Pearce, the Aussie Test star, worked on our fitness and we almost looked forward to the extra training sessions he sprang on us from time to time – he was that good. The climate I found to be ideal for playing rugby, although the grounds were too hard on occasions: although it was their winter, the temperatures were in the high 50s to mid-60s. The Aussies think this is very cold, but they do not have winters in Sydney like we do back home. It is nice to play and train with the sun on your back, and the conditions really suited my style of play.

In that first season, the Tigers were robbed of the opportunity to play in a Grand final for the first time since 1969 when referee Mick Stone disallowed my try in injury time against Canterbury Bulldogs, claiming that the pass I had received was forward. Television replays proved otherwise.

Every couple of weeks or so Frank Stanton and his wife would invite two or three players to his house for tea. His man-management skills were exceptional, and after Adele and I had been in Australia for four or five weeks, he invited us to come over with Garry and Donna Jack and Ross Conlon and his wife. Frank told me of the time he met Phil Larder in 1983. Phil had been a schoolteacher before taking up the position of Director of Coaching in Great Britain, and I don't think Frank was too impressed with teachers. Anyhow, Phil had asked to see Frank in action as Australian coach, and Frank knew full well that Phil was connected in some way with the Great Britain set-up. Frank told me he had discussed his methods in great detail with Phil, but admitted that only 50 per cent of the information he had passed on to Phil was workable – the other 50 per cent was bullshit!

7.

TACKLING THE KIWIS

THAT WINTER IN 1985, a strong New Zealand touring party landed in Great Britain, and I had cause to reflect with some satisfaction on the matches I played against them. Under new coach Maurice Bamford, I was selected for the first Whitbread Trophy Bitter Test at Headingley on 19 October alongside Ellery Hanley in the centre. Lee Crooks was at prop, and with Joe Lydon on one wing the team was confident of success. Leading 6–0 after only three minutes through an Andy Goodway try goaled by full-back Mick Burke, we then allowed the Kiwis to fight their way back into the game. Captain Mark Graham led by example, scoring one try and driving his team on for wingers O'Hara and Bell also to touch down. Before the break Ellery went over for a second Great Britain try, again converted by Burke, which left us 12–14 down at the restart.

Both Graham and Crooks departed through injury in the second half as we threw the ball about in front of a 12,591 crowd and a live TV audience both in the UK and Down Under. Burke and Joe Lydon kicked penalties and prop Kurt Sorensen touched down for the tourists before Joe finished off an outstanding, length-of-the-field movement in the 72nd minute to touch down under the posts. It started when Des Drummond collected the ball just five yards from our corner flag, rounded O'Hara and swerved his way up to the 25 before parting to scrum-half Deryck Fox. Substitute forward Chris Arkwright then joined in before releasing Ellery down the touch-line. His 50-yard dash took him beyond Dean Bell and, holding off full-back James Leuluai, he managed to lob the ball infield to Joe in support for the touchdown. This brilliant try, we felt at this stage, had won the match for us.

However, New Zealand disagreed and retaliated with strongman Kurt Sorensen bursting through to send James Leuluai over by the posts with three minutes remaining on the clock. Stand-off Olsen Filipaina did not miss, and his second conversion won the game 24–22. For my part I had been one of the chasers who had followed up Deryck Fox's kick to give us territorial advantage in those last few minutes – an area of our game plan on which Maurice Bamford had spent some time with us. Regrettably Dane O'Hara got free of my attempted tackle to make good yardage and create the eventual platform for their winning try.

The dressing-room mood after the game was mixed. We had lost, and a number of us were gutted. Coach Maurice Bamford wisely let the dust settle before instilling into us the fact that the game could have gone either way. We had been punished for a couple of mistakes, and a forward pass had been missed by the Australian referee, Mr Barry Gomersall – and after all, a few months earlier New Zealand had twice been robbed of Test victories against Australia in the last few minutes. Maurice told us the series was still there to be won, and we would win it.

Four days later I was given the chance to seek revenge, along with four other Great Britain team-mates from the first Test. Yorkshire played New Zealand at Bradford, and in front of just 3,745 hardy fans Peter Fox coached us to victory by 18–8. I can recall few more bitterly cold nights on a rugby field. The forwards battled gamely, no doubt glad to be in the thick of the action in such freezing weather, while our half-backs shone too with Ellery Hanley, at stand-off, returning to Odsal for the first time since his record move to Wigan. He scored one try and dropped a goal, and with scrum-half Deryck Fox making two tries and kicking two goals to win the Man of the Match award, we had something to celebrate. Our props enjoyed different emotions after the game as Jeff Grayshon, the veteran Bradford forward, played robustly enough to win a Test recall, but Trevor Skerrett had the misfortune to suffer a fractured cheekbone. With Dave Creasser in the centre alongside me and two wingers from the lower divisions in Carl Gibson, then of Batley, and Andy Mason of Bramley, it was a very satisfying Yorkshire triumph.

The second Whitbread Trophy Bitter Test was to be one of the highlights of my Test career. Domestic and international exploits in my first two seasons as a professional had put me firmly in the limelight, and I was beginning to appreciate that the British sporting public held and expressed very strong opinions concerning sports stars. I was still learning the game, and I found it difficult to ignore the criticisms of some fans. I was to realise that it was par for the course in the UK, as I often heard of similar experiences from other sporting superstars I had admired over the years.

After the loss of the first Test at Headingley I took some stick both from the critics and from some supporters. The members of the rugby league press I have always tried to accommodate and, with very few exceptions, I have been grateful for their honest assessments. In that game I had missed a tackle on Dane O'Hara in the movement that eventually led to James Leuluai clinching the game with his touchdown three minutes from time. Coach Maurice Bamford spoke only briefly to me after the game regarding that tackle following the kick and chase. Although I felt my place was in jeopardy, he selected me for the second Test at Central Park, Wigan. Maurice had stood by me, and I was grateful and wanted to repay his faith in me. I had to prove myself, and this was the first occasion I had experienced in rugby league where the pressure was really on. The 11th New Zealand tourists were a formidable bunch, coming off the back of a 3–0 whitewash of Great Britain back home the previous summer, followed by the closest of series with the mighty Australians. The Kiwis paraded possibly the greatest pack of forwards they had ever assembled, featuring the fearsome Sorensen brothers, Kurt and Dane, the powerful Kevin Tamati, two inspirational leaders in Mark Graham and Hugh McGahan, and lively hooker Howie Tamati – an awesome ensemble. Behind them, in James Leuluai, Gary Kemble, Dean Bell, Dane O'Hara and livewire stand-off Olsen Filipaina, they had the pace and the craft to take advantage of their forward dominance. I was well aware of the talent in the backs, as a number of them were Hull team-mates of mine. The coach, Graham Lowe, was one of the shrewdest who could fire teams up and make them play above themselves, so we were under no illusions.

Graham Lowe's men were installed as favourites after the first Test, as the media failed initially to appreciate the progress that the Great Britain coach and team were making. Maurice Bamford had made just one change, bringing in Jeff Grayshon at prop, and he reminded us of the closeness of that first encounter. The first 15 minutes were tense as our forwards fought for supremacy. The front row of Grayshon, Watkinson and Fieldhouse were in the thick of it, not giving the Kiwis any psychological advantage. Penalty goals were exchanged before the game began to open up, as both sides were confident that their backs were potential match-winners, and our skipper, St

Helens loose forward Harry Pinner, was finding more and more room to display his ball-handling talents.

I broke the deadlock with my first try. Long passes behind the scrum from Fox and Myler found Ellery Hanley, and Ellery and I worked a crossover move. He used his upper body strength and pace to suck in a couple of tacklers, hold them up and ride the collision before giving me the ball to exploit the gap he had created. The pass was perfectly timed, and I hit the ball at speed to go in from 25 yards out. I look back on all the artistry of rugby league that was in the move. First of all, the passer tries to hold off the tacklers, engaging more than one of them to create the gap. The receiver then hits the gap, and the ball is passed at speed. A centre's main function is to create space and try-scoring opportunities for his winger, but when a break is made in midfield he must also try to be on hand to continue it or to finish it off with a try of his own.

My second try on the half-hour mark was a different affair. Our second row forward, Ian Potter of Wigan, managed to intercept a loose Kiwi pass on halfway. Prop John Fieldhouse scurried away from acting half-back down the middle, and I made straight off downfield to back him up, believing that a try was on if he could just find me with a pass. The big forward did not let me down, and I went in from 35 yards, avoiding Graeme West on the way. Joe Lydon converted to make it 12–2 at half-time, when coach Bamford told us to imagine that we were trailing and badly needed the next score. Within two minutes of the restart I had scored my third try in the space of 27 minutes to put us 18–2 ahead.

Harry Pinner was not the largest loose forward to represent Great Britain, but he did his share of tackling. More important, Harry created play and schemed openings for all his team-mates. Every top side had such a player in those days, and Harry was a superb ball player and a brilliant handler who could time and deliver a pass better than any forward of the time. Harry and the equally gifted Tony Myler combined in midfield in a runaround movement, pulling in the Kiwi centres, Leuluai and Gary Prohm, sufficiently to allow Tony to release me into the gap with the sweetest of one-handed passes. I was timing every run to perfection now, with my confidence flowing and my team-mates on fire.

Though Bell pulled a try back, rounding substitute full-back Shaun Edwards, we kept the scoreboard ticking over through a Pinner drop-goal.

My record-breaking fourth try arrived four minutes from time courtesy of a classic break by Pinner, supported by the powerful Tony Myler. His pass was delayed perfectly to release Ellery Hanley and I was on Ellery's shoulder for him to put me in, beating Gary Kemble to the line. I well recall the reception the 15,506 fans gave me as I walked back with the team to halfway. None of us wanted the game to end, and the dressing-room scene was special as coach and players shed tears of joy – veteran Jeff Grayshon included, after what was his 12th cap at the age of 36 years and eight months! Champagne flowed as we had broken a run of ten consecutive defeats against Australia and New Zealand. The fact that I had equalled the Great Britain record of four tries in a Test, and broken the record for points scored in a Test against New Zealand, was secondary that night.

SECOND TEST AT CENTRAL PARK, WIGAN, 2 NOVEMBER 1985

GREAT BRITAIN 25   NEW ZEALAND 8

1.	Mick Burke	Gary Kemble
2.	Des Drummond	Dean Bell
3.	Garry Schofield	James Leuluai
4.	Ellery Hanley	Gary Prohm
5.	Joe Lydon	Dane O'Hara
6.	Tony Myler	Olsen Filipaina (captain)
7.	Deryck Fox	Clayton Friend
8.	Jeff Grayshon	Kurt Sorensen
9.	David Watkinson	Howie Tamati
10.	John Fieldhouse	Dane Sorensen
11.	Andy Goodway	Graeme West
12.	Ian Potter	Sam Stewart
13.	Harry Pinner (captain)	Hugh McGahan
14.	Shaun Edwards	Fred Ah Kuoi
15.	Chris Burton	Ricky Cowan
T:	Schofield 4	Bell
G:	Lydon 4, Pinner dg	Filipaina 2

SUBSTITUTIONS:

SUBSTITUTIONS:

Edwards for Burke (43 min)   Ah Kuoi for West (48 min)

Burton for Goodway (74 min)   Cowan for Stewart (70 min)

Referee: B. Gomersall (Australia)

Attendance: 15,506

The match was particularly satisfying for me, because we had been hammered in all three Tests in New Zealand in 1984. In this match we had completely outplayed them and this was a turning point for British rugby league in the Test arena. We were a Test force again, and new coach Maurice Bamford took credit for excellent team selection and management. For my part it was a great experience to score four tries in a Test match and equal the great Billy Boston's feat, also against the Kiwis in Auckland in 1954. Jim Leytham had scored four against Australia at Brisbane in 1910, while Alex Murphy also touched down four times at Headingley against France in 1959.

And so we moved on to Elland Road for the third Test of an enthralling series. Over 22,000 spectators witnessed the sad sight of the referee losing control as the Kiwis' game plan of violence and intimidation almost succeeded. This fixture was also designated a World Cup qualifying game, and with so much at stake the Kiwis abandoned their high-speed, running rugby for old-fashioned, forward-dominated attrition. For Great Britain Tony Myler dropped out through injury and Ellery moved to stand-off, with Shaun Edwards introduced at centre.

The game was full of controversy, starting with our second-row forward, Andy Goodway of Wigan, being stretchered off following a head-high, off-the-ball tackle by Kurt Sorensen after 20 minutes. Kurt was merely sin-binned for five minutes, but Andy took no further part in the proceedings. Lee Crooks replaced Andy and was soon in the thick of things. Some 32 minutes into the game Mark Graham scored the only try, diving in after playing the ball to himself. Referee Barry 'The Grasshopper' Gomersall was at the centre of this disputed try. We felt the touchdown had not been completed correctly, only to learn after the game that the referee would have given a penalty try anyway in the belief that John Fieldhouse had interfered at the play-the-ball! We went in at half-time trailing 6–0, and Maurice Bamford told us to keep our heads and not to get drawn into the physical side of the match.

Sadly this was not to be as, in the 63rd minute, the patience of some of the Great Britain players expired and a violent brawl ensued involving ten players. No end was in sight, and it was left to two police officers to enter the field and halt the conflict. The referee explained after the game: 'It is my stated policy to let play carry on when there is a brawl. If all 26 players had been involved I would have intervened immediately, but Britain had the ball and a three-to-two advantage. After the brawl I was not too concerned over who went to the sin-bin. It could have been any two!' It was in fact Jeff Grayshon and Kurt Sorensen who departed for ten minutes, while hooker Dave Watkinson went off for five stitches to an eye wound, and Pinner and Potter also needed stitching before the final whistle!

The referee was no help that day. Even with a penalty count of 20–7 in our favour, including nine for foul play, we never got the protection we ought to have had. Sub Lee Crooks was our hero with three penalty goals as we drew 6–6. His final effort in the last minute, from the touch-line, deserved to win the game for us, but only gave us a draw. Shortly after the match finished we had the usual celebration dinner for the end of the series, but this was a very subdued affair in view of the serious brawl that had erupted. Lee was awarded Man of the Match, and John Fieldhouse Man of the Series. As an international unit we felt we were now up there with the best, and looked forward to proving so against the Australians. We had drawn the series and were hopeful of putting together a sequence of unbeaten Tests.

The hangover from the last Test was felt when Hull FC lined up to face the Kiwis just eight days later at the Boulevard in their final tour game. Referee Gerry Kershaw from Easingwold near York sent off five players in the first half. Kershaw was heavily criticised for overreacting by sending off first Lee Crooks and Clayton Friend, then hookers Shaun Patrick and Howie Tamati, and finally dismissing Filipaina for 'dangerous kicking'. Hull had led 10–0 only to fall 33–10 to a powerful second-half display by the tourists. Despite being one man short, they showed the sparkling passing and support play we knew they were capable of. I missed much of it: I scored a try and goal before being stretchered off.

Fortunately the injury was not as severe as I first thought, and although I missed a number of Hull games over the Christmas and New Year I was included in Maurice Bamford's squad for the two Whitbread Trophy Bitter Tests against the French in the spring of 1986. The first was another World

Cup qualifying game, taking place at Avignon on 16 February. The Test squad was nicknamed 'The Family', as Maurice stuck largely with the same playing staff who had done the job against New Zealand. Wigan pair Shaun Wane and Henderson Gill were the only changes, in place of the unavailable Andy Goodway and the injured Joe Lydon. Our preparations were badly hampered by snow: we had just one video session at our Huddersfield hotel and one indoor loosener on the day we flew out, while in France our one session took place on a small football pitch.

Great Britain turned round 10–2 ahead thanks to an Ellery Hanley try and three goals from Lee Crooks. But the French performed impressively throughout, with full-back Gilles Dumas converting his own try and kicking a 62nd-minute penalty to earn them a hard-fought draw. Dumas sliced wide a decent drop-goal opportunity and missed a penalty kick in the last few minutes, while Lee Crooks did the same with a difficult 45-yard kick before the final whistle. Three players were sin-binned by Aussie referee Kevin Roberts: French prop Max Chantal (no, not the singer!), Tony Myler for tripping, and Lee Crooks for kicking out in the tackle.

This was only the third draw between the two countries in 46 meetings, but I could have won the game for us shortly after half-time. I touched down under the posts after a short pass from Lee Crooks, only for the effort to be ruled out as the pass was called forward. Ian Potter was awarded Man of the Match for his defensive work, despite five stitches in a head wound.

Two weeks later we took on the French again, this time at Central Park, with five changes forced on us largely through injuries to Hanley, Burke, Grayshon and Pinner. Back came Joe Lydon, and in came new caps Tony Marchant, David Laws, Kevin Rayne and Neil James. Maurice Bamford emphasised once more the need for us to keep our composure, and we were only penalised four times throughout by Kevin Roberts. The new boys shone and highlighted the strength in depth that British rugby league had at this particular time. Des Drummond and I scored tries in the first half, but it was the efforts of Halifax's Neil James and Castleford centre Tony Marchant, both of whom not only scored but also distinguished themselves in the tackling department, that gave us a 24–10 win. New skipper David Watkinson led the tackle count, and second row James was named Man of the Match. Our unbeaten run was further extended, and Maurice picked a 29-man squad for summer training in preparation for the visit of the Australians in October 1986.

8.

AUSSIES IN '86

A 28-MAN AUSTRALIAN squad arrived in October 1986 determined to emulate the 1982 'Invincibles' by winning every one of their 13-match itinerary. Alhough this was the shortest tour they had undertaken, the Australians nevertheless conducted another clean sweep. Financially the tour was a great success, with attendance records broken and tour receipts surpassing all projections. Five 'Invincibles' made this tour also, and interestingly they were all backs: skipper Wally Lewis, Gene Miles, Mal Meninga, Peter Sterling and Brett Kenny. No surprise, then, to find that I have chosen four of them in my Greatest World XIII later in this book.

Their first confrontation was with Wigan, where a record 30,622 crowd saw the home team fight back after trailing 20–2. The final 26–18 scoreline in favour of the green-and-golds gave our Great Britain coach Maurice Bamford great heart. However, high-scoring wins over Hull KR, Leeds and Cumbria followed, and it became clear that this squad was as strong as that in 1982 and its depth was awesome. Every position had class players competing with one another.

Great Britain's squad preparations had gone very well, and as we ran out on to Manchester United's Old Trafford pitch – the 'Theatre of Dreams' – for the first Whitbread Trophy Bitter Test match, little did we imagine that the dreams realised that afternoon would all belong to Australians. We kicked off full of confidence, highly motivated and unbeaten in our last four Tests, in front of a fiercely partisan, record 50,583 crowd. Even the driving wind and rain of Manchester seemed to be in our favour. But the opening 40 minutes ended with us trailing 16–0, having played poorly to say the least. Our game plan involved tactical kicking to gain territory and push the Kangaroos back, but in reality our kicking game never got off the ground, so to speak. With continual handling mistakes compounding the situation, we missed our chance to put them under any sort of pressure. You cannot afford to give any team an advantage at the start of a series, let alone the powerful Aussies.

To our credit we rallied after the interval, and I pulled back a try. Then Joe Lydon, controversially selected at full-back, went in following a scorching 65-yard run to score the first try by a Great Britain full-back in Tests against Australia, and the best of the game. But Australia did not allow us back into it for long. Miles twice, Michael O'Connor and Garry Jack all came up with touchdowns before I picked up a second at the death. Defeated by 38–16, and conceding seven tries in the process, it was a real knock-back.

Maurice quickly decided that we may have been unfortunate and immediately announced that there would be no team changes for the second Test. The media and general public were astonished to hear it, although the players selected were both relieved and delighted that Maurice had stuck by them. In retrospect, however, it was the wrong thing to do: Maurice's strategy might have worked against New Zealand, but Australia were another division above both of us in Test terms.

Halifax, St Helens and Oldham were all swept aside as the Aussie tour really got into gear, and when 8 November came around we were under no illusions about the task ahead. But 30,808 people got behind us at Elland Road as we strove to gain a foothold in the second Whitbread Trophy Bitter Test. And for 28 minutes we were in contention, trailing by just two points. We even had the chance to go ahead when Tony Myler broke clear, only to be halted short by a Wally Lewis ankle-tap. Then we had a further chance to take the lead minutes later when Myler again went clear from outside our 22. With just full-back Garry Jack ahead, and support arriving in the form of myself, Tony Marchant and Henderson Gill, the whole arena was shocked to see Myler kick the ball over Jack's head and out through the in-goal area. A golden chance had gone begging.

Perhaps our confidence was affected, for shortly afterwards a planned move involving prop Kevin Ward and Deryck Fox failed giving Noel Cleal, the Kangaroos' second row, the chance to put loose forward Bob Lindner over near the posts. This Australian side only needed one opportunity, and they took it. They proceeded to rack up six tries in their 34–4 victory, with just the one from us as I again scored with a few minutes remaining and the game as good as over. The Aussies celebrated another famous Ashes success, while Maurice Bamford attended a very emotional post-match press conference and suggested a number of team changes in an attempt to lift the Great Britain team for the final Test in a fortnight's time.

There was little sign of any hangovers following the series win as the tourists defeated Widnes, Hull and Bradford Northern, conceding just four points in total from two penalty goals. Great Britain went into the third and final Test at Wigan with several new faces, and came fighting back. As with the previous Test series, however, we were to fall foul of a foreign referee, and this time the honour fell to French official Julien Rascagnères. I don't wish to single out referees for blame, as I have always believed that mistakes are made honestly and that they even themselves up over a season or so in a career. But this third Test threw up a number of controversial decisions that went against us at vital times.

We were very motivated: with nothing to lose and a whitewash to avoid, we were playing with great pride. Our error rate was drastically cut down, and for almost all the game we were at least the equal of the unbeaten green-and-golds. As early as the second minute we had to accept that the official had missed a forward pass from prop Greg Dowling to Gene Miles, who touched down under the posts. Notwithstanding that setback, Andy Gregory, introduced at scrum-half, was giving Aussie Peter Sterling a torrid time, and with Harry Pinner back to his best, prompting and teasing for openings, we grew in confidence. Even a second Australian try from loose forward Bob Lindner could not keep us back. After 28 minutes on we were back in business as Pinner put Tony Myler into a gap. I fought to reach him and was rewarded with a slick pass to put me over. Henderson Gill added the goal points, and we went in just 12–6 down.

We opened the second half where we had left off, and Pinner again orchestrated an opening, this time for Lee Crooks who brought on David Stephenson, the Wigan centre, and he sent me in for my second try of the afternoon and my fifth of the series. Then in stepped the referee once more to rule that a fracas between our second rower, Chris Burton of Hull KR, and the Australian captain Wally Lewis, warranted a ten-minute sin-binning for Chris, but only a finger-wagging for Wally. This allowed the Aussies to regroup, and as their winger Dale Shearer chased a hopeful kick through he was pulled back by John Basnett, his opposite number from Widnes. The kick was too long, and we had players covering in deep positions, but the official astonishingly awarded Australia a penalty try!

Joe Lydon, whose tactical kicking had been instrumental in helping us match the Aussies territorially, then converted a penalty, and I sneaked over a rare drop-goal as we clawed our way back to 15–18. It was not to be a happy ending, though, as Wally Lewis jinked through in his inimitable way with seven minutes remaining to take his side out to 24–15.

Defeat was hard to bear. We had more than matched the Australians, and with the rub of the green would surely have won. I was named Man of the Match but felt that there had been massive contributions from Gregory, Lydon, Pinner and Goodway. Some pride had been restored, but the tourists still went home unbeaten and would be remembered for that. While Wally Lewis was named Player of the Series and half-back partner Peter Sterling had shown what he was capable of, I felt we were closer to competing with the Aussies in the pack than we had been in previous years.

TEST AT CENTRAL PARK, WIGAN, 22 NOVEMBER 1986

GREAT BRITAIN 15   AUSTRALIA 24

	Great Britain	Australia
1.	Joe Lydon	Garry Jack
2.	Henderson Gill	Dale Shearer
3.	Garry Schofield	Brett Kenny
4.	David Stephenson	Gene Miles
5.	John Basnett	Michael O'Connor
6.	Tony Myler	Wally Lewis (captain)
7.	Andy Gregory	Peter Sterling
8.	Kevin Ward	Greg Dowling
9.	David Watkinson	Royce Simmons
10.	Lee Crooks	Paul Dunn
11.	Chris Burton	Mal Meninga
12.	Andy Goodway	Brian Niebling
13.	Harry Pinner (captain)	Bob Lindner
14.	Shaun Edwards	Terry Lamb
15.	Ian Potter	Les Davidson
T:	Schofield 2	Miles, Lindner, Lewis, penalty
G:	Lydon 2, Gill, Schofield dg	O'Connor 4

SUBSTITUTIONS:

Potter for Burton (63 min)

SUBSTITUTIONS:

Davidson for Dunn (73 min)

Lamb for Meninga (78 min)

Referee: J. Rascagnères (France)

Attendance: 20,169

The Test series against the 1986 Kangaroos may not have been outstanding for the British players, but the best moment for me came after the second Test. We had just been walloped by the Australians and I had scored a consolation try at the end of the game. The player I believed to be the best in the world at that time, the great Australian scrum-half Peter Sterling, came up to me and asked me to swap my Test shirt for his. To me it was just unbelievable, because I was still making my name in the international arena. Peter and I had some good times at Hull, and we had plenty of respect for each other as players, but for this guy to come up to me to swap jerseys was a real highlight – I am still proud to have it framed at home. To have Sterling's jersey, the best player I ever played with or against – among the best in the world, was a genuine honour.

Before the end of the year Maurice Bamford tendered his resignation as coach of Great Britain on the grounds of his wife's ill health. The RFL initially wanted him to remain in the post for the two Tests against France in January and February 1987, but then consulted with team manager Les Bettinson before offering the post to Mal Reilly of Castleford with immediate effect. Several Test players were ruled out of the French games through injury, and Mal Reilly made seven changes from the third Test side of the previous November for the World Cup-rated clash at Headingley.

In came winger Mark Forster from Warrington, and new half-backs in the Wigan pairing of Ellery Hanley at stand-off and Shaun Edwards at scrum-half. In the pack David Hobbs of Oldham and Castleford's hooker Kevin Beardmore were joined by Roy Haggerty of St Helens and Warrington's Mike Gregory. Amazingly, after claiming five of our six tries against the Aussie tourists, I was unable to score even one of our nine touchdowns as we won 52–4. The in-form Shaun Edwards ran amok as we pulled out all the stops to match the tally of 52 points that the Kangaroos had scored against France in December. Mike Gregory, Edwards and Hanley each bagged two tries, with

Goodway, Lydon and Forster also going over. Lydon added eight goals, and all was set fair for 8 February and the return Test in Carcassonne.

Once again, however, we found ourselves on the wrong end of a weak performance by the match officials. The French rugby league authorities had decided to sack their influential Australian coach, Tas Baitieri, and the French players provisionally refused to turn out in Carcassonne. It was just four hours before kick-off time when ex-coach Baitieri managed to change their minds. To say that they were wound up is an understatement, as they charged into us from the off. Referee Mick Stone must have wished he was back home in Sydney barbecuing! I certainly have no recollection of a fiercer game, barely within the laws, and coach Reilly was grateful for the final whistle and a 20–10 win. Early in the second half Mike Gregory sustained a broken cheekbone after a swinging right hook from prop forward Rabot – yet both players were sin-binned for ten minutes. In fact Mike was unable to continue, and Paul Dixon entered the arena as sub. Ten minutes later the other French prop, Aitlères, was sent off for kneeing me in the back as I was tackled. Otherwise there was little positive to note: I had a try disallowed, and our new half-back pairing of club-mates Shaun Edwards and Andy Gregory was not considered a success as we eventually made our way back home.

9.

CLOSING TIME AT THE BOULEVARD

HULL MANAGING DIRECTOR Roy Waudby panicked in December 1985 following defeats at St Helens and Swinton. He held an emergency board meeting, and Arthur Bunting was sacked. This was after the coach had taken Hull to 19 cup finals, 16 of which they had won! It was apparent that there was conflict among the directors of the club, one of whom, Mike Page, wanted Arthur to stay. In the end Mike had to leave the Hull board. Arthur Bunting was succeeded as coach by his assistant, Kenny Foulkes, and we finished mid-table in the championship, losing four of our last five games. Our local rivals, Hull KR, had knocked us out of the first round of the Challenge Cup, and it was clear that winds of change were starting to blow.

Hull were without the services of Peter Sterling for the 1985–86 season, and we took a little time to get going. We were unfortunate to draw Hull KR away from home in two cup competitions. They knocked us out in the first round of the Yorkshire Cup in September, in a close game, by 10–12, and we were unable to gain our revenge in the New Year when they beat us 22–6 at Craven Park in the first round of the Challenge Cup. After that Yorkshire Cup defeat we had won six out of seven league games to be handily placed in the top four. However, the events of December intervened, we conceded too many points in our remaining games and the season ended in disappointing fashion.

In June 1986 Hull appointed former Hull KR hard man Len Casey as their coach, and as you can imagine this caused quite a stir among the Airlie Bird fans. The 1986–87 season was one of contrasts, of rewarding cup campaigns and very ordinary league form, particularly over the last dozen or so games. We did, however, reach the final of the Yorkshire Cup. In the first round lowly Bramley took us all the way, holding on at 22–22 until an up-and-under was converted into a touchdown by Gary Divorty, and we went through 29–22 in the end. Another home tie saw us beat Wakefield Trinity 21–12 to line up a tricky semi-final at Odsal against Bradford Northern. A difficult game was made all the harder with the dismissal of Hull forward Steve Crooks after half an hour. But Steve's namesake Lee and 'Knocker' Norton rallied the Airlie Birds, and we came through to book our place in the final, 16–12.

We were chasing our fourth Yorkshire Cup in the last five years, but were underdogs as we faced Castleford at Headingley. Again we gave ourselves a mountain to climb when Andy Dannatt was dismissed in the first few minutes for an alleged head-butt, immediately followed from the field by Lee Crooks into the sin-bin for dissent. Down to 11 and then 12 men, we decided to throw the ball around and back our creative abilities. This policy worked for a period, and we led 18–12 at half-time. Castleford's promising hooker Kevin Beardmore then stamped his impression on the final, scoring two tries, and we were chasing the game thereafter. The critics reckoned Hull FC had played their part in an outstanding Yorkshire Cup final, even though we lost 24–31.

In the John Player Trophy first round we overcame Salford at the Willows by 27–12, and I picked up two late tries in the last four minutes. Our 48–22 second-round win against Blackpool Borough saw me score my 100th try in the game, and the quarter-final tie at Odsal against Bradford Northern was especially pleasing: I notched three touchdowns including two interceptions, one from 90 yards out, as we went through to the semi-final on the back of a 20–8 success. Drawn then against Wigan at Headingley on 20 December 1986, we outplayed them for some time and led by 11–6 following Gary Pearce's try and conversion, only to fall to Ellery Hanley's late try, going down 11–12.

The end of the 1986–87 season saw a major change to the regulations of professional rugby league. A new system for players' contracts was approved, with the introduction of an independent transfer tribunal to oversee the movement of players between clubs. This new system meant that a player was free to move to another club when his contract ended, although his old club would be entitled to claim a transfer fee. If the two clubs involved in the transfer did not agree on the fee, then the tribunal would be called in to arbitrate. The idea was to bring the game's regulations into line with those of other sports, such as professional football, but it caused only controversy and disharmony at Hull when Lee Crooks and I were offered new terms.

At Hull, Lee and I were the highest paid players on £10,000 per year. Now most players feel they should be on better contracts and, naturally enough, their boards of directors don't often see it that way: contracts are agreed on the basis of the players who are the best, in the opinion of the board, receiving the best rates. At the start of the 1986–87 season Hull had signed stand-off Gary Pearce from Welsh rugby union club Llanelli. There was nothing more certain in rugby league in those days than that players would find out the contractual arrangements of other players – or at least that they would have a pretty accurate idea. In the case of Gary Pearce, Lee Crooks and I were led to believe that Gary's contract was £20,000 per year. As this was double the amount we were receiving, we felt entitled to approach the Hull board and ask them to reassess our contracts. We did not go over the top; we simply asked them to tear up the old contracts and to increase our annual earnings to £15,000 each. After all, Gary Pearce was unproven in rugby league, and both Lee and I were Great Britain internationals.

Our contract proposals were turned down by the Hull board at the same time as we heard rumblings that the club was in a spot of financial difficulty. This seemed to be borne out by the personnel changes that were taking place, and by the impression that the club was losing some of its ambition. There had been changes on the board, and the atmosphere around the club was not as it had been a couple of years ago. While both John Rawlings and Peter Darley had significant presences at board level, the major shareholder at the club was Roy Waudby, who seemed to be pulling all the strings. Mike Page had been Roy's major opponent in the aftermath of the dismissal of Arthur Bunting, and there was one thing for sure: Mike was a black and white fan through and through, he loved the club. At this time he was trying to put together a consortium of businessmen to come up with a financial package to take the club over and bring back the good times, but Roy Waudby did not wish this to come about. Certainly it was unfortunate for Hull that the attempted take-over fell through. Coach Len Casey found it difficult to raise the team's morale as the board began to sell players on with a view to easing the financial burden.

Lee Crooks and I never really settled after the arrival of Gary Pearce, and although Len Casey tried his best to keep the two of us at the club, the Hull board made the first move: they sold Lee Crooks to Leeds rugby league club in June 1987 for a sum in the region of £150,000. This was a record transfer fee, and the deal went through while Lee was in Australia, meaning that the club had to arrange for him to fly back to sign the forms. Lee didn't want to leave Hull: he was a home-town boy and a big favourite at the club, and was very reluctant to move. I feel sure that the club could have kept one of its major assets had it wanted to go forward – but in truth the Arthur Bunting sacking was one of the major turning points.

I was also in Australia during the summer of 1987, contemplating my future at Hull FC with Lee Crooks sold and a weaker playing squad. I was approached in Sydney by Maurice Bamford, who was the Leeds coach at the time and who outlined to me the ambitions of the club's directors. Chairman Bernard Coulby was a lifelong Leeds rugby league supporter who wanted to bring back the good times, and Maurice was full of praise and enthusiasm for the new board and the direction it wished to go in. He told me that not only had Lee signed for Leeds, which I knew, but that he had also signed the Australian Test centre Peter Jackson, who had been playing with Canberra. This was followed in July by the signing of Marty Gurr from Australian club Manly, while Maurice also confirmed Leeds' interest in the New Zealand All Black rugby union forward, Mark Brooke-Cowden.

When I returned home from Australia I reluctantly put in a transfer request to the Hull board – and they turned it down flat. I knew then that my heart was no longer in the club and I could not see myself turning out for the Hull team again. In August 1987 Leeds offered two players in part-exchange for my services, my old schoolboy pal David Creasser and international second-row forward Roy Powell. It was the interest of my home-town club Leeds that had sponsored my desire to move, and I was disappointed both that my transfer request had not been granted and that Leeds' offer was rejected.

I took advice and went into dispute with the Hull club, withdrawing my labour. The Hull chairman had a close working relationship with rugby league correspondent Dick Tingle of the *Hull Daily Mail*, and I was crucified by the local paper on a regular basis. This had the effect of turning the Hull supporters against me, and I found this particularly hard to bear. I had given the club over four years of service, but the enjoyment I hope I brought to the Hull fans was quickly dissipated by the treatment I received at the hands of

Messrs Waudby and Tingle. I didn't feel it was warranted, and I was never given the opportunity to put my side of the story. There were many things I would have liked to have said but, unfortunately, the Hull public was given only one side.

A couple of months passed by, and I employed a solicitor to represent me before an RFL tribunal as I wished to claim that I was now a free agent and able to move. A transfer fee could then be agreed between the Hull and Leeds clubs. The chairman of the tribunal was Mr Ronnie Teeman, a solicitor and a member of the Rugby League Council, while Hull FC were represented by Mr Tony Sugare – also a solicitor. The hearing went against me, and my application to be declared a free agent was turned down.

Finally, in October 1987, Hull FC ended the deadlock and I signed for Leeds for a then world-record fee of £178,250 – breaking the level set when Leeds bought Lee Crooks earlier in the year. It is worth mentioning that Hull FC would not release me until I repaid my first contract payment for that season. I had to repay £3,700 plus interest and the Hull board went so far as to send me a sheriff's letter demanding settlement.

In the end I was desperate to get away from Hull as I hadn't been enjoying my rugby and I wanted now to look ahead and make the most of my career with my home town club. That said, at the same time I was sorry to leave the place where I had enjoyed my first years in the professional game and played in such an outstanding side. The experienced professionals at the Boulevard had made such an impression on me that I had at one stage wished to play for Hull for the rest of my career – but it was not to be. While there was some good young talent to come through at the club, at the time I felt personally that the directors had lost the plot when Arthur Bunting was released. A good coach is like a good bank manager: once you find one, you want to move with him.

10.

FINALLY HOME TO LEEDS

HAVING SIGNED FOR LEEDS on 23 October 1987 for a world-record fee of £178,250 (a vast amount of money in those days, and some people might say I was worth just the £250 – but that's a matter of opinion) I just wanted to start playing rugby league again. I had been involved in a bitter dispute with Hull FC, and I just wanted to get back on the field and put it all behind me.

My fitness wasn't too bad as I had been training in the meantime with a local amateur side, Bison Sports, and I was simply short of top-match fitness. Funnily enough, Bison had applied to Hull for permission to seek an amateur playing permit for me. Needless to say Hull had turned them down flat, but Bison were bang out of order – they had not even asked my permission, let alone Hull or BARLA. I had been helping them by taking training sessions with their coach Ernest Skerrett, Trevor Skerrett's brother, at their ground down Pepper Road in Hunslet.

The Sunday following my signing, I made my début for Leeds against the touring Auckland side from New Zealand. A large crowd was looking forward to my début, and in turn I was looking forward to a long and prosperous career with Leeds rugby league club. The team had made a decent start to the season, and with several new signings now including myself, the supporters were returning in large numbers. They realised that the directors under Bernard Coulby had real ambition, and what had previously been average crowds of around 5,000 were beginning to grow. Leeds was a big club and had been in the doldrums for far too long.

The Leeds dressing-room was totally different from the one I had left at Hull. To begin with Leeds had a younger squad, very much less experienced than the ones at Hull FC, and relying on senior players such as Lee Crooks, Australian prop Peter Tunks, Ray Ashton, veteran loose-forward David

Heron and now myself for advice and help. At Hull the team had been full of international players who regularly passed on good advice, and youngsters such as myself just sat back and took it all in. Now it seemed it was my turn to share my expertise and professional approach with the younger players at Leeds, as the Hull players had done with me.

The Leeds dressing-room comedian was Colin Maskill, although Colin was always one to look after his weekly wage! As for the rest of the squad, the spirit was excellent, and none of the youngsters had an ego problem. That said, Vince Fawcett was one youngster who seemed to have a big future at Leeds, having been blooded in the first team at an early age and represented his country at Colts level. But, as with so many youngsters, he felt at this point that he had arrived and stopped putting in the hard work. His timekeeping proved a problem for the coaching staff on more than one occasion. He was once invited by Malcolm Reilly to a training weekend with the Great Britain youngsters at Lilleshall. When I was called up in my early days I made certain I arrived at the meeting place half an hour before the due time. On this occasion Vince should have been at the Bentley Arms in Rothwell for a pick-up at 9 a.m.; when he arrived at 9.30 a.m., the party had already left. Knowing Malcolm Reilly as I do, I am sure that was the start of the fall from grace of Vince Fawcett after such a promising beginning. Vince wasn't the first promising youngster to miss out because of his attitude and he certainly won't be the last.

My début at Headingley had gone well for 65 minutes. I had managed to score two tries, the first after ten minutes with an interception. I enjoyed that try because I picked off a long pass by Gary Freeman, the New Zealand Test half-back. I was also a participant in the worst brawl I had ever experienced in my career in rugby league. All 26 players were involved – although I made sure I was on the fringes of it, trying to pull people apart. There had been some provocation of a verbal nature going on in the game, and in the end the Kiwis overreacted to it – although once the brawl had died down, there were no further repercussions. Although Leeds lost 25–29, we should really have won that day.

In the 65th minute I was tackled awkwardly and went over on my ankle in front of the main stand. There was some ligament damage, and I had to be carried off. The crowd were not slow in coming forward to advise the inhabitants of the Leeds directors' box to see if they could stop the cheque to

Hull. They were concerned that a world-record fee had been paid for a player who might only contribute 65 minutes to the season! As it turned out the damage was not as serious as was feared at the time, and I was able to play again just over a week later in the league match at home to the mighty Wigan. We drew 18–18 in front of over 14,000 spectators, with Lee Crooks, Dave Creasser and I scoring tries and Crooks and Creasser kicking three goals between them.

Another close game at home to St Helens saw us win 24–21 before we set out on the John Player Special Trophy road. Our first-round tie was at Whitehaven, and we were trailing 14–10 late in the game when Australian centre Peter Jackson gained an obstruction try as he attempted to chase a Lee Crooks kick. We went through 18–14 and entertained Halifax the following week, when almost 14,000 spectators saw us win 20–10. We then travelled to Springfield Borough in round three and came away from another tight game, winning 22–12. A big win against Castleford in the league at Headingley, 44–0, was just the confidence-booster we needed before we travelled to Bolton Wanderers' football ground to take on Wigan on 12 December 1987 in the semi-final of the John Player Special Trophy. We were struggling early on, having lost Lee Crooks with a dislocated shoulder and conceding a try to Stevie Hampson, their full-back. Back-rower Paul Medley then went over for a try, goaled by Colin Maskill, and after a Ray Ashton drop-goal I added a further try. Hooker Maskill completed the try-scoring to go with his conversions, and we were through to the final with a 19–6 win.

The final itself was a feast of rugby league from start to finish. We played St Helens at Central Park, Wigan, and really should have won the game. But Saints' centre Paul Loughlin scored two tries that day, and we were pipped 15–14. Some say that scrum-half Neil Holding's drop-goal in the first half was the differential that gave St Helens the cup; I am of the opinion that the crucial moment came when referee Fred Lindop – not a great lover of Leeds – allowed Paul Loughlin's second try when there clearly seemed to be a double movement in the act of scoring. But Fred used to pride himself on being 'Johnnie on the spot', and over the course of a season you can expect refereeing decisions to even themselves out, some going in your favour and some going against you. The unfortunate thing was, this one went against us in a cup final.

I also remember towards the end of the game that we worked ourselves into an excellent field position, but failed to go for a drop-goal. This would have given us a replay, but I guess that our scrum-half, Ray Ashton, was confident enough that we were capable of scoring another try to settle matters there and then. As we returned to the Wigan dressing-rooms after the game, we were all sick at heart. It did not help that our coach Maurice Bamford stormed in and laced into Ray Ashton. Maurice knew that we had missed a golden opportunity at least to gain a replay – but sometimes the wrong option is taken with the best of intentions, and it just doesn't work out.

There then followed a quite astonishing moment. One of the Leeds directors, Joe Warham, came into the dressing-room. Believe me, Central Park after losing a cup final is not the place to be: nobody wants to know you, the press aren't interested, and there is an agonising silence made all the more eerie by the echoes of the celebrations going on outside. Joe came in carrying six bottles of champagne, just to say that he felt we had competed very well and we had taken the club to a cup final and played our part in an exciting game of rugby league covered nationally by BBC Television. I can assure you that not a bottle of that champagne was opened; we just didn't feel it was the right time. I don't know what happened to it, but it's a good bet that the cleaners at Central Park enjoyed their weekend. Joe had the right sentiment but had chosen the wrong time and the wrong place.

After the cup final loss we went straight into the Silk Cut Challenge Cup campaign, where our first-round tie took us to the amateur side Kells in Cumbria. They had qualified through the preliminary rounds, and I knew them well from my BARLA days. Ties such as this are never straightforward, but Maurice Bamford seemed to be particularly on edge. As a coach Maurice was inclined to shout and bawl at his players from time to time, and the odd cup of tea would be used as a missile – that was his style. We met at Headingley at ten o'clock in the morning for the long trip and had organised a hotel in which to rest up before enjoying our pre-match meal. It was a very cold, wet and windy night on the north-west coast. Kells' ground was in Whitehaven, and it was a case of going up there, making sure we got the job done, and returning home as soon as possible. Overall the game went pretty much to plan, and we managed to win 28–0 – a result which reflected the hard work that the amateurs put in, for this was really their cup final. John Lyons was our scrum-half that day, and I felt he had a good game – in fact, a Man-of-the-Match performance. But for some reason Maurice disagreed and gave John one of the worst roastings I have ever seen from a coach to a professional player in a packed dressing-room after victory. We were all quite astonished by this, and John was pretty low on the long journey home by coach. The Australians playing with Leeds at the time particularly felt that Maurice had gone over the top and had displayed poor judgement in front of the rest of the team.

The players did not approach the Leeds directors about the incident, but the chairman of the club asked how things were in the dressing-room and if everything was all right. It must have been clear to him that something had been going on; the chairman was told in no uncertain terms that it was not a happy dressing-room, and the players believed that Maurice had lost it, that the pressure had got to him. Bernard Coulby wanted to make sure that everyone was pulling together and was doing his hardest to try to bring success back to the Leeds club. He didn't want things being spoilt, and I believe it was that game that persuaded him to make plans to bring in a new coach.

We took on Castleford at Headingley in the second round in front of almost 15,000 fans, who enjoyed another spectacular game of rugby league. Paul Medley was really flying at this stage of the season, and he went in for a hat trick of tries. We led 16–4 at half-time, but classy Cas fought back strongly and we were hanging on by our fingertips until I went in for a late try and we ended up winning 22–14. We then drew Wigan in the next round and fought for a place in the last eight in front of a massive Central Park crowd of over 25,000. After we had taken an early lead with Paul Medley and me touching down, Wigan ran away with the game to romp home 30–14.

Although we had been knocked out by the eventual cup winners, our league form dropped off and we became highly inconsistent. Then in the middle of April Maurice Bamford stepped down as team manager and was appointed as Leeds' commercial manager with Ray Abbey taking over as coach on a temporary basis to the end of the season. Meanwhile, Bernard Coulby had apparently been in negotiations with a leading international coach, and there were many rumours flying about the club as to who Maurice's replacement would be.

Ray was a super assistant coach for Leeds, but he did not get the permanent appointment as he was not a big enough name for such a big club. That must have been the only reason, for he performed his duties very creditably with the A team and the youngsters at Headingley. When a new head coach was appointed, Ray was released from the staff altogether. I am pleased to say he is still involved with coaching and doing a sterling job with Neil Kelly at Dewsbury Rams.

The saddest part of the season came for me on 6 April, when the Leeds team travelled to Hull for the league encounter between the two sides. This was the first time I had been back to my old club, and I could not believe the reception I received. I found that the sports pages of the *Hull Daily Mail* had been building the game up on the back of my return to the Boulevard, and their second highest crowd of the season gave me a dreadful welcome. As I got off the bus I was spat at, and from walking to the dressing-room until climbing back on the bus again at the end of the game I was subjected to the most disgusting verbal abuse. It wasn't just coming from adult supporters either, but was also being directed at me by youngsters, which I found quite disturbing. When I left the field at half-time I was spat on again and the same happened at full-time. After all the service I had given to the Hull club over four years and the entertainment I had provided the fans, I was appalled. That sort of attention certainly wasn't justified. To some extent I blame the local press for not giving me the chance to put my side of the story across when I was in dispute with Hull FC, but allowing themselves to be used by the chairman to protect the interests of the club rather than offering a balanced view.

I went back to Hull with Leeds on several more occasions, and every time I received similar treatment. The game as a whole has made great efforts to improve itself as a spectacle which attracts families, but the Hull supporters, or a section of them, have done nothing to further the good name of rugby league in this respect. It does sadden me, for I have two children who enjoy attending matches I am playing in, but I would never take them to the Boulevard. And I have met many rugby league fans who follow their teams both home and away, but who declare that they have been to the Boulevard just once and will never go again.

Leeds' 1987–88 season ended with a disappointing Premiership Trophy defeat at the hands of near rivals Bradford Northern, as we were outplayed 32–18 in front of 7,000 fans. Early in May, however, chairman Bernard Coulby was able to announce that he had found the coach for Leeds, and that man was Malcolm Reilly. When I heard the news I was delighted, and even more so when it was confirmed that Malcolm would be bringing in former Headingley stalwart David Ward as his assistant. David Ward's association with Leeds went back many years as he served the club magnificently as a player and as captain, and he had recently been doing a very good job as coach at Hunslet with Peter Jarvis. The Leeds club was now well and truly on the up, and although Malcolm would be dedicating part of his time to his role as Great Britain coach, the Leeds players were confident that he would bring success back to the club in the next few years.

Malcolm soon stamped his own authority at Headingley as we won through to the John Smith's Yorkshire Cup final in October 1988. We lost just two of our first 13 games of that 1988–89 season, a run which included our Yorkshire Cup campaign. Bramley were our first opponents in the competition, and a crowd of over 4,000 at McLaren Field saw us win a preliminary tie by 38–16. A difficult first-round match followed at home to Bradford Northern, and we progressed narrowly 24–21. Bradford Northern were leading 21–8 when 'super sub' Paul Medley came on and sent full-back Gary Spencer over before scoring himself and then combining with Dave Heron to give David Stephenson the match-winning try. Paul earned the Man-of-the-Match award for just 23 minutes' play, but how well deserved it was.

Another home draw in the second round, and this time we knocked Wakefield Trinity out of the cup, with Paul Medley again on the score-sheet. We then played Hull two weeks running, losing a league game away 12–14 before beating them 12–8 at Headingley in the semi-final after trailing 8–0.

The huge Australian prop-forward Sam Backo scored one try after coming on as sub with eight minutes left, and I had the satisfaction of scoring the other. Mal Reilly was really making us play at this time, and we were delighted to reach Leeds' first Yorkshire Cup final since 1980.

The week before the Yorkshire Cup final we entertained Wigan at Headingley in a Stones Bitter Championship fixture. This game ranks as one of my top ten, for I managed to score four tries, two in each half. After the game the Wigan scrum-half Andy Gregory told me that Graham Lowe, their coach, had especially stressed to my opposite number Ged Byrne the need to 'keep a tight rein on Schoey, don't give him any room'. We won the game 22–14 with what was an excellent all-round team effort, and I just happened to be in the right place at the right time that afternoon. This was proof to us that even the mighty Wigan were not invincible.

Our Yorkshire Cup final opponents at Elland Road, Leeds, on 16 October were our old rivals, Castleford. There were 23,000 packed into the stadium to witness another classic rugby league encounter. Castleford were unbeaten at the time and top of the league, and we knew we would have to play to the very best of our ability if we were finally to get our hands on the trophy again. Before both teams had really had time to warm up, I had managed to intercept a long pass and sprint 90 yards for the first touchdown. A second try followed for me later on in the first half, while Castleford replied through Giles Boothroyd and John Joyner. We went in at half-time 15–12 up. Early in the second half it was another 90-yard interception try between the posts, this time by Carl Gibson, that set us on our way to victory. As had become the norm, Paul Medley came on as sub and went in after a looping pass from Aussie stand-off Cliff Lyons,to add to Gibson's second as we ran out winners 33–12 and collected the cup. It was a proud moment for all of us, and a cracking start to Malcolm Reilly's career at Headingley.

The coaching job at Leeds was and is a huge challenge. This is a big city club, and with success come large crowds and financial support through corporate hospitality and sponsorship. The 1988–89 season went pretty well for Malcolm, bearing in mind that he was also Great Britain coach, as we reached the quarter-finals of the Silk Cut Challenge Cup before being knocked out by the in-form team, Widnes, in a match which attracted a colossal crowd of 26,303. Widnes ended up winning the Stones Bitter Championship, while we finished third behind them and Wigan – a fair achievement in Malcolm's first year. We should have progressed further in the Premiership Trophy but were knocked out 15–12 at home to Featherstone Rovers in a tight first-round game.

I had a brief spell in Australia following a recommendation to Western Suburbs by Ellery Hanley. I played eight games that summer before returning to Leeds. Our pre-season work with Malcolm went very well that summer, although we were defeated by Wakefield Trinity at Headingley in our first game of the 1989–90 campaign. We then travelled to Barrow, winning 32–10 in what turned out to be John Holmes' last game. To everybody's surprise Malcolm decided the day after that he wished to resign. I am still not sure as to his reasons, but the timing was all wrong for us: a new coach would have to come in with preparations complete, new signings made and the season under way. Possibly Malcolm realised that the Leeds job was big enough to undertake on its own, and because he always sought to make a success of anything he undertook to do, he wished to concentrate all his energies on the

Great Britain challenge. In a way, he showed great courage in making the decision he did. The success Malcolm has enjoyed subsequently, not only with Great Britain but also in Australia with the Newcastle Knights, would to my mind make him a strong candidate to return to the coaching position at Headingley should a vacancy arise in the next few years.

That Barrow game, incidentally, was my one and only appearance in the same team as the Leeds legend, John Holmes. John was heavily involved with the A team at Headingley, playing and assisting with the coaching, but on this particular day he had been called up at short notice to play the first team at Barrow. My abiding memory of that day is of John sitting fully clothed in collar and tie in the dressing-room until 20 minutes before kick-off, when he leisurely stripped off, changed and ran out on to the field with us. He did not loosen up in any way or make any real attempt to communicate with his fellow team-mates. When I spoke with his contemporaries, David Ward, Alan Smith and John Atkinson, they confirmed that this was precisely his pre-match ritual in his regular playing days. And it was a routine which clearly worked for John, as he played over 600 games for the Leeds club. It would be interesting to observe him participating in the modern warm-ups before Super League matches. Many of us who played in the 1980s and early 1990s would be exhausted before kick-off today!

The Leeds directors acted swiftly by appointing Malcolm's deputy, David Ward, to the post of head coach. This was a great move in my view, and the players and fans were delighted to have a person at the helm who was Leeds through and through. The team spirit under David was excellent, the best I have known, and that was his way. He wasn't the best tactician, but he had inspired those he had played with and captained through his passion for the game, and that quality was undiminished when he took over as coach. To me, a great team spirit goes 75 per cent of the way towards success at the top clubs. David immediately appointed Norman Smith to be his assistant and gave John Holmes the task of coaching and managing the A team alongside Paul Gill. This backroom staff knew the Leeds set-up inside out, and I was looking forward so much to taking Leeds to the top where they have always belonged.

We met at Wigan on four occasions that season drawing 10–10 and taking them to a replay in the Regal Trophy, before going out at Central Park 0–8. With seven Stones Bitter Championship games left, we lost 14–21 at home, Creasser and Farcett touching down for Leeds. Winger Mark Preston scored

Wigan's winning try and with just three games remaining he came back to haunt us again with a brace of touchdowns, as we lost 12–16 at Central Park. This televised game was hard fought with Carrill Heugh scoring for us and Colin Marskell kicking four goals. Four points separated us at the end of the season, but it could so easily have been the other way around.

It was the following summer that the Leeds board almost lost their new coach. I remember Leeds entering a prestigious seven-a-side rugby league tournament around the time that we had been told of a Kenyan called Eddie Rombo, who was a flying winger. The directors decided to give Eddie a trial and played him in the sevens team. To me, seven-a-side is a Mickey Mouse game, not too closely related to the 13-a-side rugby we played week in and week out. But Eddie certainly showed that he was fast in that tournament, and the Widnes coach Doug Laughton was to be found discussing him with a number of people there, including members of the Leeds board. The impression was that this player could be the next Martin Offiah, and Leeds were determined not to miss another star: the directors panicked and signed Eddie Rombo in a blaze of publicity straight after the tournament on the Monday. When we next reported for training, it was clear David Ward had not been party to the signing.

I believe David marched into the boardroom and offered to resign, claiming that the directors did not have faith in his ability to manage the team and were interfering in his work. He felt that the club couldn't just give the guy a trial in a seven-a-side setting, and then offer him a three-year contract. By all means give him half a dozen trial games, and then – but only then – make a rational judgement. The players supported David Ward and persuaded him to stay at the club. We had taken Wigan to the wire in the 1989–90 Championship, finishing runners-up, and we hoped to go one better the following season. We believed that if the board backed David financially in the close season, enabling him to bring in three or four more players of quality, we could take that championship away from the cherry-and-whites.

Season 1990–91 was to be David Ward's last as coach of Leeds. Bradford Northern knocked us out of the Yorkshire Cup in the first round in August by 16–24, and a recruit from local rugby union, Simon Irving, made his début that day. I well remember Simon's first training session with us: he made the mistake of having an early tea before joining us at 7 p.m., when the extra intensity of pre-season work made its mark and Simon brought up his tea! He learned very quickly, and never ate before training again. That summer we also welcomed the New Zealand rugby union international full-back, John Gallagher, who came to the club with an outstanding pedigree in the 15-a-side game. Sadly, he was never able to hit the same heights in rugby league, although that may have been due to a very heavy tackle he took early on while playing for Leeds against St Helens.

We played the 1990 Australian tourists at Headingley in October and gave them their hardest game outside the Test matches, eventually going down 10–22. We were starting to run into form, although we had been unable to win at Widnes or Wigan, when the directors decided that the coach and his playing staff should spend four days away in Blackpool in the build-up to our second-round Silk Cut Challenge Cup tie away to Bradford Northern. Looking back, I believe it was a mistake to take the full 25-man squad, and I will explain why. We stayed at a fine hotel, the Pembroke, and were joined there by a couple of the directors, Alf Davies and Michael Stockdale – which admittedly seemed strange at the time. When David announced his team on the Friday evening to play Bradford Northern on the Sunday at Odsal, clearly ten of the 25 players had to be left out. Unfortunately these players, or a number of them at least, decided there was no point attending team meetings and went out on the drink. The two Leeds directors may well have taken this as a lack of support for David Ward as club coach, and this may equally have contributed towards the decision they took at the end of the season.

We lost to Bradford on the Sunday by 5–0. We went on to finish fifth in the Stones Bitter Championship and visited Castleford in the Premiership Trophy – a match which brought me into conflict with my old pal Lee Crooks. Very early on in the game I intercepted a low pass by Castleford's John Joyner and went in under the posts from 75 yards out. To my horror, my team-mate Phil Ford met me as I turned to walk back and said, 'Make sure you don't lose it, Schoey – he's disallowed it!' On hearing this I was stunned for a second, then I charged back 70 yards to referee Jim Smith to ask: 'Why have you disallowed the try, ref?' Jim's reply was simply, 'Knock-on, scrum defence.' I then verbally expressed my true feelings in no uncertain terms. The Castleford captain then entered the debate, as my old friend and ex-team-mate Lee Crooks advised the official, 'Don't let him speak to you like that, ref. Put him in the sin-bin to cool down.' I told Lee to keep his mouth shut, but it was too late: Jim Smith sent me to the sin-bin for ten minutes.

I am pleased to say that I had the last laugh, scoring the winning try under the posts after evading three Castleford defenders – including dear old Crooksy. Shortly afterwards, the final whistle blew, and I immediately looked round for Lee to shake his hand with a big smile on my face. He was nowhere to be seen!

We progressed to the semi-final, and a visit to the Boulevard to play Hull FC. For 78 minutes of the game we were by far the better team, only to be beaten at the death when their Australian scrum-half Greg Mackey launched a high bomb. Our full-back John Gallagher dropped the ball under the posts for Hull to score a try that put them through to the Premiership final. Once again under David Ward we had come close, but not close enough.

Shortly after that semi-final defeat in the Premiership Trophy, Alf Davies asked if Adele and I would go on behalf of the Leeds club to the RFL's end-of-season awards dinner. At that time Bass Brewers were the club sponsors and my wife and I were to be guests of Bass that evening. The awards dinner was held in Manchester, and I cannot say that I was too bothered about going, so my wife and I called in at the Town Hall Tavern on the way over. That evening Tom Collins was fighting in Leeds Town Hall, and the Town Hall Tavern landlord, Laurie Graham, offered me two tickets. It was Adele who suggested that we both really ought to go to the awards dinner and not let the club down, so in the end I turned the tickets down and we drove across to Manchester. We were greeted by David Howes and Tracey Barr from the RFL, who were both delighted to see us, and we had the best of evenings on the Bass table as they made us very welcome.

The awards began with the Second Division Player of the Year, followed by the First Division Player of the Year, the Young Player of the Year, the Top Try-scorer, Top Goalkicker, Top Points-scorer, Top Referee and, eventually, the Top Coach. This last award went to John Monie of Wigan; Dougie Laughton had been nominated, but was not at the dinner to receive his prize.

Then finally it came to the most prestigious annual rugby league award, the Man of Steel. The BBC's Harry Gration was master of ceremonies, and he began by telling everyone that the 1991 Man of Steel had represented his country ten times over the last 12 months and had played a leading part in the success of the 1990 tour Down Under. I was overwhelmed, for I suddenly realised that Harry was talking about me. This award came completely out of the blue, and indeed, if it hadn't been for my wife Adele, I might not even have been there to receive it.

I accepted the award and dedicated it to David Ward, the Leeds coach, who had played me at stand-off half and stuck by me, allowing me to establish myself there not only with the Leeds club, but eventually also for Great Britain. I thanked my team-mates at Headingley who had supported me throughout a successful season with the club. How tragic, then, that seven days after this dinner Leeds made the announcement that David Ward had been sacked and would be replaced by Dougie Laughton. My nightmare was about to begin: as they say, what a difference one week can make.

The manner in which David found out he had been relieved of his position was nothing short of disgraceful. At the end of the Premiership final between Hull and Widnes at Old Trafford, the television summariser for the BBC, Alex Murphy, announced that, 'This is Dougie Laughton's last game as Widnes coach – he will be taking over the Leeds job tomorrow.' How interesting it would have been if we had beaten Hull and taken on Widnes at the Premiership final! Clearly the Leeds board had moved for Dougie Laughton some weeks earlier – but the way that David Ward found out was very unprofessional, not being told, but hearing from Alex Murphy on the TV. It seems that one Leeds director, Harry Jepson, did not know that David was to be replaced either.

The players whom David had coached over the previous two seasons were shocked and saddened, for we felt that he was getting the job done. The board would no doubt argue that they wanted somebody with a proven track record, and at Widnes Dougie Laughton had that. But I felt he was the wrong man for the job at the time, and that David Ward should have been given another year at the very least. David remains involved in the professional game at Batley Bulldogs, the Northern Ford Premiership side, and he still refuses to comment on the events surrounding his departure from Headingley, nor will he openly criticise the club he served with such dignity and commitment.

I also heard from a reliable source that not only had Roger Millward been interviewed twice by the Leeds chief executive for the position of head coach, but he had then been told the job was his! Did Roger turn the offer down? If he did, he certainly owes me! How much more could Leeds and I have achieved if the fates had been kinder and Roger had been appointed instead of Dougie Laughton? This is where my nightmare was to begin.

11.

ALMOST TOPS UNDER REILLY

AFTER TAKING CHARGE of the Great Britain set-up in January 1987, coach Mal Reilly had to wait some 15 months before embarking on his first major campaign with the 18th British Lions tour Down Under. This was preceded the previous autumn by a 42–0 whitewash of Papua New Guinea on 24 October – the Kumuls, as they were known, being on their first-ever visit to Great Britain. I missed that Test through injury, but two Whitbread Trophy Bitter Tests with France followed in early 1988, and while coach Reilly used these three games to look at several players on the fringe of international selection and 25 players in all were called up, I was selected for both French matches.

I touched down twice in Avignon, the second a 95-yard interception with seconds to go. This gave us a record win, 28–14, against the French on their own soil, although we were never at our best, making numerous handling errors and finishing badly. Indeed, the speed of our wingers, Des Drummond of Warrington and new cap Martin Offiah, was crucial to our defensive effort as they got back to stop a number of French breaks that could have cost us dear. Both also touched down, with Martin's the first of what was to be many. The Test was remarkably penalty-free, and forwards Hugh Waddell of Oldham and Roy Powell of Leeds did their tour chances no harm at all.

Two weeks later we triumphed 30–12 at Headingley, again without ever reaching the heights. Skipper Ellery Hanley scored two tries, while I notched one try, thanks to Ellery, and kicked five goals with Andy Gregory and David Plange of Castleford completing the try-scoring. Wigan's Stevie Hampson was named Man of the Match for his attacking play from full-back, and Castleford's hooker Kevin Beardmore topped the tackle count. On 5 April coach Mal Reilly named 23 of his Great Britain squad to tour Papua New

Guinea, Australia and New Zealand that summer, with Joe Lydon set to join up in June after completing some exams. Three further places were left open subject to fitness assessments.

No sooner were the names announced than Steve Hampson broke his arm; he proved unable to join the tour at a later stage, as was originally planned. A few days later Andy Goodway withdrew, citing the demands of his new restaurant business as the cause. Next to miss departure were Joe Lydon, already due to join up late, and Des Drummond, both of whom were the subject of legal proceedings involving alleged assaults on spectators. Finally, Andy Platt, the St Helens prop, injured his ankle and could not travel with the rest of the squad. This trend was unfortunately to continue as the tour progressed. It was always going to be a gruelling and challenging trip, but even before a ball was kicked we were under tremendous pressure. In addition the tour organisers had given us a Test match for our first fixture and, with it, World Cup ranking points at stake.

We set off from home shores on 16 May, the day after the Stones Bitter Premiership finals. Mal Reilly was very ably supported by tour manager Les Bettinson, business manager David Howes, assistant coach Phil Larder, Dr Forbes Mackenzie, and physiotherapist Geoff Plummer. The squad spent more than three days reaching Papua New Guinea, before acclimatising for just three more days. Defeat at the Lloyd Robson Oval in Port Moresby would have been a serious setback. The heat was oppressive, and with 12,000 vociferous fans inside the ground and many more in the trees overlooking the stadium, we needed to be at our best. But we could not have had a worse start as Shaun Edwards suffered a knee injury after just seven minutes, jetting home for a cartilage operation on 4 June.

We had been given valuable medical advice and never missed an opportunity to take in liquid during the game. The plan was to score as often as we could in the first 40 minutes, and then cope as best we could in the second half. This worked well to begin with: Andy Gregory put myself and Paul Medley in for early tries, both goaled by Paul Loughlin, and Henderson Gill then went over wide out. Paul Loughlin was taking longer and longer with his conversion attempts as we carefully conserved our energy. Despite a solo effort from Dairi Kovae, their full-back, we scored two more converted tries before the interval, through Mike Gregory and myself. Although we went in 28–6 up at half-time, the scene in the dressing-room was nothing short of alarming. Players were struggling to breathe normally, and some were physically sick. It took so much out of you simply to change into a dry shirt. I don't know where Malcolm and Dr Forbes Mackenzie got so much ice from, but it was most useful in cooling down towels to wrap around us. With 17 minutes remaining the Kumuls had come back to within eight points of us, and for the last ten minutes we played by instinct. Skipper Ellery Hanley pulled off two brilliant try-saving tackles before his long pass put me away, and I drew the full-back to put in my centre partner, David Stephenson. This try finally broke their resistance, and Henderson Gill raced over five minutes from time to seal a far from comfortable 42–22 win.

My first taste of Papua New Guinea had been quite a culture shock, with the many scenes of poverty and violence. We were confined to our hotel during the visit, and the local news was full of tribal conflict, violence towards women, and even cannibalism. Little did I know how close I would come to experiencing the violence at first hand on my next tour Down Under. Our other fixture was in Lae and resulted in a comfortable win over Northern/Highland Zones by 36–18. I was given the captaincy for the first time, while Martin Offiah marked his tour début with three tries and Phil Ford chipped in with two. Ellery Hanley came on as sub and set up a try for me, and with Lee Crooks successfully overcoming the humid conditions for his first full 80 minutes in six months, the management were glad we were over the first hurdle.

We flew on to Australia and started well with a big win in Cairns over North Queensland, 66–16. I was rested for this fixture as Martin Offiah introduced himself to the home fans with four outstanding tries. Mike Ford came in at scrum-half to score three tries, followed closely by his namesake Phil Ford with two more; two from Paul Medley and one from Paul Dixon completed the try-scoring. Match-day, 27 May, was also the date on which Mal Reilly agreed to join Leeds as their new coach with effect from the end of the tour, so we had a double celebration that evening.

Moving down to Sydney we came up against Newcastle Knights, our toughest test to date, and triumphed 28–12. Scrum-half Andy Gregory was outstanding as he helped Kevin Ward to a try before combining with Ward to send Offiah racing through for a second. Despite a Newcastle fightback, skipper Ellery Hanley touched down twice before Offiah sealed matters with his second. The Australian media were rather subdued after the game: they had slagged us off from the beginning, and a Newcastle defeat had not been in their scripts.

Four days later in Tamworth, our euphoria proved to be misplaced as we suffered our first defeat of the tour and Great Britain's heaviest outside Tests for 68 years, going down 36–12 to Northern Division. This five-try hammering just a week before the first Test was the last thing we needed. As skipper I was devastated, and Mal Reilly locked us all in the dressing-room afterwards and gave us a real verbal lashing for half an hour. This country fixture was not our most competitive on paper, although the inadequacies of our itinerary were about to be emphasised as our next match was just two days later, on 7 June against Grand Final winners Manly.

Bearing in mind that the first Test was to take place four days later, on 11 June, we were under the cosh. Most of our Test team were rested at Brookvale Oval, and we went down 30–0 against a less than full-strength Manly side. Five tries were conceded, and Great Britain were nilled for the first time in Australia outside the Test arena. We were playing into the hands of the pommie-bashing Aussie press, who promptly forecast a walkover in the forthcoming international.

The first Test, the 100th between the two countries, was dubbed the Centenary Test, and was a big part of Australia's bicentennial celebrations. But the match did not develop as the home fans had anticipated. Our coach was not one to lack confidence in his own ability, and he conveyed to us his belief and desire. We worked on getting into Australia's faces from the start, not allowing them to settle or play the football we knew they were capable of if we gave them time and room. The plan was executed well, and for 60 minutes we were never behind. Paul Loughlin kicked a penalty after 12 minutes, and just before the break skipper Ellery Hanley produced a dummy and shuffled sideways, crab-like, before handing off Peter Sterling and plunging over to take us out to 6–0.

Malcolm warned us to expect Australia to raise their game from the restart, and they did exactly that. Their coach Don Furner sent Peter Sterling back on for the second half despite a shoulder injury, and he began to combine with Wally Lewis to throw the ball around while the rest of his team-mates backed one another up at speed. Sterling set up giant Canberra prop Sam Backo from close range in the 50th minute by means of a miskick, and then Peter Jackson, the Canberra centre, went in despite our claims for obstruction, both tries being converted by Michael O'Connor. The 12–6 scoreline was not comfortable enough for the Aussies and Wally Lewis knew this, dropping a goal with 11 minutes left on the clock. A late Jackson try and a 17–6 victory flattered the Kangaroos, particularly as a Great Britain try had been refused at 12–6 for a forward pass from Ward to Andy Gregory.

Kevin Ward was named Man of the Match, although nothing could salve his dejection and that of the whole touring party. Platt, Dixon and Beardmore also tackled out of their skins, and yet we were one down with two to play. While pride had been put back in the Great Britain jersey, it was also the first time a British squad had lost three successive matches on tour.

My personal disappointment was compounded just four days later in Brisbane. Eight minutes into the game against a Combined Brisbane XIII, I scored a try, and five minutes later my tour was over. I suffered a fractured cheekbone and once again returned home early from Australia. Great Britain won 28–14 and went on to win three more provincial games in Rockhampton, Toowoomba and Gympie before returning to Lang Park in Brisbane for the second Test.

Although we went down 34–14 our two tries by Phil Ford and Martin Offiah were rightly acclaimed as the best of the match. Both were long-range efforts and typified the classy backs in the side. The final score did not fully reflect the efforts of the team, and Andy Gregory was named Man of the Match, although he finished in the sin-bin. Mal Reilly conceded that he may have put too much emphasis on motivation, as we conceded numerous penalties for rugged play. This was our 15th successive Test loss to the Kangaroos, and the final Test was just 11 days away. Taking our mounting injury list into account, the squad were down but not out.

Once again our tour itinerary stacked the odds against us. Four days before the third Test we had to play a President's XIII in Canberra and the Aussies took great delight in fielding their strongest side of players not involved in the forthcoming Test. The strength in depth Down Under was emphasised as Great Britain went down by 24 points to 16. In very British rain and mud we shipped tries from Meninga, Lazarus, Alexander, O'Brien and Bradley, all of whom were to become players of international renown. Phil Ford displayed outstanding running from full-back with two sparkling tries, and the depleted tourists fought back hard but to no avail.

By this stage, a total of ten players had withdrawn from the original tour party through a combination of unavailability and injuries suffered both before and during the tour. But the third Test was to be Great Britain and Malcolm Reilly's finest hour. His pride, self-belief and determination were fuelled by the taunting quotes of the Australian management in the days before this final game. The Sydney Football Stadium contained just 15,994 spectators on 9 July 1988, and they were to witness one of the great Test triumphs.

On the eve of the match two more players withdrew, stand-in hooker Paul Groves from St Helens and his cover, Widnes's Richard Eyres. Back-row forward Paul Hulme moved in as fourth-choice hooker, and Hugh Waddell made his tour début in Tests. The coach and his back-up staff prepared the 15 players as meticulously as ever and passed their mood of confidence through to the lads. Tackles were made, and the big Australian forwards backpedalled as Andy Gregory pinned them in their own half with well-judged kicks. The backs showed their talent, and the in-form Phil Ford at full-back was denied a good claim for a touchdown before Martin Offiah went over 16 minutes into the game, thanks to that man Andy Gregory and the mighty Kevin Ward. The irrepressible Ford then jinked his way past four green-and-gold jerseys to touch down by the posts, Paul Loughlin goaled, and half-time came with a 10–0 lead.

Wally Lewis tried to drive his team back into it after the interval scoring himself as he pulled clear of Phil Ford's despairing tackle. O'Connor goaled to make it 10–6. Andy Gregory had given Peter Sterling a torrid time in the first half, and the Parramatta scrum-half had been replaced at half-time by Gary Belcher. Lewis clearly missed his classy half-back partner, and Mal Reilly's lionhearts were not going to accept second-best. Gregory fooled the Aussie defence with a grubber kick from which Henderson Gill scored, and with another Loughlin goal we led again by ten points. A Sam Backo try, goaled by O'Connor, reduced the lead only for a confident Loughlin to stride clear three minutes later to put in Gill for his second try. Who can forget 'Hendy's' sensational celebrations after this brilliant touchdown!

The final score of the series was one of the best, with Andy Gregory beating several defenders deep in his own half before releasing second-row forward and namesake Mike Gregory 70 yards out. Martin Offiah was outside him, but Mike made it easily to the posts, with both Wally Lewis and Wayne Pearce trailing in his wake. The British fans in the ground went wild

ABOVE: Delighted to be named captain for the New Zealand Test series
BELOW: Training's more enjoyable under Dean Bell

ABOVE: 1991: This is the closest Doug Laughton and myself were during the four years Doug was at Headingley. This is where my nightmare begins

OPPOSITE PAGE: Myself, Adele, Jonathan and Danielle delighted about the announcement of my OBE for services to rugby league

Working hard for Great Britain at a training camp at Catterick Army Barracks

ABOVE: Scoring an interception try in the semi-final for Leeds against Leigh

BELOW: Carl Gibson, Paul Dixon, Roy Powell and myself – the team spirit that David Ward inspired at Leeds

ABOVE: 1984: Myself, Frank Myler and Joe Lydon
getting set to take on the Aussies in 1984

OPPOSITE PAGE: 1984: Delighted at scoring my first try for
Great Britain against Australia at the
Sydney Cricket Ground

Peter Sterling – the best player I've played with, or against

as Loughlin added the two points, and we hung on for nine more minutes to beat the Australian XIII soundly by 26–12.

My regret at missing the latter stage of the tour disappeared, as I felt so much pride in Malcolm and all the players out there. As a coach he proved with this win that Great Britain were in good hands, and he must have enjoyed the after-match press conference and the chance to give it to the team's critics in the media. One in particular, Peter Fellingoss, an Australian hack, came under deservedly heavy fire after being barred from our dressing-room and from any contact with management or players.

It is worth recording, too, the significance of the win. It was Great Britain's first in Australia for 14 years, and ended a run of 15 consecutive Aussie successes. The victory was our first against Australia for over a decade, and our 50th in total against the old enemy. Oh, and it had been designated a World Cup-rated fixture. The two points gained meant that we needed just one more from our final game of the qualifying competition in Christchurch on 17 July to make it through to the final.

Mal Reilly's battered squad immediately moved on to New Zealand, overcoming Wellington 24–18, and just eight days after the Sydney Test we were facing the Kiwis in Christchurch. But the weather conditions hindered our back division, and we were pipped 12–10. Talking with some of the lads on their return home, it was clear that they were very disappointed to have missed out on an appearance in the World Cup final. The rub of the green did not go their way in Christchurch, with referee Mick Stone from Australia ruling out an Andy Gregory try for a forward pass and hardly penalising the home side at all in the second period. Ellery Hanley went off with a bad facial injury in the second half as the Lions pressed for the one chance that would tie the game and earn the single point we needed. Mistakes were made, and Paul Loughlin could not repeat his excellent goalkicking performance of the Sydney Test. It was New Zealand, then, who went forward to the World Cup final, losing 25–12 to Australia in Auckland on 9 October 1988.

On 21 September 1988 I was one of four Leeds players to represent Yorkshire in the Rodstock War of the Roses at Headingly. We managed to triumph 24–14, and I intercepted a Derek Pyke pass for our final try. The following month at Headingley I turned out for Great Britain as we took on the Rest of the World and won 30–28. Once more I managed our final touchdown. Regrettably, a leg injury from the Roses clash ruled me out of both Tests with France and the summer tour to New Zealand.

In March 1990, Mal Reilly selected a team to take on the French in Perpignan. We won 8–4 but found France a well-prepared side as they looked forward to a summer trip to Australia. I kicked two goals, but few players performed at their best that day. Three weeks later, in the return at Headingley, Malcolm made several changes with the forthcoming tour to New Zealand and Papua New Guinea in mind, selecting Gerald Cordle, the Welsh winger from Bradford Northern, Carl Gibson of Leeds and Karl Fairbank, also of Bradford Northern. Poor Gerald was destined to become one of the small band of one-Test wonders, as the French deserved to win 25–18, and the experimental half-back partnership of Castleford's Graham Steadman and Shaun Edwards did not click at all.

A number of top players withdrew from that summer's tour party including Hanley, Platt, Hampson, Loughlin and Edwards. With an average age of less than 23, the Lions were once again cast in the role of underdogs for the three-Test series against New Zealand that would be preceded by the banana skin of two Tests in Papua New Guinea. I was asked to be skipper Mike Gregory's vice-captain and was honoured to accept. I felt fit mentally and physically and was looking forward to a cracking – and this time, I hoped, complete – British Lions tour.

We arrived in Papua New Guinea and immediately began acclimatising following a long journey. In my case I had left Rothwell, South Leeds, 42 hours earlier, and within 45 minutes of reaching our hotel in Port Moresby we went on a training run. It damn near killed us all! We found that little had changed for the better since our last visit – in fact, the general situation seemed far worse. You wouldn't even send your mother-in-law there, as Ian Botham might have remarked! The country is like no other I have ever visited, and I can remember the tour management being very concerned over the financial arrangements. The local officials at the games were more concerned with being seen in the club bar than they were with ensuring that spectators entering the ground through the turnstiles actually paid.

The troubles off the field were repeated on the terraces at the matches we played, which was really quite frightening. During our second match, against the Northern/Highland Zone in Lae, the police fired volleys of rifle shots over the crowd and let off tear-gas canisters – but unfortunately the police were panicking as much as the players, and the canisters were thrown all over the place. The Lions team all huddled together in the middle of the field and were quickly joined by the rest of the touring party from the benches. It appeared that the police were trying to stop the locals entering the ground, but as a result those people in the ground, when faced with the tear-gas, were now trying to get out of the ground. Somehow we finished the game, although there were pockets of trouble continuing in the half-empty stadium. Had any players tried to leave the field I am sure we would not have seen them again.

Unbelievably, we had further problems during the first Test at Goroka. On the way to the Danny Leahy Oval our coach (the motor variety!) was surrounded by natives, and we could not move. Malcolm Reilly bravely stepped off the coach and tried to persuade the crowd to clear a passage so that we could get to the ground in time to play. Shortly after the match started, the rifles and tear-gas appeared again as fans throwing stones outside the ground had to be cleared away. But the gas blew back across the stadium, and the detrimental effects of it and the three-minute stoppage it caused may have been a contributory factor in the 20–18 defeat we suffered after leading 18–8. I had been selected as stand-off, which was a new experience for me on the Test match stage, and I must admit to having a poor game.

After more tear-gas and riots in our next match against Islands Zone in Rabaul, we sought revenge on the field in the second Test at Port Moresby. I was much happier with my performance in the 40–8 victory, creating four tries and scoring a very satisfying touchdown myself from 50 yards out. Thankfully the game was trouble-free both on and off the field, and we were relieved to make our escape to the calmer climes of New Zealand.

It was the New Zealand leg of the tour that gave me my greatest satisfaction. After my disaster at stand-off in the first Test in Papua New Guinea, it seemed that I could do no wrong in the series that followed against the Kiwis.

Shortly after we reached New Zealand the Widnes full-back, Alan Tait, had to return home suffering from a groin injury. It transpired that upon his return, Alan was asked to give a newspaper interview in which he criticised the fact that the players had had very few days off and the lack of social activity on tour. This was probably because Alan was more used to being away on rugby union tours, where the social side of things was more significant. This was his first rugby league tour abroad, and manager

Maurice Lindsay and Mal Reilly had made sure that their approach was extremely professional and detailed. The players had little time to socialise, and Alan was simply not expecting this. Maurice Lindsay wanted to take action against Alan for his comments, and asked me to back him up with regard to the businesslike purpose of our tour and our preparations.

We were a very inexperienced touring party, and after a narrow victory over the President's XIII, 23–22, we struggled, losing to Canterbury Select by 18–10 and a strong Auckland side by 24–13. This last was considered our hardest game outside the three Tests, and unfortunately the weather played a hand as the pitch soon became a paddy-field. The first half was particularly violent: there were three bust-ups between the sides before the referee took any action. Although we had lost, the tour management felt that the forwards led by Roy Powell and Wigan's Denis Betts had worked hard in the conditions, and our preparations were proceeding well for the first Test. Three days later we confirmed that impression when the midweek side defeated Kiwi Colts 22–10, which gave the whole squad a boost before Palmerston North.

Again I remember most of all the awful weather we had to endure in that first Test. Mal Reilly selected me at stand-off, and I believe I repaid his confidence in me as we won a close game 11–10 after trailing twice. Skipper Mike Gregory and Paul Dixon carried the fight to the New Zealand forwards, but we were already trailing 4–0 after ten minutes when I was able to break a tackle and release wingman Jonathan Davies for our first touchdown. A Kevin Iro try followed for the Kiwis, though we were able to draw level just before half-time as I released Paul Dixon, who then put Carl Gibson over – a real Leeds effort, this. We had planned our strategy around a good kicking game in order to pin New Zealand in their own territory as much as possible, and in the second period this worked like a dream. The only score of the half was a drop-goal I managed to put over after 57 minutes which enabled us to win the first Test 11–10.

Three more games followed before the second Test in Auckland, and despite losing to Wellington – the first international team to do so – we took wins against the New Zealand Maoris and a Taranaki Invitation XIII. The attendances for these games were poor, and I believe the tour overall was not a great financial success.

The second Test was another close affair. We were still regarded as underdogs by the media, but once again we proved them wrong – this despite a number of decisions by the Australian referee Bill Harrigan going against us, to give an overall penalty count of 14–3 in the Kiwis' favour. As a result, their full-back Matthew Ridge kicked five penalty goals, but it did not prevent us from winning 16–14. I sold a dummy after 33 minutes to go in under the posts, and Denis Betts forced his way over early in the second half to give us a 12–8 lead. New Zealand came back with a Mark Horo try and a penalty goal, but the game was settled in our favour seven minutes from time with a typical show of speed and finesse from our winger, Martin Offiah. Martin had joined up with the party at the start of the New Zealand leg of the tour, and his class was clearly evident as he sped over from 40 yards out to give us the victory we deserved in both the match and the series. New Zealand had pushed us all the way, but great credit must go to Malcolm Reilly for motivating and guiding such a young squad to two Test victories.

The third Test in Christchurch was yet another close affair, and this time Martin Offiah was cast in the role of villain. Shortly after kick-off a length-of-the-field move by Great Britain should have been finished off by Martin under the posts, but as he went to touch down one-handed he lost the ball and the six points with it. It made all the difference in the end, as we went down 21–18. Although we trailed 20–6 early in the second half, late tries from Roy Powell and Martin Offiah brought us back into it, but were not enough to pull the game out of the bag. I was disappointed that we did not win all three Tests in New Zealand, but I enjoyed my stand-off battle with Tony Kemp to score an early try thanks to another dummy.

It seemed that most of the options I chose during the series came off. After selling a dummy to score a try in our 11–10 win in the first Test, I managed to use the dummy to even greater effect in the second Test. My try in that match was the result of the same gambit, and I repeated the move in the third Test to similar effect – also using it to set up Roy Powell later in the game. The dummies worked like a dream: it seems that only the New Zealand TV commentator could see them coming, and he was trying to warn his fellow countrymen, to no avail.

All three Tests had been nip-and-tuck, but a touring party that nobody had any great hopes for had won a series in New Zealand. Not only that, but players such as Mike Gregory and Jonathan Davies had truly arrived on the international rugby league stage. Afterwards our coach Mal Reilly was clearly looking forward with relish to the forthcoming visit of the Australians in 1990.

He also told us in no uncertain terms that we could beat the Kangaroos and that nothing would give us greater pleasure in our careers. He believed that those players who had not made the tour would really have to prove themselves if they were going to break into the Great Britain team to play in the three Tests in the autumn, and this lifted us all. Malcolm worked very hard to give his players the confidence to play to the best of their ability.

When the plans had been made for the Papua New Guinea and New Zealand tour, the management had felt that it would help team morale if two breaks were organised for the players. The first took place before we arrived in New Zealand, when we spent four days in Cairns on the northern coast of Australia. This proved to be a great mistake, for the whole squad hit the beer for two solid days. When our sponsors announced that a trip to the Great Barrier Reef had been arranged for day four, it was a real setback for them to find that no one in the party could take any more alcohol, and the planned refreshments had to be returned!

The second tour break was actually planned for after the New Zealand Test series. We were booked to stay on the Pacific island of Hawaii for a few days before flying home to our families, wives and girlfriends although, as you can imagine, the great majority of us just wanted to get back to Britain as soon as we could. A number of us were carrying injuries, and a number of us were short of funds. Our tour manager Maurice Lindsay disappeared at this point, not bidding us farewell but simply returning home. The stopover was a very quiet affair in spite of our successful tour, and we foolishly travelled back home in beach shirts and shorts. That went down like a lead balloon with our wives and families as we disembarked from the coach at the Bentley Arms in Rothwell!

My room-mate on the tour was Bobby Goulding, who had had a great season with Wigan and was the youngest-ever Lions tourist. As vice-captain I was given Bobby to keep an eye on, to take care of, and we have been the best of friends ever since. Bobby played the dangerous Kiwi half-back Gary Freeman off the park and came of age in the series. He did, however, encounter a problem on the tour. He was out enjoying a few beers in a bar round the corner from our Auckland hotel with Paul Dixon, when a couple of Kiwis provoked him. The pair allegedly received undue physical attention in return, and the police were called. Both players were arrested, and I well recall Paul Dixon phoning me in my room at 3.30 a.m. to tell me that Bobby was still in custody, although Paul himself had been released. A couple of hours later the bedroom door opened, and Bobby walked in and burst into tears. This upset me greatly, and after I had given him what for, I agreed to speak with Mal Reilly and Maurice Lindsay on his behalf.

Both Malcolm and Maurice did all they could for Bobby. They wisely chose not to send him home, knowing that the publicity would have been very damaging and that the New Zealand press would have made even more of the incident than they did. I was told at the time that Malcolm had been in a similar position in 1970 when he toured with Great Britain in Australia, no doubt born of his passion to beat the Kangaroos. Bobby made a brief court appearance and, with excellent support from Malcolm and Maurice, the matter was swiftly closed. From that day on the senior players and I made sure that Bobby always went out with us as part of a large group. The management could take great credit for the dignified way in which they looked after the players, and I am sure that this contributed to the success in the Test series.

I do not know how true it is, but I was told that Shaun Edwards, who had missed this tour through injury, was upset to hear that I was playing well as Great Britain stand-off, and his father put photographs of me in a number 6 jersey in Shaun's kitchen to try to motivate him to take my place for the forthcoming Kangaroo Test series!

And so we moved on to the first British Coal Test at Wembley on 27 October 1990. Australia, coached by Bobby Fulton, walked out in front of a record crowd for a Test in Britain, some 54,569 spectators, and with their unbeaten record intact so far on tour the Kangaroos looked the part. They did not appreciate, however, that Malcolm had chosen a highly motivated and confident Great Britain team. He felt no compunction in selecting several big names who had missed the Kiwi tour, but he also kept his promise to the younger players who had come of age in New Zealand. The emotion of the large Wembley crowd as they sang 'Land of Hope and Glory' really got to me, and, I believe, to the rest of my team. Our forwards – Karl Harrison, Lee Jackson, Paul Dixon, Denis Betts and Roy Powell – tackled as if their lives depended on it, which shocked the Australian forwards who had been used to having things all their own way. But their defence in turn stood up to our probing, and it was clear that something special would be needed to break the deadlock.

Ellery Hanley was the man to turn the game early in the second half with a clever kick that he himself collected. A speedy play-the-ball, and centre Daryl Powell whipped the ball out to Paul Eastwood, the Hull winger, who used his pace and strength to dive under despairing tackles from Hancock and Cartwright and score in the corner. We led 6–2, but the Australians retaliated and the powerful Mal Meninga went in after a sharp break from centre partner Mark McGaw. But we were not to be outdone, and once again an Ellery Hanley kick caught the Australians out. This time the kick was high, and Kangaroo full-back Gary Belcher was taken by surprise and did not collect the ball cleanly, allowing Martin Offiah to pick up the rebound and score by the posts. Paul Eastwood converted this try, and we led 12–6. Further good play by the Great Britain forwards then gave us a position where I was able to drop a goal, to give us that extra point which left the Australians needing two scores to win.

The last 15 minutes they threw everything at us, and the Cronulla centre McGaw once again used his power to pull clear of several tackles and touch down for Australia's second try, which was goaled by Meninga. One point in the game now, and the Australians were beginning to play as we had expected they would do. The only difference was, we believed that we would win this game. Mal Reilly had worked with us before the game on the principle that the Australians moved up very quickly when their opposition were in possession. To take advantage of this, Malcolm felt we should employ a chip over their defensive line every so often. This had worked already in the game for Ellery Hanley, and with nine minutes remaining I was fortunate enough to have the perfect opportunity to put another chip over. I raced through and caught the ball before releasing Daryl Powell. With only Andrew 'ET' Ettingshausen in front of him, Daryl waited before timing his pass to Paul Eastwood to put the wingman in for his second try.

I can remember walking back to the halfway line and drinking in the atmosphere within the stadium. The red, white and blue was everywhere, and our first win over Australia for 12 years was now a reality. Paul Eastwood, who had proved to be our match-winner, collected his 14th point in the game with a last-minute, touch-line penalty goal, and I can clearly recall Paul turning round as soon as he had kicked the ball to jog back to our half of the field, knowing that a winning seven-point lead had been established. The whole team had played their part, and it seemed as though the whole country had been involed in what was an outstanding victory at Wembley. We celebrated at Stringfellows nightclub in London that evening, and I knew then that all the hard work and encouragement of my early years at Hunslet Parkside had paid off.

FIRST TEST AT WEMBLEY, 27 OCTOBER 1990

GREAT BRITAIN 19   AUSTRALIA 12

1.	Steve Hampson	Gary Belcher
2.	Paul Eastwood	Andrew Ettingshausen
3.	Daryl Powell	Mal Meninga (captain)
4.	Carl Gibson	Mark McGaw
5.	Martin Offiah	Michael Hancock
6.	Garry Schofield	Ricky Stuart
7.	Andy Gregory	Allan Langer
8.	Karl Harrison	Steve Roach
9.	Lee Jackson	Kerrad Walters
10.	Paul Dixon	Martin Bella
11.	Denis Betts	Paul Sironen
12.	Roy Powell	John Cartwright
13.	Ellery Hanley (captain)	Bob Lindner
14.	Shaun Edwards	Greg Alexander
15.	Kevin Ward	Des Hasler
16.	David Hulme	Dale Shearer
17.	Karl Fairbank	Glenn Lazarus

T:	Eastwood 2, Offiah	Meninga, McGaw
G:	Eastwood 3, Schofield 1dg	Meninga 2

SUBSTITUTIONS:
Ward for R. Powell (45 min)
Fairbank for Harrison
  (72 min)

SUBSTITUTIONS:
Lazarus for Bella (72 min)
Hasler for Cartwright (72 min)

Alexander for Langer (79 min)
Shearer for Hancock (79 min)

Referee: A. Sablayrolles (France)
Attendance: 54,569

The second Test took place at Old Trafford, Manchester, on 10 November, and we came so close to avoiding defeat by the Kangaroos in a Test series for the first time in 20 years. Another huge crowd turned out, with over 46,000 looking forward to a Great Britain display as passionate as in the first Test, and they were not let down. At half-time we trailed 4–2, after Australia had crossed the only try of the first period through winger Dale Shearer, and we had a Paul Eastwood penalty goal in reply. The forward exchanges had been intense, but we felt in the dressing-room we were in with a great chance. Shortly after the interval the Leeds second row Paul Dixon used all his strength to go over, and we had taken the lead. Back came the Australians, and their reply was immediate: winger Andrew Ettingshausen finished an intricate handling move by kicking infield, and Cliff Lyons was there to take the ball and touch down. Mal Meninga converted the try, and the Kangaroos once again had the initiative. We had lost Martin Offiah with a knee injury shortly after the break, but it was his replacement, Paul Loughlin, who exploited one of the few mistakes the Australians made when he intercepted a long pass by scrum-half Ricky Stuart to sprint 40 yards down the left wing, touching down just too far out for Eastwood to convert the try.

It was 10–10 with ten minutes remaining, and we were manfully holding on as this tremendous game played out its last act. With the final whistle due any second I kicked deep into the Australian corner, believing that we only had to contain them and successfully defend their last set of six tackles to draw the match and, at the very least, the series. Sadly this was not to be, for Ricky Stuart made amends for his earlier mistake by dummying Lee Jackson and charging 70 yards down the right wing. Mal Meninga forced his way through to support Stuart, pushing opposite number Carl Gibson out of the way before taking a final pass to touch down for the winning try.

This 14–10 defeat brought the series level, and our dressing-room was as quiet as a tomb. It had been a great Test match, although none of the Great Britain players looked on it as such at the time. Skipper Hanley had done all he could to win the game, and Paul Eastwood was inconsolable after missing two conversions. While Meninga had only managed one goal himself for Australia, his try had been crucial. It should be acknowledged that the Kangaroos had made numerous changes from the first Test, and these had paid off, demonstrating their strength in depth. Their vice-captain and hooker, Benny Elias, was outstanding, as were forward colleagues Lazarus, Sironen and Lindner.

The Australians made no mistake in the third Test at Elland Road, winning the series 2–1 with a comfortable 14–0 success. Ellery Hanley was always to the fore for Great Britain, but the tourists made sure that they marked him tightly. Their half-back pairing of Cliff Lyons and Ricky Stuart was the decisive influence, and we simply could not make enough yardage with the ball to pose any real threat. We had competed up to half-time, conceding just one try to Andrew Ettingshausen, but second-half tries by Meninga and Elias ensured that we could not get back into the game. Once again the Kangaroos had triumphed.

The series as a whole turned out to be the greatest of successes for rugby league. Media coverage exceeded all expectations, and Test attendances reached a new high. Financial records were broken, and the average crowd for the 13 tour games was also the highest ever seen. Ellery Hanley for Great Britain and Australian back-row forward Bob Lindner were named as their respective teams' Men of the Series, and Mal Meninga was named as BBC TV's Overseas Sports Personality of the Year to underline the progress that rugby league had made on television.

That third Test at Elland Road in 1990 left me with a lasting impression of Ellery. As the final whistle blew he stood there unable to make a move, simply drained. Throughout the game the Australians had targeted him as a serious threat, and whenever they had the opportunity to pile into him in the tackle they did so. The more Ellery tried to keep his feet and use his upper body strength, the more the Australians piled into him. His sheer character and his own particular style of rugby stood out that day.

The following spring we took on France twice in the British Coal Test series and triumphed in record style. The first encounter in Perpignan was a one-sided affair, with Martin Offiah, Shaun Edwards and I each scoring two tries as we won 45–10. I was feeling off-colour, but still had two further touchdowns ruled out! The second meeting at Headingley was even more of a runaway success, highlighted by five tries from 'Chariots' Offiah which set a new record for scoring in Tests. The Great Britain team clicked from the start, and all 11 tries were scored by the backs. This game was one of the most satisfying of my career, as I was the playmaker at stand-off when we scored so many well-executed touchdowns, and I am proud, looking back, to see that I won the Man-of-the-Match award – ahead of five-tries Offiah! That French side was not as bad as the score suggests: we simply were unstoppable on the day. Sadly for all of us, including Malcolm Reilly, the next tour Down Under was over a year away. Had we been going in May 1991, I think we would have been in with a real chance of winning the Ashes back.

The World Cup-rated British Coal Test against Papua New Guinea was our next international, on 9 November 1991 at Central Park, Wigan. As captain I led out a strong Great Britain side which was on a hiding to nothing. The Kumuls had already lost to Wales 68–0 and to Great Britain's Under-21s 58–0, and our 56–4 win in front of just 4,000 people was something of a non-event. Although this was the first occasion on which I had captained Great Britain, in my 37th Test, I was simply concerned that we came away with two World Cup points. We fulfilled that ambition in a solid all-round display in which eight of us shared ten tries.

12.

NIGHTMARE TIME WITH LAUGHTON

ON 24 MAY 1991 Dougie Laughton was unveiled as the new Leeds coach. As well as replacing David Ward at first-team level, the board also sacked John Holmes and Paul Gill, the very successful A team coaches, and John has not been to a Leeds game since.

The arrival of Dougie Laughton immediately brought about a policy of change as he proceeded to rip the heart out of the first-team squad. After we had finished as runners-up to Wigan in the previous season it was my belief that few changes were needed, and I had the chance to express that. The new coach sat down with me in the main stand at Headingley prior to the 1991–92 season and asked me: 'How do you think I should manage the team this coming campaign?' Grateful to be consulted, I advised him that this was a large juggernaut of a club. While Dougie had achieved outstanding results at Widnes, with the greatest respect that club was a small operation compared to Leeds. The sad part was, Leeds had underachieved for so many years, and a number of coaches before Dougie had failed to turn the great potential into success. I said I felt the only way to approach the coming season was with patience: it was important that he did not rush in and try to stamp his identity on the team at once, but that he should gradually tackle the challenge.

Unfortunately, Dougie did not heed my advice, and no fewer than 24 players departed within his first two seasons, not all of whom became bad players overnight. Most important, I believe the team spirit was badly damaged: all top sides have a vital team spirit, and ours was not to recover. The coach was often heard to remark, 'I will remove the Schofield clique. They think they run the club!' But the so-called clique I was part of *was* the club! Heron, Dixon, Maskill, Creasser, Gibson, Divorty, Wane, Molloy, Roy Powell, Spencer, Phil Ford and Lord – were all good mates and we battled for one another, both on and off the field. But Dougie did not like the fact that his predecessor, David Ward, had created such a great team spirit at Headingley and that he was merely inheriting it. The irony was, under Dougie Laughton I was to experience the worst team spirit of my career! All the chopping and changing of the squad was no doubt the reason for that, for the new players would keep company with one another, while the older players that were left tended to stick together too.

In autumn 1991 there was the ongoing saga of Ellery Hanley – was he going to sign for Leeds or not? At the same time there were two other questions to be asked: would I be staying or going, and who would be club captain? Colin Maskill and I were invited to represent Leeds at the launch of the 1991 season hosted by sponsors Stones Bitter and held at the Dragonara Hotel. There were players there from all the different clubs, as well as Maurice Lindsay, chairman of Wigan and one of the leading figures of the game. At this time our relationship with each other was excellent, particularly as Maurice had been the Great Britain manager on the 1990 tour to New Zealand. The ceremony went well, and afterwards Dougie Laughton went chasing Ellery, while Maurice approached me. He had already been quoted by the media as saying that Leeds could have Ellery as he felt that Wigan had got the best out of him, and he had also apparently suggested to Leeds that they could have Ellery and Wigan would pay an extra £25,000 to secure my services. That was quite a compliment in a way – and now Maurice approached me in person to see if I was interested in joining Wigan, and offered me a three-year contract worth £100,000 per season.

Colin Maskill couldn't believe the amount of money I'd been offered – it was far more than I was being paid at Leeds. I told Maurice that I would see what happened – but Leeds was my club, and out of loyalty I was going to stay there. With Wigan being the side they were, I guess people reading this might be surprised. But everyone knows that the most decorated player in rugby league is Shaun Edwards, and Maurice was looking for Shaun and me to form Wigan's half-back partnership. Now, after 17 years in the game, I haven't got a single winner's medal – and who knows, if I'd signed for Wigan in 1991 I could have had a bucket-load. But my loyalty to Leeds meant that I didn't want to leave, even though the financial rewards on offer to me were a lot higher than the ones I was currently receiving.

During pre-season training that year, 12 of us arranged to play golf on our day off, Monday. After a round at Roundhay golf club we adjourned to the Chained Bull on Harrogate Road in Leeds, before proceeding to the Horse and Jockey in Castleford. This was one of those meeting places – the Garden Gate in Hunslet was another – where rugby league players would gather on their day off. It became known as the 'Monday Club', and was our way of unwinding after the physical and mental exertions of the weekend game. Players from Cas, Featherstone, Wakefield, Leeds, Dewsbury, Hunslet, Halifax and many other clubs would come together for a drink, to swap advice and wind each other up! I believe there were similar circuits in Lancashire at the time – although clearly the modern game no longer can accommodate such excesses. Fitness levels are so much higher, and personal training programmes are very common. Perhaps this contributes to there being fewer personalities in today's sports.

This particular Monday was no different from any other: we finished up in the Langtree Park in Cas, famous for its karaoke nights, and I can clearly recall our own Steve Molloy on this occasion winning the talent contest. The next morning at training in Horsforth, we could tell that Dougie was not happy at all. He had got wind of our long day out and gave us all a good rollicking – for not inviting him to join us at 'The Rocket'! Much laughter ensued, before a voice at the back shouted, 'Dougie, it's called the Horse and Jockey, not the Rocket!' It was funny at the time, but looking back it may have been the start of the resentment that Dougie obviously felt towards the spirit within the squad.

I had picked up an ear infection in Papua New Guinea in 1990, and this was recurring more and more frequently. During the 1992–93 season, after having consulted with our physio, Seamus McCallion, and club doctor Paul Lanfear, I visited a specialist, Dr Ian Fraser, who put me on a three-month course of drops. This treatment failed to improve matters, and the specialist decided an exploratory operation was needed. I consulted with Leeds chief executive Alf Davies, who suggested that my health should come before my rugby. So, after we had played Widnes in the 1993 Silk Cut Challenge Cup semi-final and been walloped 39–4, I told Alf that I would be going into hospital on the following Monday. This meant I would miss two matches – the Widnes league fixture which had been rearranged for the midweek after the semi, and the Wakefield match at Headingley on the following Sunday.

That Sunday afternoon I called into the dressing-room before the

Wakefield game to wish the lads well – and was met with silence. Even the customary nervous banter was missing. Before I had time to find out what was going on, Dougie put his head round the door, asked me what the fuck I was doing, and told me to wait for him in his office. This broke the ice in the room; it was clear that the team knew what was coming. Dougie informed me: 'You're suspended for two fucking weeks and fined £300 for missing two games without good reason.' In response I told him that the club were well aware was the need to have the exploratory operation, and that they would it be receiving a further specialist's report recommending major surgery in the close season.

My own GP, Dr Terry Crystal, who is, incidentally, the England rugby union team's doctor, had been very surprised that I had been able to play at all with what was a serious ear condition. He was sure my balance must have been affected on the field, and was shocked to hear that the club's medical team had allowed me to play on for so long without further specialist consultation. Meanwhile, Dr Fraser advised that the poison from the infection was working its way through to my brain, and I would have died within 12 to 18 months if I had not had treatment. Little did he know my brains were actually in my boots, so I could have lasted rather longer!

Despite the specialist's report the suspension stood, and I was barred from Headingley for two weeks. What hurt me most of all was not that I missed games for Leeds, but that I also lost my Great Britain place for the international with France at Headingley the following Friday. I had been selected as captain, and when I advised David Howes at the RFL of the situation, David confirmed that he had no option but to rule me out as I was under club suspension. How costly this proved can be seen by the fact that I only hold the world record for the number of appearances for my country jointly with Mick Sullivan!

This incident underlined the power Dougie Laughton had at the club in 1993. As chief executive, Alf Davies should have cleared me, and both the club doctor and physiotherapist were made aware of and supported the need for my exploratory op.

Later that season Dougie once more revealed his animosity towards me. On this occasion we had finished training in the morning and, as we often did on a lunchtime, Colin Maskill and I drove down to Stoggy's bar on Burley Road for a few frames of pool before I collected the children from school. As we left Headingley we had seen Dougie walking towards his car, so we took a different route to Stoggy's – but as we were parking we saw Dougie driving down the street. No sooner had we set up the balls and ordered a Guinness and a lime and soda than a Lancastrian voice shouted across the bar: 'Schoey, you're a fucking c***!' Now Masky is a quiet lad, but on this occasion he felt he had to intervene. He told the coach in no uncertain terms that he was out of order, and if any discussion was needed it should take place within the confines of his office and not in a public bar – or words to that effect! Sadly Dougie did not see it that way, and he proceeded to rant and rave at me, saying he was going to see that I was sacked. I suggested that the Leeds directors might have a different view, particularly as they would have my contract to pay up, to say nothing of unfair dismissal. And for four hours it continued like that, with Dougie slagging me off in this bar, while I gave as good as I got in return. The more he drank, the worse it became, and the manager, Brian Stockdale, and several customers who came and went were all gobsmacked. Eventually I left him in the pub at 5.45 p.m. If Dougie didn't know I couldn't stand him before that episode in Stoggy's, he did afterwards.

Needless to say, over the following day or so I heard nothing from Dougie or the club. I was told that an ex-player, Paul Pickup, had got wind of the encounter and had phoned Alf Davies the following day to express his disgust at the coach's behaviour. But the club treated it as if nothing had happened, and because I had a couple of years to go on my contract I didn't need to make more of the incident. I understand that several clubs subsequently enquired after my availability, only to be put off by the size of the transfer fee being quoted. I was determined to outstay Dougie in any case, but the whole sorry affair took its toll on my confidence, and my form became inconsistent. I always took training seriously, but perhaps at times I overdid it, spurred on by my desire to show the coach that I was invaluable. I realise now, however, that no one player is indispensable.

I don't want to give the wrong impression: we did have our lighter moments. Towards the end of Dougie's reign at Headingley, he asked me to play scrum-half in order to allow young Graham Holroyd the benefit of the experience of playing stand-off. I had some difficulty in feeding the scrums, and was called into Dougie's office the following week. 'There's nothing to it,' said Dougie, 'I'll show you how to cope.' He then pulled a chair out from the side of his desk and bent down with a rugby ball before shoving it through the legs of the chair. 'This is how easy it is, just try for yourself. You're welcome to use the chair any time!' I cannot believe to this day that I actually did pick the ball up and proceeded to do as he had done, feeding the chair for a couple of minutes! I can just imagine Dougie chuckling as he recalls this particular coaching session.

If Dougie had one asset, it was his ability to persuade the Leeds board to spend money on buying top players and to pay them well. I do not know all the financial implications of Dougie's tenure, I only know that most of the players whom Dougie brought in would not have moved to Leeds without improving their terms of remuneration. No doubt the Leeds club needed success in order to cover such costs, and I am sure the Challenge Cup final appearances in 1994 and 1995 must have helped to some extent.

But this policy was continued year in and year out, building up potentially ruinous financial pressure, and it eventually led the Leeds Cricket and Athletic Company Limited, to give the club its full title, to seek new investment. On the verge of collapse, in 1996 the club was bought out by Mr Paul Caddick, in partnership with Gary Hetherington, formerly of Sheffield Eagles.

Graham Lowe approached Leeds through chief executive Alf Davies and asked if I would be released to join the club he was coaching, Manly, Down Under for the summer of 1993. Dougie refused to release me, giving no reason for his doing so. I sought legal advice for restraint of trade and was told I had a strong case, although defeat could cost me up to £20,000 in legal costs. I wisely decided not to proceed. Our relationship remained heated, and I did not want to inflame the situation further, nor did I want to fall out with the board.

Other players suffered harshly too, with the late Roy Powell, the Great Britain second-row forward, being refused a testimonial for services rendered to the Leeds club, and then finding that his contract was not renewed by Dougie. The team was now split into several factions, and Dougie was unable to motivate the squad. We then found that he had a 'mole' in the dressing-room, reporting to him any gripes or moans that a particular player might have.

At the start of one season I was asked to appear on Sky TV as a panellist on the rugby league magazine programme *Boots 'n' All*. Leeds struggled in the first few weeks, and my co-panellists took the opportunity to introduce some humour into the proceedings by winding me up. This gave the panel a human side, and I'm sure that the fans of all the other clubs looked forward to our banter each week. That was until Dougie threw a wobbly, no doubt riled at my modest TV profile: he phoned RFL headquarters and asked them to pull strings to have me removed from the panel as, in his view, the club's image was being damaged by the mickey-taking. Sky reluctantly released me and, lo and behold, four weeks later the replacement panellist was revealed as none other than Mr Douglas Laughton, the Leeds coach!

One of Dougie's most misdirected ideas was to take the Leeds squad off during pre-season training to an Outward Bound centre in Wales. He revealed to us before departure his belief that this was the best way for the players to come together as a team. We were cut off from civilisation for five whole days with nothing to occupy ourselves during our leisure hours! This wasn't the bonding success that DL thought it would be!

The second pre-season Welsh 'safari' proved particularly eventful: far from bonding us all together, the trip led directly to the sacking of Bobby Goulding! It is difficult to put down in print the circumstances surrounding Bobby's dismissal without thinking of that great philosopher, Fred Karno! While the players were Outward Bound, Dougie stayed in his own caravan with his family nearby, and the catering was covered by a mate of Dougie's. After four days in an old house with just three bedrooms shared by 24 players, we were all getting on each other's wires, and the coach finally accepted that we needed to unwind on the final night with a few beers at a local pub in Anglesey. That particular night we all had a good session, and one or two locals started to resent our presence as the evening went on. Inevitably they picked on the smallest member of our squad, Gareth Stephens, the son of our assistant coach. Bobby was never one to pass confrontation by and visited Gareth in the loo: 'If you need any help, I'm your man.' Now Gareth was in direct competition with Bobby for a place in the team, and was sufficiently wound up over this to shock Bobby with his reply: 'Fuck off, I can fight my own battles without your fucking help!'

This was not what Bobby wanted to hear, and he was now giving the impression of a human volcano, about to erupt. One or two of us recognised the signs and tried to defuse him, to no avail. Then in stepped Dougie to employ his man-management skills, the success of which must be judged by what followed. Bobby went back to the centre and damaged both wing-mirrors and doors on Dougie's car before spending £100 on a taxi to take him straight home that evening to Widnes! I wouldn't mind, but Dougie and Bobby always had a good social relationship, and still do as far as I know.

The Leeds board of directors were informed, and Bobby was immediately suspended. Back home that weekend I received a phone call from Bobby, and I agreed to try to mediate on his behalf. I spoke with Alf Davies and passed on Bobby's apologies, but it did no good: he was sacked, perhaps for one off-field indiscretion too many. All right, Bobby had a bit of a reputation, but I still felt that he should have been given one last chance.

Dougie may well have been capable of picking the top players by and large, but his coaching philosophy was to send us all out together and expect us simply to get on with it. I remember that he signed French scrum-half Patrick Entat, for we were short of a playmaker at the time and Patrick was a good little half-back. Suddenly, Dougie stopped picking him, and once out of favour Patrick never had another chance with us. Dougie was a big fan of young Graham Holroyd who was brought into the side to replace Patrick, although Graham never really established himself as the number 1 scrum-half at the club – not least because he was a stand-off! He was an accomplished goalkicker, but rather light for the game of rugby league at the top level.

After signing Tony Kemp in the summer of 1995, Alf Davies went over to New Zealand with a view to bringing in Dean Bell as Dougie's deputy. This was because Ellery Hanley had announced that he was to leave the British game and had accepted a lucrative contract Down Under with the Australian Rugby League. With Ellery having been doing most of the coaching in recent times at Leeds, his departure meant that the club now needed a new assistant for Dougie, and Alf, having known Dean Bell very well, obtained the board's approval to make an approach.

I don't know for sure what made Dougie Laughton resign on the day that Dean Bell's appointment was announced, but he possibly felt that Dean's professional attitude towards his job and responsibilities might make him suffer by comparison. Dean would have worked out Dougie straightaway – you only had to look at their very different approaches to the role of head coach. At the time I had a new two-year contract waiting to be signed but I was not keen, particularly if Dougie Laughton would be coaching at the club over that period. My family and I were having a few days' break away in September in Great Yarmouth when I passed a Leeds fan on the sea front, and he told me that he had heard Dougie Laughton had just resigned. I made my way to the nearest telephone and called up Alf Davies and asked him if it was true that Dougie had gone. When Alf confirmed this to be so, I told him to get the two-year contract out and I would sign it that weekend. I am sure that if Dean Bell had not been appointed, I would have left Leeds and Dougie might still be there now – although that is purely speculation.

As a result of the difficulties in which the club found itself, Dean Bell and the new football manager Hugh McGahan had little money to spend on new players in their first season. But Dean's most important signing was not a player: he immediately appointed American Edgar Curtis as conditioner. Edgar had been the Olympic coach for the Bulgarian national powerlifting squad! He came over now from Auckland Warriors in New Zealand and immediately made his mark. Leeds had recently fitted out a new gym at Headingley with £25,000 worth of equipment, but Edgar took one look and told them that it was not suitable for a professional rugby league club. Within a fortnight he'd been to Sweden and ordered and installed free weights in place of the basic machines we had been using over the previous 12 months.

What had been fairly low-key training sessions under Laughton's regime were replaced with more regular and intense sessions and new training methods. This new disciplined approach had an immediate impact on all the players: we were keen to train, and we did so with smiles on our faces. We all looked forward to improving our own performances, and within as short a time as eight weeks Dean Bell and his staff had stamped their own professional attitude on the club. Team spirit in particular picked up considerably at this time, though sadly the team itself was breaking up. This proved to be the unfortunate legacy of what had been a nightmare under Dougie Laughton, not only for myself but for the club, its board and fans.

13.

STILL NO SILVERWARE

ON HIS ARRIVAL at Leeds in the summer of 1991, Dougie Laughton approached me to discuss my thoughts on the possibility of the club signing Ellery Hanley. I told Dougie that Ellery and I went back a fair way, having played together with Great Britain Under-24s in 1983, toured together with the British Lions the following year, and then again in 1988. I had the highest regard for Ellery as a player, and I told Dougie to go for him. Dougie confirmed that the captaincy was not at issue – but we are shortly to find out how long that lasted!

On 6 September 1991, Dougie signed Ellery for Leeds from Wigan for what was reported to be a world-record fee of £250,000. It was a record that would last less than four months, as Martin Offiah moved from Widnes to Wigan for a reputed £440,000 on 3 January 1992.

On 8 September Ellery made his début against Hull in a 20–14 victory. A crowd of over 15,000 were at Headingley that day. A week later Hull got their revenge in the first round of the John Smith's Yorkshire Cup as they defeated us at the Boulevard 16–11, and I came in for the usual abuse from a section of the Hull crowd.

There followed a dramatic U-turn by Mr Laughton after that first game of the season, the win over Hull. Dougie called me into his office and told me, 'I'm making Hanley captain, so you can like it or lump it!' No further explanation was offered, and he walked straight out of his office before I could gather myself, leaving me dumbstruck, shocked and upset. If the delivery of the news was meant to cause me maximum grief, I can assure him it certainly did. If I disliked Dougie before this episode, I certainly hated him afterwards. I have always tried to be honest and forthright, sometimes to my detriment, but I also value man-management as a major asset in professional team sport. No explanation was ever forthcoming, and there probably was little reasoned argument for his decision. Perhaps Ellery had suggested the change – but I do not believe Ellery was all that bothered about the leadership.

Ellery and I had different personalities, but I would like to think that there was a mutual respect between us. We were never likely to socialise together, but he would always be one of the first names I would pencil into my greatest rugby league team! We were both proud to be professional players, confident in each other's abilities, and we gave everything together for Leeds, in spite of the lack of team management.

In Dougie's absence from the training field, Ellery and I found ourselves coaching the squad together, but my confidence was jolted and I found it more and more difficult to lift myself. My form slipped, and I overcompensated in training. Ellery himself did not use fitness techniques like the rest of us: just a simple medicine ball for him, and it proved very effective. His upper body strength was exceptional and well suited to the physical power that is needed in international rugby league. Playing alongside him I found that he was invariably on hand to support most breaks and run in the tries. His experience would see him move into offside positions ahead of play, anticipating what would happen in order to be there on the shoulder of the Leeds player who made the initial breakthrough. The slower he became later in his career, the further upfield he needed to be – but rest assured that he was invariably there.

Ellery's move to Balmain in 1995 signalled the beginning of the end for Dougie, as the team needed a motivational and tactically aware coach who could make up for the deficiencies of the manager. Dean Bell was the man who took over from Ellery in this respect, and his arrival was simultaneous with Laughton's departure. In many ways it was tragic that Leeds never got the best of Ellery, especially playing in tandem with me. Ellery's playing record was formidable, and with the pair of us firing on all cylinders under a coach of the calibre of Frank Stanton, Mal Reilly or Arthur Bunting, Leeds would surely have overtaken Wigan as the number-one team of the 1990s.

In only his ninth game for Leeds, Ellery Hanley broke his jaw in three places in a violent tackle by Hull's Andy Dannatt, an incident that overshadowed our Regal Trophy second-round win at Hull. Tries by Hull old boys Gary Divorty and myself, and two goals from Simon Irving saw us through by 12–4. Referee Brian Galtress missed the Ellery incident, but Joe

Warham, the Leeds official and also a member of the Rugby League Council, cited video evidence and the RFL board referred the case to its disciplinary committee. Hull failed in their attempt to have the High Court reject the use of video evidence, and on 12 December Andy Dannatt was suspended for eight matches. Ellery, meanwhile, suffered an injury that ruled him out of 12 first-team games.

A week before, in the first round of the Regal Trophy, we had had a good win at Warrington by 17–8, with my contribution being a solitary drop-goal. Round three saw us face Castleford at home and cruise to a comfortable 24–4 win, including two more Schofield drop-goals! As was the nature of the Regal Trophy in those days, the semi-final followed just six days later, and a crowd of just over 7,000 packed into Bradford City's football ground to see us beat Salford 22–15, with yours truly scoring the first try.

In the Regal Trophy final against Widnes on 11 January 1992, we suffered a record 24–0 defeat – the first of several record defeats we were to incur under Dougie Laughton. I had been struggling with flu from the weekend of the semi-final, and Les Holliday, the Widnes loose forward, led his pack to dominance in the game. We failed to defend the high ball, although the referee did not give our full-back, Morvin Edwards, much protection as several times he was hit in the air, attempting to catch the ball. This gambit led to at least one try, by Holliday, and Davies, Tait and Sorensen added others to complete our misery.

Less than a month after the final, you may be interested to recall that Wigan sent a team on behalf of Great Britain to the Nissan World Sevens competition in Sydney, Australia. Although this caused problems with cup and Great Britain fixtures at home, it emphasised the strength of the Wigan side at this time as they lifted the trophy having seen off the competition of the best of the Australian club sides. Martin Offiah was named Man of the Tournament, a status which he underlined in the final, scoring four tries to defeat the Brisbane Broncos 18–6 at Sydney Football Stadium on 9 February.

Our 1992 Silk Cut Challenge Cup campaign was brief. We swept aside Bramley at McLaren Field in the preliminary round on 21 January by 36–12, with one try to Schofield. The first round proper saw us defeat Ryedale-York at home 48–6, only to be knocked out in the second round by St Helens 32–12, once again on our own patch.

In spite of losing Ellery for over two months our league form was good, as we won every game in November, December and January – our only defeat in any competition in those three months coming in the Regal Trophy final. We were top of the Stones Bitter Championship table in December, only to fall away badly after that and finish fifth behind Warrington, Castleford, St Helens and the mighty Wigan. The wheels fell off in a big way, as our campaign ended with only four wins in our last 15 games. On three of those occasions we failed to score a try – at home against Castleford, Wigan, and even Wakefield Trinity. Our final game was humiliating, a Premiership Trophy semi-final defeat on 10 May at Central Park, Wigan, by 74 points to six, the highest score ever conceded by Leeds. I take no great pleasure in recording the fact that Martin Offiah produced one of the most outstanding individual performances ever seen on a rugby league field, scoring ten tries in that particular game. Amazingly, this feat had been performed twice before, in 1905 by George West, the Hull Kingston Rovers winger who set the rugby league record with 11 against Brookland Rovers; and then in 1951 by Lionel Cooper, the Australian winger playing for Huddersfield against Keighley.

This game, needless to say, does not rank in my list of top ten games. I am certain that it will figure in Martin Offiah's, though. 'Chariots', as he was affectionately known, was simply uncatchable that day. Dougie had selected young Leigh Deakin on the wing to mark Martin, but after 30 minutes he had no choice but to substitute him. At that stage we already trailed 26–0, and Martin had picked up a hattrick to go with two tries from centre Dean Bell. The substitute was Great Britain winger John Bentley – but this made no difference, as Martin went in for a further two tries before half-time! For a game of such importance it must have been unbelievable to watch, let alone play in, and I was only grateful to have been selected at loose forward that day and not in the backs! In the second half Martin gave up his role on the wing and started roaming all over the pitch following the ball, and the further five tries he scored in so doing simply underlined his great class. I have no hesitation in naming Martin Offiah in my World XIII. Ironically, a shell-shocked Leeds side scored the last points of the game when Paul Dixon powered through and touched down, Colin Maskill goaling.

Perhaps it wasn't so surprising when you consider how Dougie Laughton ran the team. Our normal training programme began on the Monday after the Sunday fixture. No compulsory sessions were organised for the Monday, although a number of us used to go swimming at the Leeds International Pool. Ellery Hanley was one who would have preferred not to visit the pool – but I would emphasise that Monday was usually the day after a game, and there was no compulsion to train. Tuesday was the fitness day, and Ellery took charge of this with help from Alan Tait and our club conditioner. We would start at 10.30 a.m. and finish at 12.15 in the early afternoon. Wednesday was another day when nothing was organised, although we could come in for weight training if we so wished – but, again, the Leeds club had no compulsory activity for us that day.

On Thursday we would meet again and commence at 10.30 a.m. with warm-ups, followed by ball work which involved planning and practising set moves, the calling of which was entirely in my hands. Once again the Thursday morning's training generally finished at 12.15 p.m., and the afternoon was free for the players. Friday was another day off, and with the Sunday fixture in mind we would come in on Saturday morning at the usual time, 10.30 a.m., to undertake further ball work when I again organised the moves we were to practise. When the session finished at lunchtime, Dougie Laughton would come in and put on a videotape showing our opposition for the following day. He would then leave the room, and the players would sit, have a light lunch after the training and watch our opposition on the video screen. Invariably they would drift off after lunch, well before the videotape had finished and nobody seemed to be too concerned.

I have always felt that this was a disgraceful way to operate, particularly if you bear in mind that at this stage of our careers at Leeds we were all full-time professionals. Dougie had signed a number of big names and simply left it to us to organise ourselves. The Leeds public were simply unaware of the limited amount of training the players were putting in under Dougie. I suppose it is human nature that if there is no compulsion for players to turn up, then generally they will do as little as they can get away with. Wednesday, for instance, became a golf day for me. But the length of the training sessions that were organised was the most alarming aspect of our professional careers under Dougie Laughton. No wonder we were never able to catch up with Wigan. As a player, it was impossible to generate the sort of training we should have been doing, and neither Ellery Hanley nor I were ever in a position to challenge the Leeds head coach over his methods. Looking back perhaps we should have done; but the Leeds board had given Dougie Laughton their full support, and he in turn expected us to go out and perform every Sunday in spite of the minimal preparations – and so that's what we tried to do.

14.

NEARLY MEN OF '92

IN MAY 1992 I set out on a record fourth tour with the British Lions, being part of the largest group of players ever to leave together. We were to play fewer matches on this tour, but the intensity of them was to be greater than ever before. Seventeen matches including six Tests and five Sydney Premiership club sides lay ahead. Only a couple of players dropped out after the tour party was named, Jonathan Davies through injury and Bobby Goulding under suspension. They were replaced by the St Helens winger Alan Hunte and the Featherstone scrum-half Deryck Fox.

The tour captain was Ellery Hanley, but there had been some doubt as to his fitness before we left. He last played for Leeds on 26 April and had struggled with foot and hamstring injuries. I was named as tour vice-captain and, with Ellery Hanley still short of match-fitness, I captained Great Britain in his place for the first game against Highlands Zone in Goroka, Papua New Guinea, on 24 May. We triumphed 24–15, even though St Helens second-row forward Sonny Nickle was dismissed on his Lions début and we struggled to come to terms with the decisions of referee Luxie Metta. Centre Paul Newlove showed outstanding form in this game before succumbing to the effects of the intense heat. The second fixture against Islands Zone was also won, by 38 points to 20, despite temperatures again in the 90s. The opposition arrived late for this fixture, and we ended up playing 35 minutes each way as the local airport had no floodlights and we were due to fly out to Port Moresby that evening! Both props, Lee Crooks and Wigan's Kelvin Skerrett, performed well, with second row Karl Fairbank scoring two tries.

I was moved to centre for the Test match that followed, to allow Daryl Powell to play at stand-off alongside Shaun Edwards. We made far too many handling errors, and the Papua New Guinea team pushed us all the way. After 21 minutes they were 8–0 ahead with tries from Elara and Tani. Paul

Eastwood then pulled a try back, and Wigan loose forward Phil Clarke touched down just before half-time to give us a 12–8 interval lead which also included two penalties struck by Paul Loughlin, the St Helens centre. Mal Reilly tore into us at half-time, but further indecisive play in the second half allowed their centre Wagambie to touch down after following up a high kick that bounced awkwardly between Paul Eastwood and full-back Steve Hampson in the in-goal area. The try was converted giving them a two-point lead, and it was not until eight minutes from time that we put together a decisive passing movement to put Martin Offiah in for the first of his two tries. He scored his second just a couple of minutes later, and on both occasions Paul Loughlin had combined with me to make the initial break. The 20 points to 14 victory had been hard work for us, and as we moved on to the second leg of the tour in Australia confidence was not at its highest.

We beat a strong Queensland Residents XIII by 14 points to 10 in a tight game in Townsville, having been unable to select seven forwards through injury as the hard grounds were already taking their toll. The second tour game in Australia saw us beat Canberra Raiders 24–12, although sadly they had a Winfield Cup match scheduled for the following day and so fielded a virtual reserve side. We then encountered a strong Illawarra Steelers team, finally overcoming them by 11–10.

The first Ashes Test followed against the Kangaroos at the Sydney Football Stadium, and attracted a capacity crowd of over 40,000. Malcolm had prepared us well, and we took the game to the Aussies from the start. But we suffered injuries throughout the game to such an extent that we finished with just 12 men, having used all four of our substitutes. Martin Offiah provided our greatest threat with his pace down the wing, and Australia were thankful for full-back Andrew Ettingshausen who managed to force Offiah narrowly into touch on several occasions in the first half. Mal Meninga opened the try-scoring, popping up three times in support of a break from the Australian 22-metre line before touching down in the 30th minute. Wishart's conversion gave the Australians an 8–2 interval lead.

We felt aggrieved to be down at all at half-time and came out full of confidence for the second half, only to concede a second try to Meninga. When the Kangaroos' second-rower Paul Sironen powered over at the start of the final quarter, it was clear the game had drifted away from us. The number of injuries eventually told on us, and the Test was one of the toughest games of rugby league I had played in. Although we had lost 22–6 in Sydney, we all looked forward to taking on the Australians again at the highest level in Melbourne.

Next we defeated a New South Wales Country XIII 24–6, with Paul Eastwood scoring a try and kicking six goals in another physical encounter. At one stage we only had two recognised forwards on the field, and Joe Lydon spent much of the last quarter in the second row. Our only non-Test defeat on tour was to follow as we went down 22–16 to Parramatta. My opponent at stand-off was the experienced Brett Kenny, and he certainly had a fair game that day. Martin Offiah raced in for two tries, but will recall with less pleasure the challenge laid down by the Parramatta winger Lee Oudenryn to run the length of the field, the winner to take £1,000 in cash. To everyone's astonishment Martin was beaten in this race.

The next game, the last before the second Test, saw Ellery Hanley make his first tour appearance in a 22–0 win over Newcastle Knights. Sadly, Ellery was to last only nine minutes before limping off after damaging his hamstring once more, and leaving the tour. Although the Leeds club doctor had felt that Ellery was not fit to tour in the first place, the management had taken quite a gamble by including him in the squad. Perhaps they felt that the Australians would gain a psychological advantage before the series started if Ellery withdrew in May, as the Aussies had such a high regard for him. The game itself saw the midweek squad continue their unbeaten record, giving four tour replacements a run-out in Hull back-rower Steve McNamara, Wigan winger David Myers and the Sheffield Eagles players Mark Aston and Paul Broadbent.

The second Test at Melbourne on 26 June was to go down as the greatest Test match I ever played in, and I am sure this also goes for the other 16 players who represented Great Britain that day. It was all the more pleasing for myself as I had been appointed tour captain in Ellery's place.

Taking over the captaincy of Great Britain was the pinnacle of my career. I was aware of the likely appointment, but very proud for myself, my family and all those who had helped in rugby league. I was determined to do my best, both on and off the field, in the game I loved. Our coach had selected the Wigan pack in its entirety, and I was back at stand-off half. We were roared on by 8,000 British supporters in a full house of over 30,000. Heavy rain had made conditions under foot quite slippery, and Mal Reilly stressed to us that we could not afford to miss any tackles, but if we worked hard and kept in the faces of the Kangaroos, then they would make mistakes. Every player played to his full potential in the first half, and the Australians felt the full force of the British Lions' tackling. Two Paul Eastwood penalties set us on the way before Phil Clarke went past two green-and-gold defenders to touch down. With the try converted by Eastwood, we were 10–0 up.

Shaun Edwards at scrum-half was having an outstanding game, and it was his kick over Ettingshausen that allowed Paul Newlove to follow up and dive over after half an hour, with Eastwood again converting. We continued to pile into the Australians, and then it was my turn to enjoy a moment to remember. After 35 minutes I chipped the ball through from some 12 yards out and sprinted round a couple of Aussie forwards and into the in-goal area, where 'ET' somehow slipped as he tried to smother the ball. This enabled me to dive and touch the ball down before it rolled dead. From under the posts Paul Eastwood had no trouble in kicking his fifth goal, and we went in at the interval leading 22–0. We had surprised ourselves, but the scoreline was fully justified and now it was a case of making sure that the Kangaroos did not get back into the game.

Mal warned us that they would throw everything at us in the second half, spurred on by pride alone, and so we began the final 40 minutes as we had started the game. Nine minutes in, and the forwards had driven into Australian territory enabling me to drop a goal. Eventually our line was broken, as first Bob Lindner and then Chris Johns scored tries to pull back to 23–10 with 20 minutes to go. But we were not to be outdone, and with seven minutes remaining the players prepared to celebrate when Martin Offiah made a try for Graham Steadman, the Castleford full-back. Graham had always been a tricky player to defend against, and he showed his class now by squeezing in at the corner for Paul Eastwood to put over an incredible conversion. Leading 29–10 we knew victory was ours, and Martin Offiah put the tin lid on it by curving round the outside of Ettingshausen to touch down and make the final score 33–10. This equalled the highest winning margin by Great Britain over Australia in all Ashes Test matches.

The match had been played at the Prince's Park in Melbourne, the home of Aussie Rules football, but the British supporters made so much noise that we felt we were playing back home. The pitch itself had a cricket square in the middle, which was harder than the rest of the field where more grass had

Receiving applause from the Headingley faithful after scoring a try for Leeds

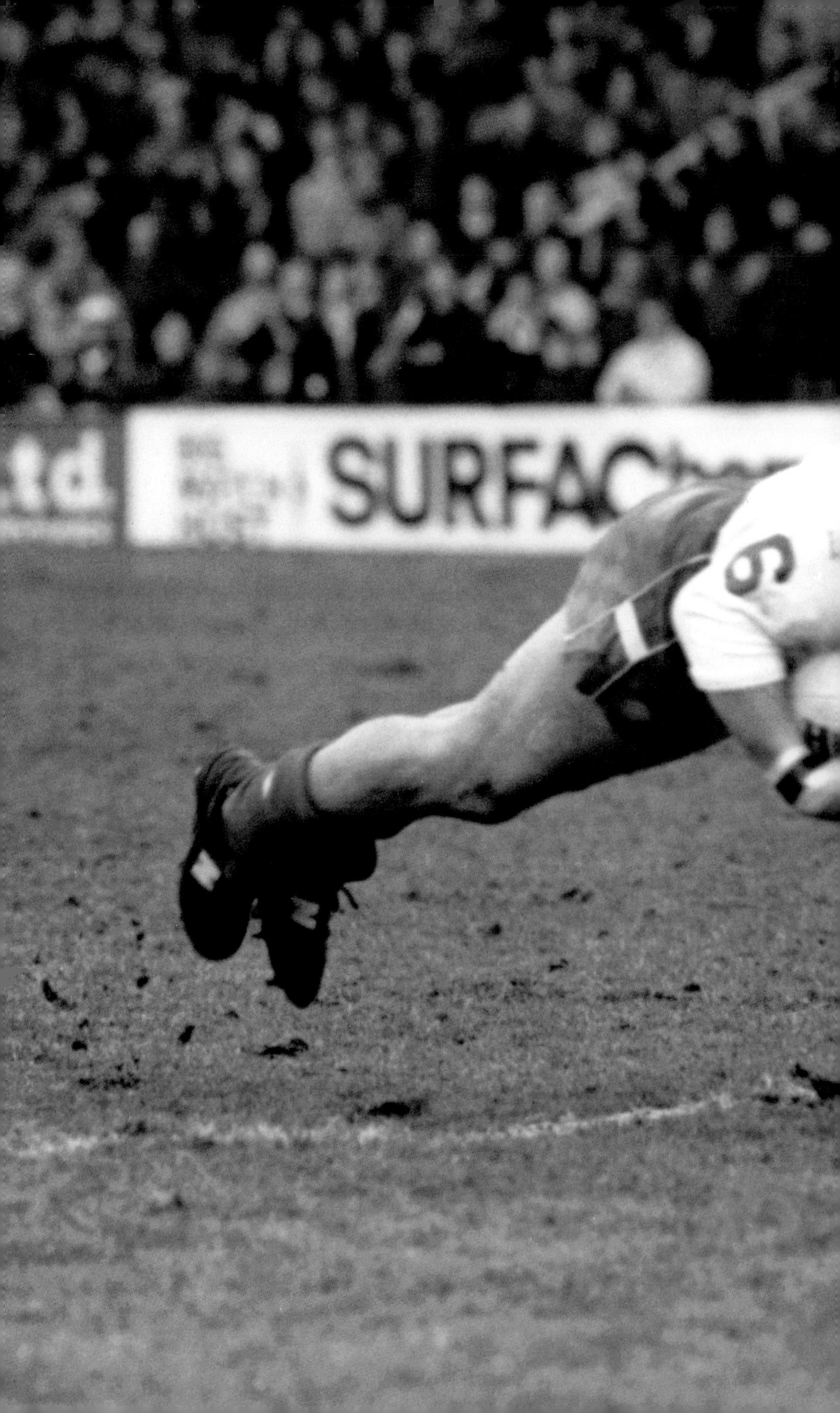

td.
SURFAC

Scoring a try for Great Britain against
France at Headingley

**Colin Maskill, the Leeds hooker: 'Come on
Schoey, you've not run far enough to be that tired!'**

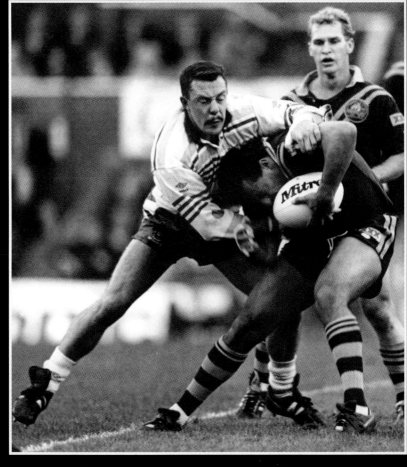

Tackling Laurie Daley during the Leeds v Australia match of 1990. Allan Langer is in support

**Scoring the winning try against Wigan
in the John PlayerTrophy semi-final at Bolton**

ABOVE: **Sustaining a knee injury in the last Test match against Australia at Lang Park in 1992.**

BELOW: **Myself with Colin Maskill in support, breaking the St Helens defence line**

**With Martin Offiah in support, I make a
break against France at Headingley**

been left on. It was these conditions that had played a part in my try, particularly as 'ET' lost his footing in the in-goal area when trying to get to the ball. There is little doubt that the plan to play the Wigan pack together paid off, for they all knew each other well and supported, covered and tackled for each other from the start, laying the foundations for this fabulous victory. At the final whistle I remember looking at the Great Britain bench and being quite shocked at the size of the smiles on the faces of Mal Reilly, his assistant Phil Larder and our tour manager, Maurice Lindsay. Once in the dressing-room we realised how much we had taken out of ourselves in containing the Aussies, and many of us just sat there thinking of the impact this win must have had back home. I know many people watched the game live on Sky TV after breakfast, and as the magnitude of the victory sunk in, that evening proved very emotional for all of us.

SECOND TEST AT PRINCE'S PARK, MELBOURNE, 26 JUNE 1992

	AUSTRALIA 10	**GREAT BRITAIN 33**
1.	Andrew Ettingshausen	Graham Steadman
2.	Rod Wishart	Paul Eastwood
3.	Laurie Daley	Paul Newlove
4.	Mal Meninga (captain)	Daryl Powell
5.	Michael Hancock	Martin Offiah
6.	Peter Jackson	Garry Schofield (captain)
7.	Allan Langer	Shaun Edwards
8.	David Gillespie	Kelvin Skerrett
9.	Steve Walters	Martin Dermot
10.	Paul Harragon	Andy Platt
11.	Paul Sironen	Denis Betts
12.	Bob Lindner	Billy McGinty
13.	Bradley Clyde	Phil Clarke
14.	Brad Mackay	Gary Connolly
15.	Glenn Lazarus	Paul Hulme
16.	Chris Johns	Joe Lydon
17.	Kevin Walters	Karl Harrison

T: Johns, Lindner   Clarke, Newlove, Schofield,
                                      Steadman, Newlove, Offiah
G: Meninga   Eastwood 6,
                                      Schofield dg

SUBSTITUTIONS: SUBSTITUTIONS:

K. Walters for Jackson (8 min) Harrison for Skerrett (61 min)
Johns for Wishart (40 min)   Hulme for McGinty (61 min)
Lazarus for Sironen (56 min)   Connolly for Newlove (65 min)
Mackay for Harragon   Lydon for Powell (73 min)
(67 min)

Referee: D. Hale (New Zealand)
Attendance: 30,257

Accompanying us on the Lions tour were between eight and ten thousand supporters, and I was fortunate that one of them was my father. Dad went out to watch the last two Tests, and that second Test was such a proud moment for me knowing that my father was on the ground. I was only young, and for a member of my family to be present, actually in the crowd that day, was fantastic.

One moment in the aftermath of this great win sticks with me today. We were back at the hotel and the champagne was flowing. Sky Sports commentators Eddie and Stevo were there with their producer, Neville Smith, and they were congratulating the lads. I had managed to get my father and his party into the hotel and into the reception. I can remember introducing Stevo to my dad, and he said to dad, 'You must be proud of your son tonight, the way he's played for his country.' And my father just came up to me and gave me a pat on the backside and said, 'Well done tonight, son.' At the time I thought dad could have shown a little more emotion, but as I said earlier in this book, he is not an emotional man. You wouldn't know he was my father: he's very quiet, he studies the game, and he would always pinpoint the things that I had done first before giving me any praise. I just felt on this occasion that a little bit more emotion would have been nice – but that's the way my father is. It didn't spoil one of my special memories – not just the highlight of winning the game, but the thought of him being there to see what was a record win against the Aussies. And it could have been worse; it could have been Stevo who patted me on the bottom!

I also received a telegram from Liverpool comedian Jimmy Tarbuck, which said: 'Congratulations on a magnificent victory over Australia and good luck for the third Test!' It was so good to receive such a note when we were far away from home representing Great Britain.

Our second-string side kept up their unbeaten record under skipper Deryck Fox's inspiration with a 28–10 win over Gold Coast at Tweed Heads. We then moved on to Brisbane, where the third Ashes Test and the series decider took place on 3 July in front of 32,000 rugby league fans, the majority of whom were Australian and out for revenge. They were not accustomed to facing the prospect of losing a Test series to Great Britain on their own soil, and the media had really built the game up. In the event the match was not a classic, and the first half ended with Australians leading 8–4, four penalties to two. They put us under some considerable pressure, cut out their mistakes from the second Test, and their kicking was much more accurate, which had the effect of pinning us in our own half on numerous occasions. We nevertheless felt we were in with a good chance of winning the game as we came out after half-time, only to concede a try to stand-off Laurie Daley within seven minutes. Eight minutes later we were really up against it when Mal Meninga picked up Daley's kick and powered over. Meninga was celebrating a record 37th Test cap, and with 12 points from four goals and a try was the Australian hero that night. We just could not overcome them a second time in the space of just seven days, and had to settle for a Martin Offiah try from 70 yards out with four minutes left. We went down 16–10 but had more than played our part in a fantastic Ashes Test series, and were now looking forward to winning the Test series in New Zealand.

We seemed to be everybody's favourite to win the first Test on 12 July in Palmerston North. The Kiwis were a young and inexperienced side at Test level, and we had just run the Australians so very close. Tony Kemp scored early on for New Zealand before Shaun Edwards replied in kind, and an exchange of penalties saw the score at half-time 8–6 to us. A stunning try set us on our way early in the second half with Martin Offiah heavily involved, taking an awkward pass from me and putting Phil Clarke in at the corner. Paul Eastwood converted from the touch-line, and with 14 minutes to go we were 14–6 ahead.

The home side then put us under intense pressure, as full-back Matthew

Ridge launched a bomb that his opposite number Graham Steadman could not collect. Winger Paul Eastwood had only to kick the ball dead but missed it completely, allowing centre Richie Blackmore to fall on the ball for a try converted by Ridge. Our two-point lead was then taken away ten minutes from time by a penalty from second row Gavin Hill, and with five minutes to go the ball bounced kindly for the Kiwis on our 22-metre line and Daryl Halligan, on as substitute for Matthew Ridge, coolly dropped the winning goal.

It goes without saying that Malcolm Reilly was more than a little disappointed, for he felt we should have made short work of the New Zealanders. Seven days later we had the chance to put things right in the second Test in Auckland, and this time we came out on top with a 19–16 victory. Once again the Kiwis played passionately and managed to open up a 10–0 lead in the first half before our hooker, Lee Jackson, touched down by the posts after Denis Betts had timed his run on to my pass to perfection. The reliable Paul Eastwood converted, and we went in at half-time 10–6 down. We came out firing on all cylinders in the second half, and after Denis Betts went over in the corner, goaled again by the irrepressible Paul Eastwood, we saw a vintage touchdown from Martin Offiah after clever play by Daryl Powell. This was Offiah's 21st try in 26 Tests, and with Eastwood inevitably kicking the goal, followed by my drop-goal, we had a nine-point cushion. The Kiwis did score again near the end through Brent Todd, but it was too late for them to pull the game out of the fire, and we had squared the Test series one all.

In the meantime Deryck Fox had led the midweek side to two more victories in New Zealand 14–8 over Auckland and 17–6 against Canterbury. The performance of a number of players in these second-string fixtures outlined the strength in depth that Great Britain had to call on in 1992. We flew home in good spirits after the New Zealand Tests with our pride restored.

After missing the 1988 event by the skin of our teeth, Great Britain qualified for the Stones Bitter World Cup final on 24 October 1992 on points difference from New Zealand, by virtue of the number of points we had accumulated in our victories over Papua New Guinea. I was named captain, proud and delighted with the honour of leading Great Britain in a World Cup final. The sponsors were delighted for the final was to take place at

Wembley Stadium. A record international attendance of over 73,000 people saw a close, physical encounter between ourselves and our old rivals Australia. Our coach Mal Reilly had moved me to centre to accommodate Shaun Edwards at stand-off half alongside Deryck Fox, but Shaun was soon in the sin-bin. He was extremely fired up that day, and in the context of the game we needed everyone to fulfil their potential and maintain concentration.

There was only one try scored in the whole game, and at half-time we led 6–4 through three Deryck Fox penalties. Mal Meninga had replied with two penalties for Australia, and man for man we had held them. The breakthrough which clinched the World Cup for Australia came 12 minutes from time: St Helens winger Alan Hunte knocked on well inside our own half, and following the scrum the Australians moved the ball forward before spinning it out to Brisbane Broncos centre Steve Renouf, who evaded an attempted tackle by substitute John Devereux to score wide out. Meninga added the conversion, and we were trailing 10–6. Up to that point we had stuck to our game plan, with Fox kicking well and the whole team defending as a unit. After the Renouf try we had to take the game more to Australia, but we failed to make any further impression on the scoreline, and so the Kangaroos won the World Cup. It had been a tough, technical battle and we had come so close once again to beating the Australians when it mattered most, and were bitterly disappointed for ourselves, the management and the fans.

WORLD CUP FINAL AT WEMBLEY STADIUM, 24 OCTOBER 1992

GREAT BRITAIN 6   AUSTRALIA 10

	GREAT BRITAIN 6	AUSTRALIA 10
1.	Joe Lydon	Tim Brasher
2.	Alan Hunte	Willie Carne
3.	Gary Connolly (captain)	Steve Renouf
4.	Garry Schofield	Mal Meninga (captain)
5.	Martin Offiah	Michael Hancock
6.	Shaun Edwards	Brad Fittler
7.	Deryck Fox	Allan Langer
8.	Kevin Ward	Glenn Lazarus
9.	Martin Dermott	Steve Walters

10.	Andy Platt	Mark Sargent
11.	Denis Betts	Paul Sironen
12.	Phil Clarke	Bob Lidner
13.	Ellery Hanley	Bradley Clyde
14.	John Devereux	John Cartwright
15.	Kelvin Skerrett	David Gillespie
16.	Alan Tait	Chris Johns
17.	Richard Eyres	Kevin Walters

G: Fox 3

Renouth
Meninga 3

SUBSTITUTIONS:
Devereux for Connolly
(40 min)
Tait for Lydon (48 min)
Skerrett for Ward (52 min)
Eyres for Hanley (72 min)

SUBSTITUTIONS:
Gillespie for Sironen (40 min)
K. Walters for Clyde (45 min)
Cartwright for Sargent (63 min)

Referee: D. Hale (New Zealand)
Attendance: 76,631

15.

TO WEMBLEY AND THE PALACE

THE RUGBY LEAGUE CHALLENGE CUP took on a new format in 1993–4 with the inclusion of 64 amateur teams in the first round. As a First Division Championship side, Leeds did not enter the competition until the fourth round, where we were pitted with Rochdale Hornets away. We progressed with a win by 40 points to 18, despite a hattrick of tries from the Rochdale centre Paul O'Keefe. That preceded a home draw against Warrington, and another comfortable victory on 12 February by 38–4 saw us proceed to the sixth round and a difficult tie at home to Bradford Northern. A magnificent crowd of 22,615 saw us produce some of our best form, and we entered the semi-final on the back of a 33–10 victory. Bradford were swept away by a rampant Leeds team, and one particularly outstanding try was scored by 17-year-old Francis Cummins from well within his own 22-metre line.

We visited Central Park, Wigan, on 26 March 1994 for the semi-final against St Helens – with a poor record at that venue when used as a neutral ground. We were disappointed that we were not playing at a semi-final venue east of the Pennines, but two tries from Ellery Hanley led us to victory by 20–8. St Helens had us on the back foot for most of the semi-final, though we led 8–6 at half-time, and Alan Tait, our full-back, gained the Man of the Match award.

It meant a return to Wembley for those magnificent Leeds fans after so many years. Inevitably we were to face Wigan, who overcame Castleford at Headingley by 20 points to 6 to register their 35th successive Challenge Cup victory since 1988, and their seventh Wembley appearance in a row. But the cup final itself on 30 April 1994 was to be a great disappointment to every one of us who went to London in the Leeds colours. The Leeds public had turned out in force as we all expected, and the day itself was as always a great credit to rugby league. The weather was exceptional, and the ground was full of the blue-and-amber of Leeds, the cherry-and-white of Wigan, and supporters wearing the shirts of just about every other club in the professional and amateur games. Once more, Wembley and its unique atmosphere lives long in my memory.

The game itself was quite outstanding, many spectators have told me, but for a player on the losing side it was something I wanted to forget. Once again Leeds had almost succeeded, only to fall at the last hurdle to the outstanding pace of the world-class Martin Offiah. Martin won the Lance Todd Trophy as Man of the Match, as voted on by the rugby league journalists present at the final. He did so for the second time, joining just two other players who had achieved this honour twice: Gerry Helme, the Warrington scrum-half of the 1950s, and Andy Gregory, the cheeky Wigan scrum-half of the 1990s.

We never felt at any stage inferior to Wigan, but the pace of that one individual robbed us of the cup. His try after 14 minutes has been classed as the best individual effort ever seen at Wembley in the Challenge Cup final. Martin was just a few metres from his own line when he took the ball and accelerated past two of my colleagues – and suddenly he hit open field, and put his foot on the gas to move away from the Leeds defenders until he was faced finally with Alan Tait, the British Lion and former rugby union player. All Alan could do was give Martin the outside line and ensure that the conversion would be as difficult as possible. It is not easy for one of the victims to give the try great credit, but looking back it was remarkable.

This apart, I felt that we held Wigan throughout the game in brilliant weather, and despite Andy Farrell scoring a further try and Frano Botica kicking two goals, our fans were still singing at the break. We came back after going in at half-time 12–0 down, and Jim Fallon, our ex-rugby union winger, scored first before I managed to hand off the wonder winger Offiah to bag a second. A penalty from Graham Holroyd brought the score to 12–10 before we suffered yet another blow from 'Chariots' Offiah.

Mick Cassidy made a burst and released Offiah 60 yards out, who motored away past Jim Fallon to touch down again in classic fashion. With Botica's conversion, we had another hill to climb. Wigan substitute Sam Panapa made it even higher following a heavy tackle by Va'aiga Tuigamala on full-back Tait, although we did score the final try through young Francis

Cummins, from 85 metres out after Offiah had dropped the ball looking for his hat trick. Francis had become the youngest ever player to appear in a Wembley cup final, and the capacity crowd had been treated to a magnificent game of rugby which Wigan finished up winning 26–16.

For us all the forwards had battled well, but Gary Mercer particularly, together with Richard Eyres in the second row, did not give an inch. This was Wigan's seventh consecutive Silk Cut Challenge Cup success, and yet I feel we had been their equals in every department – except for the supreme pace of Offiah. Other records were broken that day by Mike O'Neill, for the longest playing span at Wembley; Marcus Vassilakopoulos, the youngest forward to play at Wembley; and Shaun Edwards, for most finals and most winner's medals – but at the end of the day I was going home with no winner's medal, and that hurt.

In December 1994 I took my wife Adele and my two children, Danielle and Jonathan, down to London to be with me when I received the OBE from Prince Charles at Buckingham Palace. This was the proudest day of my life, and I was doubly pleased for mum and dad.

In the autumn of 1993 I had received a phone call from Maurice Lindsay at Rugby League Headquarters on Chapeltown Road in Leeds. Now chief executive at RFL, Maurice mentioned to me that they had put my name forward to the Government department which deals with the Queen's New Year's honours list, for achievements and services rendered to rugby league. Maurice then asked me if I had received a letter from the Prime Minister on the subject. No such letter had arrived, and I promised to let him know as soon as one did. I was both shocked and grateful for even being considered, and thanked Maurice Lindsay for calling me. Our relationship had been a good one, in my view, built on mutual respect for what we had achieved.

I had forgotten about the call when, early the following May, I opened an official document from Downing Street confirming that I had been put forward for an OBE, to be made public in the Queen's Birthday honours list on 11 June 1994 – a date which is also my daughter's birthday. I could not believe it! I shot round with the letter to mum and dad, and we all spent a very difficult six weeks before the Queen's birthday, as we were not permitted to disclose the honour before the official announcement in case it was withdrawn. Strangely enough, Leeds rugby league club found out and wanted to throw a surprise party for my family and me on 11 June. The club had been approached earlier in 1994 by a Government representative seeking more details of my career, and they had simply put two and two together.

Now this is where my relationship with Maurice Lindsay took a turn for the worse. The Leeds club told me later that they had been approached by Mr Lindsay, who had somehow got to know of the planned party, and were advised in no uncertain terms that they could not go ahead with it. My wife Adele and Colin Maskill who were most closely involved, were told that it would not now proceed, but were never told the reason why.

My family and I travelled down to London, and I was invested with the honour on 6 December 1994 by Prince Charles. It was a long ceremony, lasting over two and a half hours, with many awards to be granted, but it was my proudest moment. Prince Charles spoke with me for about 12 seconds, commenting on how rough the game was. I feared he was not too clued up on rugby league and, sadly, he proved me correct when he said, 'Those South Africans must be tough to play against.' Clearly the guy was talking about the Springbok rugby union team! My son Jonathan slept through the whole proceedings, and we left in a hurry afterwards in order to catch the train back to Leeds.

That evening, the Blue and Amber Club at Headingley was having its Christmas party, and I had promised to be there. The Blue and Amber Club was formed to accommodate all Leeds' junior fans, and I used to spend much of my spare time coaching the youngsters and giving them advice to help them progress in the game – in particular, that they have to look after their kit and appreciate that dedication is the key to success. I was delighted we made it back in time, for so many youngsters and parents wanted to congratulate me and have their photograph taken with me and the medal that represented the Order of the British Empire. I was only too pleased to oblige them.

To his credit, Dougie Laughton turned up later in the evening – and then spoilt it all by not offering me any congratulations. His only comments concerned the words Prince Charles had spoken to me: 'Did he give you any advice of a carnal nature?'

In the end the Leeds club, in conjunction with Robert Charles of Yorkshire Television, produced a *This Is Your Life* special for me on 23 April 1995. John Helm compèred a great night, and I was particularly grateful to Arthur

Bunting, Mike Page and Mick Sullivan, who all travelled over from Hull. Just a handful of Leeds players attended – Gary Mercer, Kevin Iro and James Lowes!

Following the same format as 1993–94, the 1995 Silk Cut Challenge Cup kicked off again with the amateur sides being drawn against the lower-division professional clubs. For the first time in 86 years, a professional club was eliminated when Beverley won 27–4 at Highfield. In round four Wigan, the holders, managed a late equaliser to snatch a fortunate draw against St Helens, only to progress with some ease in the replay by 40 points to 24. Our entry into the competition at the same stage on 12 February 1995 saw us eliminate Bradford Northern at Headingley by 31–14. We were trailing by 12–8 at half-time and, in a very physical game, Bradford lost their way as Ellery Hanley and Gary Mercer each touched down twice to give us victory.

In the fifth round we were favoured with another home draw, this time against Ryedale-York, and a 44–14 victory included four tries by our winger, Jim Fallon. In the sixth round in March, a hat-trick of tries by Ellery Hanley saw off Workington Town by 50 points to 16, and took us through to the semi-final. We avoided both Wigan and Oldham in the semi-final draw, meeting Featherstone Rovers instead in front of over 21,000 fans at Elland Road in Leeds, with the prospect ahead of us of a final against Wigan with their 41 consecutive Silk Cut Challenge Cup victories. The two teams at Leeds United's football ground that day were:

FEATHERSTONE ROVERS

Carl Gibson; Ikram Butt, Brett Rodger, Matt Calland, Frederic Banquet; Brendon Tuuta, Mark Aston; Steve Molloy, Graham Southernwood, Jason Simms, Daniel Divet, Gary H. Price, Neil Roebuck; Mark Nixon and Leo Casey.

LEEDS

Alan Tait; Jim Fallon, Kevin Iro, Craig Innes, Francis Cummins; Garry Schofield, Graham Holroyd; Neil Harmon, James Lowes, Esene Faimalo, Gary Mercer, Richard Eyres, Ellery Hanley; George Mann and Harvey Howard.

Although Featherstone was a small mining community, their rugby league tradition was folklore. They loved the game in the village and always looked forward to taking on a big-city club such as Leeds. We knew we had our work cut out. How well I remembered them defeating the champions Hull against all odds in the cup final at Wembley in 1983, just before I signed at the Boulevard. The Lance Todd Trophy winner that day, David Hobbs, is now a colleague of mine on BBC Radio Leeds.

We were also facing our old coach, David Ward, and were certain that he would be able to motivate his players for such an important match. Ex-Leeds players Carl Gibson, Steve Molloy and Ikram Butt certainly wanted to beat their old team-mates. Ikram, who had had limited opportunity in the first team at Headingley, was a player of no mean ability, who represented the Asian community with great dignity and was a credit to rugby league. Not only that but he was an elusive winger, and for those Leeds supporters who followed our A team on Friday evenings a few years earlier, he was one of the outstanding players.

Before the semi-final, David Ward suggested that both Dougie Laughton and Leeds had good reason to curse the fact that they were contesting honours with one of the greatest trophy-winning sides ever seen in rugby league. He believed Wigan would only be overtaken when their own high standards started to slip. While Laughton had seen and done it all in the game over the last 30 years – he had been a member of the last Great Britain team to defeat Australia in an Ashes series, and as coach of Widnes he had helped to deny Wigan two championships – he would have found that managing Wigan was a piece of cake compared to the task of taking over at Leeds. It seemed clear to David that Laughton had underestimated the size of the job at Headingley.

David Ward was in good form before the game. 'We're just happy to be here,' he said, 'because everyone expects to see a Leeds–Wigan Wembley final. They are both great sides, and we're the underdogs this afternoon. We'll just enjoy the day at Elland Road and see how it goes. I was fortunate enough to captain Leeds to successive Wembley wins before the age of 25. I never managed to return to Wembley again, except in the capacity of spectator, but I'll be there again on 29 April – in one capacity or another!'

Dougie Laughton was quoted as saying: 'Let's say that I could see the writing on the wall. Just as the local butcher can't compete with the supermarket, I realised that Widnes couldn't continue to compete with Wigan when the playing field was uneven. I knew there were only a few clubs capable of matching Wigan's overall resources, and Leeds was the biggest and most ambitious of them. Taking Leeds to Wembley was one of the most satisfying experiences of my career, because the loyalty of the supporters deserved to be rewarded with success. That's why occasions such as the Cup semi-final are so important. There's so much at stake in terms of financial reward and prestige for the club, and greater exposure for the players. The hopes of thousands of fans, sponsors, players and directors, wives and girlfriends all rest on the outcome of the 80 minutes. It's always a big occasion for the whole city, and we really lapped it up last year. I was thrilled when we got the win over Saints in the semi-final because it gave everyone a taste of being back in the spotlight. We may not have won the trophy, but the side performed with credit at Wembley, and everyone agrees that we are much stronger this time around. Sadly, this was not to be the case.

We triumphed 39–22 to earn a visit to Wembley for the second year running, and another confrontation with the Wigan club. Ellery Hanley scored two tries to bring his total up to 40 for the season, and equalled the Leeds record for a forward set in 1970–71 by Bob Haigh.

The only similarity with the 1994 final was the same teams competing – for the first time ever in consecutive finals – and the exceptionally good weather. Once again the Leeds fans did us proud, but regrettably we could not raise our game even to the level of 12 months earlier. On this occasion it was Jason Robinson who scored two tries and was voted Lance Todd Trophy winner as Man of the Match, to emulate his fellow-winger Martin Offiah's achievement the previous year. It was no consolation that Robinson had been omitted from Wigan's team in 1994 – nor that, Hunslet born and bred, he had been missed by Leeds as a youngster. Referee Russell Smith denied me a try during the game, and the after-match dinner and disco in the team hotel was a most depressing affair. The cup final score was 30–10 in front of another capacity crowd.

Several of the players from Leeds and other West Yorkshire clubs occupied themselves during the summers by playing cricket for John Morgan's All Star XI, helping to raise money for charity at the same time. I enjoyed many a relaxing day in this manner with rugby mates Colin Maskill and Bobby Goulding. A number of our players were quite outstanding cricketers, and we enjoyed good results in the main. I will openly admit that I am not a great cricket fan – the ball is far too hard for me; but I did enjoy the social crack and the company of the many people who give up their spare time to raise money for good causes. I also always enjoyed John Morgan's company and am surprised that, for all his fund-raising and charitable works, he has received little formal recognition. Until his recent retirement, John was 'Ranger' – the racing correspondent and tipster for the *Yorkshire Evening Post* – and his outstanding devotion to the cause of Hunslet rugby league club, now known as Hunslet Hawks, is legendary in these parts. John even mentions the club in his after-dinner speeches, by following grace with the words, 'As we say in Hunslet – *bon appétit!*'

16.

INTERNATIONAL FINALE

IT WAS A CASE of after the Lord Mayor's Show, following the tense World Cup final against Australia at Wembley in October 1992 when Great Britain went on to meet France in the two British Coal Tests of March and April 1993. I played in the first fixture at Carcassonne, captaining a strong side to victory 48–6. I was back at stand-off half with Shaun Edwards as my scrum-half, and I managed to score three tries in addition to putting over substitute Mike Ford and Ellery Hanley. The score was a record on French soil, with the team running in 30 points without reply in the second period. We already know that I did not play in the second fixture at Headingley on 2 April, courtesy of Dougie Laughton, when Great Britain ran up a world-record score of 72–6!

We then prepared for the visit of the New Zealand rugby league tourists in autumn 1993. I was confirmed as captain for the series and felt Great Britain were becoming a force to be reckoned with. The first John Smith's Test took place at Wembley on 16 October – and our performance almost impressed our coach Mal Reilly. We did not allow the Kiwis a single score in the match, leading 10–0 at half-time and eventually running out winners 17–0. Jason Robinson scored two outstanding tries on the right wing in the first half, and early in the second half left winger John Devereux from Widnes dived to touch down following a Jonathan Davies bomb. Davies kicked one penalty, one conversion and one drop-goal to complete the scoring. Shaun Edwards had one of his best games for Britain and was deservedly named Man of the Match, although Davies ran him close at full-back, and defensively Reilly must have been very pleased with the performance of his forwards, Harrison, Chris Joynt and Phil Clarke in particular.

For the second Test, played at Central Park, Wigan, our coach invited the backs to express themselves – a complete reversal of policy from the first Test. I certainly enjoyed myself in this game, for we all clicked together and by half-time we were leading 12–6 – although this did not accurately reflect the dominance of our attacking. New Zealand had scored first through full-back Dave Watson, with Botica converting, and two tries by John Devereux, both improved by Jonathan Davies, were all we had to show for our skilful ball play. In the second half I managed to pick up a try and a drop-goal, and in the last ten minutes Martin Offiah and Paul Newlove went over for tries, both of which were goaled by Davies. We had won the second Test 29–12 and the series, but more important was the way we had played, which was pleasing not only to the Central Park crowd but also to the coaches and management of the Great Britain squad.

The third Test at Headingley saw the introduction of Andrew Farrell of Wigan, the youngest forward to make his début for Great Britain. Once more we played an expansive game which led to five tries, one of which went to Farrell. All the forwards played their part, with Karl Fairbank scoring after ten minutes and Phil Clarke touching down six minutes later. Jonathan Davies had another excellent game, picking off a Tony Kemp pass to race 90 yards and touch down, in addition to four goals and one drop-goal. Once again, though, he failed to win the Man of the Match award as this went to loose-forward Clarke. We won comfortably 29–10, although I sustained a rib injury after 11 minutes which meant that my contribution was short-lived. The match was spoiled to some extent by the late dismissal of our substitute forward, Sonny Nickle, for an off-the-ball elbow on New Zealand counterpart John Lomax.

Malcolm Reilly was probably at the peak of his powers with Great Britain at the time of this whitewash of New Zealand, and his introduction of younger players such as Andrew Farrell promised much more for the future. Later that same winter we played a John Smith's Test in Carcassonne against the French. Although we never trailed in the game we did struggle, and were indebted in the end to a try 20 minutes from time by Shaun Edwards. Shaun had suffered from food poisoning the day before the match and was a doubtful starter. In the end he turned out, and he and I combined in a runaround move which enabled Shaun to take advantage of the gap created and score with a curving run from near halfway. An earlier Paul Newlove try and, late in the game, an Andrew Farrell penalty to add to that struck by Lee

Crooks in the first half meant that we won the game 12–4 – but we owed the victory to the Edwards try. The French had worked hard and were none too pleased with Wigan referee John Connolly, particularly after he ruled a forward pass against them in the last minute. It seems that this was the first time that a neutral referee had not been appointed for this fixture for a number of years.

Malcolm Reilly resigned as Great Britain coach to take up a post with Newcastle Knights in Australia late in the summer of 1994, only a month before the Australian tourists were due to visit our shores. The favourite to replace him, Phil Larder, declined to take the position, apparently owing to the proposed involvement of the New Zealander Graham Lowe in a Great Britain management structure. Consequently, on 29 August, Ellery Hanley was appointed Great Britain's coach for the forthcoming John Smith's Test series against the Kangaroos. With the Graham Lowe idea shelved, Ellery immediately nominated Sheffield Eagles' Gary Hetherington as his assistant.

With the tourists due to arrive in October 1994, all the players in contention to face them knew that we would have to perform well for our club sides in order to impress the new Great Britain coach. Regardless of who had been involved in the previous winter series against New Zealand, with a new coach on board it was clear that we all needed to impress early in the season. My own season had started quite well, but Dougie Laughton had persisted with Graham Holroyd at stand-off for Leeds for his own reasons, and had me playing scrum-half – a position for which I could not realistically see myself being considered for the starting line-up for the first Test at Wembley on 22 October.

Shortly before the first Test squad was to be announced, Leeds were down to play the Australian tourists on a Wednesday evening. To my surprise, Doug Laughton had selected me at stand-off half for this fixture, and had advised the press that this would give me one last chance to impress the new Great Britain coaching staff. This seemed an odd comment to make given our relationship, and in the circumstances I just wondered whether he believed that the Australians would win comfortably, and my cause would be irreparably damaged. In the event the Australians did beat us comfortably, by 48–6. They played a strong side as they warmed up for Wembley, and Leeds found it very difficult to make any impact on the game. I always enjoyed playing against the Australians, but we were on a hiding to nothing that evening.

A few days later the Test squad was announced, and I was surprised to find that not only had I not been picked in the starting line-up, I wasn't even in the squad. I had played 44 Tests already, and with my experience and proven record at international level as both stand-off and captain, to say I was disappointed would be an understatement.

The Monday the Test squad was announced, I was away playing golf with a good friend of mine, the late Phil Carrick. Phil was enjoying a well deserved testimonial from his much beloved Yorkshire County Cricket Club, and I had travelled over to Oldham after training in order to support him on the golf course. I recall playing with Paul Pickup, Barry Spence and Jack Brennan: all three were keen rugby league supporters, and they knew that the squad was to be announced that day. None of us had heard any news that morning, and so we set off on our round of golf on the assumption that the RFL's media office would probably announce the squad after lunch.

We had reached the eleventh tee when I saw three guys walking across the course. As they approached, I realised that they were three well-known rugby league journalists – Alan Thomas, Peter Wilson and Martin Richards. I asked them what they were doing on the golf course, whereupon Paul Pickup advised me that he had in fact heard that I had been left out of the Test squad. Paul had been telephoned by my wife Adele that morning to pass on the news. She had had the press ringing her to find out where I was for an interview, but with me going straight from the training ground to the golf course in Oldham, nobody had been able to contact me. Adele knew how upset I would be at missing out on international selection for the first time since 1984, and felt that she ought at least to contact Paul Pickup who would then be able to tell me.

The three press lads asked me for comments and an interview. I responded that, on this occasion, I couldn't say anything before speaking with my close friend, solicitor John Penistone. I felt at the time that I was not in the best frame of mind to make a reasoned statement. I was rather upset and did not wish to say the wrong thing. It goes without saying that I could no longer concentrate on my golf, and after a couple more holes I then saw television cameras coming over the hill towards me. They were carried by two members of the Australian media who had travelled 12,000 miles to cover all the tour matches. They represented two television channels Down Under, Channel 9 and Channel 7, and they also wanted me to give an interview. I confirmed that I wasn't in a position to give them any comment at this stage, and the last six holes proved disastrous for me.

Looking back, I had been associated with the Great Britain Test squad for the previous ten years, and I did find it hard to accept that I had been unable to make it into a squad of 20 players. I understood that the Great Britain management had picked the players they felt were best suited for the series ahead, it was just the shock of no longer being part of something that I had cherished and enjoyed for so long. People had also been bringing up the issue of Mick Sullivan's world record for the most Great Britain Test caps, as I was coming so close to emulating that figure.

That evening I joined Phil Carrick for dinner and a couple of beers after the golf, but the disappointment hanging over me was intense. The following morning I spoke with John Penistone regarding my rugby career and told him that I couldn't go into training at Leeds that morning, as I felt Dougie Laughton must have had something to do with this. Ellery Hanley, the Great Britain coach, was also still a club colleague of mine, and I would have appreciated him speaking to me face to face regarding my omission. John told me that I must attend training, and so I drove to Headingley with a heavy heart. At the A.B. Sharman gates I was stopped by Alf Davies, who must have been waiting for my arrival, to try to defuse the situation between Dougie, Ellery and me. I told him straightaway I felt there was a conspiracy to stop me from achieving something I had worked very hard for over many years. I'm sure now this was not the case, but that's how I felt at the time. When I had reached my 40th cap in 1992, I set my sights on trying to beat Mick Sullivan's world record of 46. Alf simply told me I had to keep working hard, and try to concentrate on my game. I would then have every chance of being considered for one of the later Tests, he felt sure.

When I arrived in the dressing-room all was very quiet – you could hear a pin drop. All the players knew the situation, and not many words were said. In fact Alan Tait was extremely miffed himself, for he felt he had every chance of being selected as one of the full-backs, but he too had been omitted. This surprised me, as he had been playing quite well at the time, and I thought his form warranted selection. The more I reflected on my lot, the more it came home to me that for as long as I was playing out of position with Leeds, I couldn't expect to get in the Great Britain starting line-up or the squad as a scrum-half. In the weeks leading up to the Tests, there had been a debate as to who would be the Great Britain captain in this series, me or Shaun Edwards. One of the rugby league magazines even undertook a poll on this subject. Shaun had been playing very well for Wigan in his own position as scrum-half, and I could see no way of making the Test team in that position.

When we went out on the training park that Tuesday morning Dougie Laughton never said a word to me – which was probably a good thing, because I would certainly have told him exactly how I felt. In fact, a physical response might not have been considered inappropriate, so wound up was I! Alan Tait was also finding it difficult to concentrate on training and continued moaning all morning. This helped me considerably and, looking back, he may have acted in this manner to take some of the heat out of my situation. As it was, I had no choice but to come to terms with the decision of the selectors, and I got on with the job of performing to the best of my ability with Leeds.

The blow was softened when the BBC asked me to join them as a summariser for the first Test match between Great Britain and Australia at Wembley. It was a pleasure to work with Steve Rider and the *Grandstand* team, and I must say he was extremely professional and made me feel so relaxed and not at all intimidated. I did enjoy that afternoon, though I would have preferred to have been out there! Great Britain were the underdogs, but once again came up trumps, winning 8–4, in spite of losing captain Edwards early in the game, sent off for a high tackle on Bradley Clyde. Bobby Goulding came on to assume Edwards' role, and Jonathan Davies turned out to be the match-winner when he scored a magnificent try in the corner. The Australians seemed to lose some of their discipline as the Great Britain forwards got stuck in and frustrated them.

As soon as I arrived at Leeds' training ground the following Monday, I went straight to Dougie's office where Ellery was sitting and congratulated him on a fantastic win. I suggested that a surprise could well be on the cards, and that Great Britain might win the first Test series and the Ashes against Australia since 1970. After that first win I guess I was helped considerably by Shaun Edwards being sent off. Whether that was the reason or not, Ellery recalled me to the squad for the second Test as Great Britain strove to clinch the series. Looking back, the Test side he picked seemed a little negative: I was a substitute, Sheffield centre Daryl Powell was selected at stand-off half, and Bobby Goulding came in at scrum-half. Unfortunately we went on to lose the second Test that day, being on the receiving end of an inspired Australian performance and going down 38–8. I was brought on at half-time to replace Daryl Powell at stand-off, and although we lost the second half 20–4, the British press seemed to feel that my introduction had helped the Lions play with more purpose.

The third and deciding Test match was played at Elland Road, Leeds, on 3 November 1994, and once again I was on the bench in company with Bobby Goulding, Daryl Powell and Sonny Nickle. This time Ellery Hanley had decided to play Phil Clarke, the Wigan loose-forward, at stand-off alongside the returning Shaun Edwards at scrum-half. Great Britain put up a great fight for over an hour, and I entered the fray after 23 minutes, replacing Phil Clarke who suffered damaged ankle ligaments. We really took the game to Australia and were unfortunate on several occasions not to break through and take the lead. Centre Gary Connolly came close, and Chris Joynt also could have turned the game our way. It was not until late in the game that the Australians powered away from us, with tries from Wishart, Walters and Dean Pay. We had gone down gallantly 23–4, and I had equalled Mick Sullivan's world record of 46 Test appearances.

I look back at that third Test at Elland Road, the football ground in my home town, and remember with pride that the stadium was absolutely packed with rugby league supporters. The atmosphere was tremendous. I recall removing my tracksuit when I saw Phil Clarke limping very badly – I didn't wait for the call, I just took my tracksuit top off and waited on the sideline! When I got the nod to go on, I will never forget the roar of the crowd when it was announced to them that I was equalling Mick Sullivan's world record. I would have preferred such an occasion to have been a successful one, but in the end we had to settle for another 2–1 series defeat. Having played in a record six series against Australia one of my biggest disappointments is not winning the Ashes in at least one of them.

Just after the third Test the RFL held the usual end-of-series dinner, with the players of both Great Britain and Australia present as principal guests. I had been told before the dinner that the master of ceremonies, Harry Gration, had been advised by one high-ranking British official not to make any mention of my equalling Mick Sullivan's record! You can imagine how this made me feel – not so much for the absence of any announcement, more as a result of finding out that such instructions had been given to Harry. The evening was one of very mixed emotions for me, with the Australians privately congratulating me. Laurie Daley was particularly astonished to find that no mention had been formally made and no presentation given. Laurie suggested that if this had occurred in Australia, then they would have made me guest of honour at their dinner. At a later date there was a gathering in the Trust House Forte Hotel at Brighouse in recognition of my achievement, although I would have been prouder still if the Australians had been in attendance.

At the end of May 1995, Ellery Hanley accepted a lucrative deal with the Australian Rugby League and he left Leeds rugby league club, Great Britain and the preparations for the Centenary World Cup. After the Test series against the Aussies in 1994, the next international competition didn't involve Great Britain: it was England, under new management with Phil Larder as coach, who were challenging for the ten-nation World Cup in October 1995. By this stage I had already upset the apple-cart with some outspoken comments regarding Super League and the offer of loyalty contracts to some players and not to me – so I guess I wasn't surprised to be left out of a 40-man squad that was named in the summer to prepare for the tournament. At the same time I could not believe I was not one of the best 40 players in the country. If this really was the case, then I might as well forget playing rugby league altogether!

My Great Britain career was clearly coming to an end, but it would have been a great finale to my international career to go out with England in the Centenary World Cup. And with a new coaching set-up now in place at Leeds, and having seen the back of Doug Laughton at last, I thought to myself: set your sights on a World Cup place.

So I set my stall out to force my way into Phil Larder's squad. Phil had said in the press that players outside the training squad could still make the final 25 when it was to be announced later in the year. The new coaching regime at Headingley of Dean Bell, Edgar Curtis and Hugh McGahan gave me back a spring in my step at training, and Dean Bell in particular seemed to appreciate what I had achieved in my career. I played against Dean on several occasions, and he was a very good international. He and Hugh restored my confidence, especially when they gave me back the captaincy of my home town club.

I was looking forward to a good campaign with Leeds in the short 1995–96 season, the last one in winter before the summer Super League. My form after the first six weeks was pretty good, and people were saying to me, keep it up and you should be knocking at the door of the England squad. Phil Larder had appointed former Castleford team-mates John Joyner and John Kear to be his assistants, and I believe they had watched me as well as several others in the Leeds team. Phil Larder then contacted me by phone and arranged for him and John Kear to meet with me at Rugby League Headquarters on the Tuesday before the squad was to be announced on the following Monday.

On the Monday before the final squad was to be announced, Lee Crooks was celebrating his birthday with a bit of a drink in the Horse and Jockey in Castleford. I went over on the Monday teatime for a few drinks, and quite a few of us were there – myself, Crooksy, Masky, Gary Stephens and also John Joyner. John told me then that Phil wanted a chat with me, and I said that we had a meeting lined up for tomorrow. To my surprise 'JJ', as he is well known, asked me if I had the desire to play for my country any more. You can well imagine what my reply to that was! Playing for my country has always been very special to me, and to play in a World Cup, especially on home soil, was more than I could express in my reply! JJ was left in no doubt that I was definitely up for it, and he assured me that the coaching team felt my performances had been very impressive. It seemed as though I could have played myself into the squad.

So I went along to Rugby League Headquarters at 1.45 p.m. on the Tuesday and met Phil Larder, with John Kear in attendance, and at the time I recalled our first meeting many years earlier when Phil had doubted my career prospects. Now he enquired about my attitude towards playing for England, and asked me if I could stick to a game plan and play to the coach's system. I replied, 'I'll stick to whatever game plan you set, if that's what you want. I'll do whatever you feel is best for the team.'

As everybody who has watched my career will know, whether at Hull, Leeds or in a Great Britain jersey, I could bring innovation to the game. At times I would go and take responsibility myself if I felt there was an opportunity to turn a game. Sometimes it paid off and sometimes not – interceptions for instance – but more often than not, it has worked pretty well. I guess Phil was a little worried that such individualism may cost

England in the World Cup. So I said I would be more than delighted to stick to the game plan, offensively or defensively as he wished. After we'd agreed on that, he went on to explain to me where the lads would be training and where they would be based, at the Trust House Forte Hotel in Brighouse. They even congratulated me on making the final squad! They told me that a letter would be sent out to all players to arrive on the following Monday when they would be announcing the squad to the media.

The three of us shook hands after the meeting – myself, Phil Larder and John Kear. I was delighted with the outcome of our discussions, and I fully expected the letter on the Monday morning. There were three Leeds players who were hoping for selection. I was certain I was going to be one of them after the meeting; Neil Harmon, who for me was the front-rower at the time who was showing the best form; and young threequarter Paul Cook. When we arrived for training that Monday morning, Cooky had his letter and was receiving the congratulations of all his colleagues – but for me no letter had been forthcoming, neither was there one for Neil Harmon. When Phil Larder announced his squad he was asked by the press why I had been omitted, and his reply was that it had been a choice between me and Daryl Powell for the the stand-off position. According to the England supremo Daryl had been exceptionally doubtful through injury but had proved his fitness the previous Sunday for Keighley! One match in the First division, and he was to play in the World Cup!

I was surprised, but deep down I had a feeling that my comments regarding Super League and the loyalty contracts had gone against me; I had the feeling that Maurice Lindsay was behind my omission from the squad. Between Phil Larder telling me I was in on the Tuesday afternoon, and the Friday morning when the letters were sent out, someone must have got at the team management to rule out my selection. Some ten days later David Facey, the rugby league correspondent of the *Daily Mail*, asked for an interview, and I stated categorically to him what Phil Larder had said to me regarding the World Cup arrangements. I had provisionally been selected for the England World Cup squad, but after my attack on Mr Lindsay over Super League I felt that he had been behind my omission. For the comments which David quoted me as saying, I was brought before a disciplinary subcommittee of the RFL's board of directors for bringing the game into disrepute. I was asked why I'd made those comments and I told them why.

They said there was no truth in my suggestions, and I was fined £250. This happened to be the precise equivalent of the fee I had received from the newspaper for the interview, and that was the end of the matter.

The World Cup itself was a great success overall; large crowds turned out, and the sponsors, the Halifax Building Society, were very pleased. Unfortunately for England, again, we couldn't overcome the Aussies when it mattered. Although England won their opening group game against Australia, when the two sides met again in the final at Wembley the Kangaroos retained their crown as world champions with a 16–8 success.

Some weeks after the World Cup I was told by a person still very heavily involved in Super League that Mr Lindsay had indeed approached Phil Larder and John Kear. This person confirmed that something had gone on after my meeting with the coaches, and that Phil and John were told in no uncertain terms that if I was selected their positions would be placed in jeopardy. People know how Maurice ran the game from the top: perhaps those three – Phil, John and John Joyner were intimidated and didn't have the bottle to go against him. My own management team at Leeds certainly felt it was unjustified for me to be left out, and I didn't have much respect for Phil Larder after that. I thought his coaching lacked innovation, a theory which gained substance when he was appointed as coach of the Great Britain team to tour New Zealand and the South Pacific in 1996.

I don't want to sound bitter over this issue. I was so fortunate to play for and lead my country for so many years. I just had so much desire to play at international level for as long as I possibly could, and when I was given a final chance to go out on a high, only to see it taken away from me in the way that it was, it left me gutted. Now I can see that I might have overreacted, but at the time that was how I honestly felt. And I feel I should call it now as I saw it then.

17.

BEHIND CLOSED DOORS

I **FIRST MET** my wife Adele at Hunslet Parkside rugby club. She and her sister Helen were keen on rugby league, and they were Hunslet girls. We married on 1 December 1984, after having to postpone the ceremony we had originally scheduled for July owing to my first Great Britain tour selection. We have two children, Danielle and Jonathan, who both love sport. Jonathan plays with Oulton Raiders amateur rugby league club, although he's also keen on golf and football. They have followed me to many of the matches I have played in over recent years.

Sadly my wife was diagnosed with breast cancer early in 1995, and her specialist, Mr Tom Brennan, had the lump removed within a couple of days. Twelve months of radiation and chemotherapy treatment led to her receiving the all-clear. Before the illness was diagnosed, our marriage had been strained through my travelling and playing abroad for several summers, and my inability to ignore the attractions of the occasional drinking session and the opposite sex. I lived life to the full both on and off the pitch, and I can understand how difficult it must have been for her to live with me for any long period of time. While we both agreed to put aside any problems we had in order to concentrate on helping Adele to pull through her fight against the disease, 12 months after her full recovery we did agree to part, and a bitter divorce followed. It saddened me all the more that false accusations were subsequently made against me by Adele, and found their way on to the front page of the local newspaper. This was an upsetting time for all our family, relatives and friends.

Tragically Adele's cancer reappeared in 1998 and despite major surgery the medics were unable to stop it spreading. Just after Christmas 1999 Adele died from three brain tumours, the day before Jonathan's ninth birthday. The hardest thing I've ever done in my life – no matter who I played against and how big they were – was to tell our two children that their mum had died. I will never forget the moment. Both children knew that the illness was not getting better, but the shock of losing their loving mother was still something that will stay with me forever. Our two children are the greatest gift this life could afford me.

18.

INTO SUPER LEAGUE

THE LEEDS BOARD had appointed Dean Bell as assistant coach to Dougie Laughton in June 1995, and on that same day Dougie had resigned. Leeds then moved to appoint Hugh McGahan to the post of team manager, and so we approached the final winter season before the advent of the summer Super League under New Zealand management with two hugely successful former Kiwi internationals at the helm. Although there wasn't a lot of money to spend, the club recruited Mike Forshaw from Wakefield Trinity, and a big signing in prop-forward Barrie McDermott from Wigan. Speedy winger Leroy Rivett also joined the club in September, from East Leeds amateur rugby league club.

Our home form that season was excellent, apart from the 22–27 defeat by Sheffield Eagles in November. We had beaten Wigan earlier that month by 23–11, and moved to within two points of them at the top of the table. But consecutive defeats away from home at Warrington and Halifax saw us drop off the pace, and we eventually finished second, eight points behind the champions Wigan. Our wingers Francis Cummins and Jim Fallon were ably supported by Kiwi centres Craig Innes and Kevin Iro in the try-scoring stakes, with Paul Cook kicking 74 goals.

With Super League on the horizon, the season had kicked off on 20 August 1995 and finished on 21 January 1996. The first summer Super League matches were scheduled to be played over the last weekend of March 1996, and Leeds were one of 12 clubs who had been accepted into the European Super League. The others were Bradford Bulls, Castleford, Halifax, London Broncos, Oldham Bears, Paris St Germain, St Helens, Sheffield Eagles, Warrington, Wigan and Workington Town.

The first season of Super League introduced an outstanding technical development in the game: video replays were used to deal with debatable circumstances surrounding the scoring of a try, through the judgement of an off-the-field official, with the replays also relayed to the crowd on giant television screens at all the televised games. It was in my view a great step forward, and I feel sure that other sports will eventually follow rugby league in this regard. Greg McCallum, the RFL's referees' coaching supremo, has worked tirelessly to support the game in this country, and his innovation in this area must go down as one of the major achievements in sport in this country in the twentieth century. Our game is so difficult to referee, what with its speed and the technical aspects of applying the rules correctly, but the 'big screen' has made it easier in a way that is respected and valued by the supporters who attend games and who watch the Sky coverage. That said, it is now down to the referees to ensure that they take responsibility when they need to do so, rather than just relying on the video evidence. But I can assure you that many people approach me with different views over certain controversial incidents, only to find that the screen helps to sort out their arguments in their entirety. Interestingly enough, the first decision ever to be made by video replay was over an incident that took place in Paris, as the first Super League match to be screened by Sky Sports was Paris St Germain v Sheffield Eagles.

The game of rugby league in Great Britain had undertaken a massive upheaval in the spring of 1995. For some time people connected with the game, especially the chairmen and directors of clubs, have been discussing the possibility of the professional competitions being played in summer. One chairman in particular, Jimmy Quinn of Oldham, had been forthright in his views on this subject – although you could understand Oldham wanting to play in the summer because, I can assure you, come November or December you didn't want to be playing at the Watersheddings on a cold winter's night!

Rupert Murdoch had been broadcasting rugby league through his Sky Sports satellite channels for five years, and was interested in expanding his coverage of a Super League. It was said at the time that he was keen to see the game develop in the big cities, and on a national level. As we all know, rugby league has traditionally been very strong along the M62 corridor, in Yorkshire and Lancashire, in addition to Cumbria, but not in other parts of the country. The clubs themselves were not in the best of financial health, and when Murdoch's News Corporation began making enquiries to further their ambitions, it was clear that the way was open for him.

News Corporation was in the middle of an intense battle with Kerry Packer's Channel Nine in Australia for the television rights to cover the Australian game. All sorts of breakaways and alternative competitions had been proposed Down Under as the battle raged, with the clubs divided on who they should support. News Corporation believed that if they could reach agreement swiftly with the British clubs, this would help with their Australian struggles. The RFL's chief executive, Maurice Lindsay, firmly believed that the game in this country needed to be drastically streamlined, and so Rupert Murdoch put his proposals to Maurice. With a new contract system having been implemented along with full-time professionalism, salaries and transfer fees were escalating, and clubs were paying over the odds for players in some cases. If a player meets with a club official thinking he's worth £35,000 a year, and the club offers him £50,000, well, it's clear that the player will accept the club's offer.

News Corporation began their approaches to the British game early in April 1995, causing the biggest upheaval and controversy in the game's history. This was some months after the power struggle had begun in Australia between Packer and Murdoch, and Packer's Channel Nine station at this stage held the television rights to cover the Winfield Cup. Murdoch and News Corporation were in the process of retaliating by planning a new Super League competition in direct opposition to the Winfield Cup. Murdoch began by buying up many of Australia's top players, and when that failed to force the Packer-backed Australian Rugby League to renegotiate the television contract, he looked to Britain and France to become key players in a £300 million worldwide competition that would be established to isolate the official Australian league.

Murdoch's initial offer of £75 million to share among the British clubs seemed like an unbelievable lifeline, given the financial state of the game here. But the haste with which the League rushed through proposals for the new Super League, featuring controversial mergers of clubs and the introduction of summer rugby, caused widespread anger among supporters. Although there seemed to be a general acceptance that something had to be done to save the game, and that the concept of the Super League was right in principle, the idea of clubs being compelled to merge and lose their identities led to demonstrations at a number of grounds. All were peacefully carried out, but left the RFL in no doubt about the supporters' feelings.

Emotions probably ran highest in Castleford, Featherstone and, to a lesser extent, Wakefield, as the long-term rival fans joined forces in opposing plans to merge the trio into a new Calder club.

Much of the protest was directed personally against Maurice Lindsay, the RFL chief executive who had played a leading role in the revolutionary proposals. But Lindsay could point out that every club in the game had voted in favour of the Super League package. Although some chairmen started voicing doubts as soon as they left the rooms where the crucial decisions were made, the general view among the clubs was that Murdoch's cash offer was too good to refuse. And while critics accused the game of selling its soul, others believed it was saving its life.

Still the arguments raged on through the following weeks, and were extended to the House of Commons whose MPs backed the supporters in their anti-merger campaigns. It at least resulted in the game receiving unprecedented nationwide media coverage. That the public outcry had been effective became evident less than four weeks after the first announcement of the institution of the Super League, when a special meeting of clubs voted overwhelmingly against enforced mergers and reintroduced three divisions. Widnes was the only club to vote against the new proposals, while Keighley Cougars were consulting their lawyers when the vote was taken. Both clubs later decided to take legal action against their omission from the Super League. But after a month of storms, the game began to move into calmer waters as the clubs started to channel their energies into making the new set-up a success.

Amid all the arguments about the Super League and proposed mergers, the equally revolutionary move to summer rugby was accepted with comparatively few protests – although under other circumstances it would have been a major issue for debate on its own.

The international repercussions continued, with the Australian Rugby League refusing to select for representative rugby those players who had joined Murdoch's Super League, while Great Britain in turn said that they would not play internationals against non-Murdoch men. This put the traditional Ashes Test series between the two countries in serious doubt, along with British Lions and Kangaroos tours. It also resulted in the top British players being offered massive 'loyalty bonuses' to stay in this country, in the face of attempts by the ARL to lure them away to play club rugby in the Winfield Cup. Ellery Hanley, the Leeds captain and Great Britain coach, was the ARL's biggest capture, although Wigan Test winger Martin Offiah rejected a million-pound deal to join him in favour of a similar offer to stay. Meanwhile, the ARL began to look increasingly isolated, as the South Pacific nations joined Great Britain, France and New Zealand inside the Murdoch portfolio.

In Britain it was time to look to the future, and Maurice Lindsay summed up the RFL's position immediately after the meeting which retained Super League but scrapped the merger plans. 'The revisions take account of concerns raised over the past three weeks,' said Lindsay. 'I believe that we have not been able to allay the fans' fears over club mergers and the loss of the game's traditions. We have taken these steps after a great deal of thought. Now is the time for everyone involved in the game to pull together. With the backing of the fans and the considerable support of News Corporation, we can take the game into a new era while protecting the game's great traditions. The chairmen are convinced that these steps will ensure the future development and success of our great game.'

Two court rulings in Australia were also to have a direct bearing on the progression of Super League in Britain. First, on 23 February 1996, Justice James Burchett ruled that the attempt by Rupert Murdoch's News Limited to launch Super League in Australia was unlawful. Ruling in favour of the ARL, he accepted the claim that eight of their clubs had been enticed into breaking a loyalty agreement to join Murdoch's competition. Granting 36 of the 37 orders sought against Super League in the Federal Court on 11 March 1995, Justice Burchett confirmed that the competition would be banned until the year 2000. Although he rejected the move also to ban the British-dominated European Super League, his overall ruling had a damaging effect on the game in this country. For without the Australian Super League there could be no World Club Championship, an inter-hemispherical competition which was to have been the pinnacle of the new set-up. It also ruled out Great Britain's planned tour to Australia later in the year.

But the legal battle was far from over, and an appeal meant that it dragged on until 4 October, when an astonishing turnaround resulted in an overwhelming victory for Murdoch. The Australian Federal Court of Appeal reversed every one of the orders, the key ruling being that the loyalty agreement signed with the ARL by all 20 of its senior clubs, including the eight aligned to Super League, was itself illegal. The final word on the 14-month legal battle came on 15 November, when the High Court in Sydney denied the ARL leave to appeal against the appeal decision. While the ruling was a boost for rugby league in Europe, which could now plan for the World Club Championship and international matches, it left the game divided Down Under with the ARL and Super League running different rival competitions.

THE TIMETABLE OF EVENTS

4 APRIL RFL chief executive Maurice Lindsay makes an urgent, unreported trip to London for talks with BSkyB after Murdoch's News Limited make the first confirmed approach about a European Super League. Wigan's World Club Challenge match against Canberra, due to be played in June, is cancelled as a direct result of the revolutionary changes in Australia.

5 APRIL The Rugby League Council has a scheduled meeting at Headingley, Leeds. Summer rugby is to be debated, but Super League is not on the agenda. During the meeting Lindsay takes telephone calls and tells the Council of News Limited's approach. Talks are arranged between the RFL's board of directors and News Limited with the outcome to be put to a special meeting of club chairmen three days later. There is no official statement from the RFL, but news begins to filter out that the European Super League is on its way. First reports are of Murdoch putting up £50 million for a Super League to be played during summer.

6 APRIL Reports from Australia quote Murdoch's no. 2, Ken Cowley, as saying that a Super League deal has already been struck with the RFL.

7 APRIL The First Division club chairmen, together with one from the Second Division, Hull Kingston Rovers, meet with Lindsay and RFL chairman Rodney Walker at Huddersfield. The Super League details are outlined for the first time.

8 APRIL The revolutionary decision is made at Central Park, Wigan: a Super League of 14 clubs will start in the summer of 1996. The five-year deal is reported to be worth £77 million, but the shock proposal that 15 clubs should be involved in mergers starts a major controversy. Two new clubs from France would be included in the Super League, while a Welsh side based in Cardiff is planned for the inclusion in a new First Division. The Super League clubs will each receive a total of £5 million over the five years, while the First Division clubs will each get a one-off payment of £100,000.

THE SUPER LEAGUE IS TO BE AS FOLLOWS:

Existing clubs: Bradford Northern, Halifax, Leeds, St Helens, Wigan.

New clubs, including proposed mergers: Calder (Castleford, Featherstone Rovers, Wakefield Trinity), Cheshire (Warrington, Widnes), Cumbria (Barrow, Carlisle, Whitehaven, Workington Town), Humberside (Hull, Hull Kingston Rovers), Manchester (Oldham, Salford), South Yorkshire (Doncaster, Sheffield Eagles), London, Paris, Toulouse.

The First Division will be: Batley, Bramley, Dewsbury, Highfield, Huddersfield, Hunslet, Keighley Cougars, Leigh, Rochdale Hornets, Ryedale-York, Swinton, Welsh XIII.

The top four Super League clubs will take part in an annual World Club Championship with the leading Australian and New Zealand clubs. There will be no promotion or relegation between Super League and First Division for the first two seasons. An interim competition will be played during the 1995–96 winter in the new First Division, in which clubs will play each other only once.

The whole package was voted in unanimously by the 32 senior clubs. RFL associate members Blackpool Gladiators and Nottingham City also voted in favour with Chorley abstaining. Despite the unanimous decision there were misgivings expressed immediately the meeting was over, with Keighley already considering legal action over their exclusion from the Super League at a stage when they looked certain to be promoted as Division Two champions.

9 APRIL There is an air of unreality at the Sunday afternoon matches as the shock of mergers sinks in. The first protests take place at grounds where supporters fear the end of their club. Leeds chief executive Alf Davies accuses the RFL of 'holding a gun to the heads of clubs' to force through the changes. He claims chairmen were told: 'Vote in favour or you are out.'

10 APRIL ARL chairman Ken Arthurson says he feels betrayed by

Lindsay, and claims it will be the end of British Lions and Kangaroos tours. The all-party Parliamentary Rugby League Group of MPs and peers calls for a meeting with the RFL after expressing alarm at the prospect of the game being sold 'lock, stock and barrel to a private media interest'.

The Rugby League Players' Association secretary Nic Grimoldby also seeks a meeting with Lindsay to discuss how players' contracts will be affected by the Super League. There is concern over players being made redundant as mergers reduce the number of clubs.

11 APRIL Leeds announce that they will now give their full support to summer rugby after failing to win their battle to remain playing in winter. Keighley's hopes of a Super League place are raised after Lindsay says that the RFL will reconsider their case if they can raise £1.5 million to improve their ground.

12 APRIL The Halifax board make a surprise decision to seek a merger with Bradford Northern. There is also talk of Ryedale-York moving to Gateshead. Salford and Oldham fail to agree on a merger to form a new Manchester club. ARL chief Ken Arthurson writes an open letter to British supporters accusing the 'Murdoch empire of attempting to destroy a great English tradition'. The British Amateur Rugby League Association say they will continue to play in winter.

13 APRIL Keighley intend to sue the RFL after a meeting of Super League club chairmen rejects their claim to join the élite. The South Pacific nations indicate that they will support the ARL and reject Murdoch's money.

14 APRIL The Widnes and Warrington merger is called off as both clubs are allocated a Super League place after France decide to enter only one club. More demonstrations take place at the traditional Good Friday derby matches, which will be the last if mergers go ahead.

18 APRIL The Centenary World Cup is saved following a weekend trip to Australia by Lindsay to meet top Australian officials to discuss international affairs. He is, however, unable to guarantee the future of the Ashes Test series or official tours.

20 APRIL National Conference League club Chorley are to sue the RFL for compensation after being excluded from the new divisional format. Lord Merlyn Rees is to chair a specially appointed four-man committee which will adjudicate on mergers of clubs. The All-Party Parliamentary Rugby

League Group moves to refer the Super League broadcast contract to the Office of Fair Trading and the Monopolies and Merger Commission.

21 APRIL Great Britain are to make a shortened tour of Australia and New Zealand in October 1996. But the ARL says it will be unofficial, and the Ashes will not be at stake. Halifax chairman Tony Gartland resigns following strong criticism of and a hostile reaction by fans to his proposed plan to merge with Bradford Northern.

23 APRIL Top British players are targeted by the Kerry Packer-backed ARL as they step up the battle against Murdoch's Super League. Ellery Hanley, the Leeds captain and Great Britain coach, is believed to have already agreed a deal. The RFL's response is to declare that they will use the Murdoch money to pay top players 'loyalty bonuses' to keep them in this country.

Castleford pull out of their proposed merger with Featherstone and Wakefield in order to aim for Super League status on their own.

24 APRIL Keighley hold a meeting in Leeds to announce the serving of a writ on the RFL in respect of their exclusion from the Super League. They seek damages after claiming that their omission has cost them £300,000 in lost sponsorship.

25 APRIL Wigan Test winger Martin Offiah rejects a million-pound Packer offer to play in the Winfield Cup and pledges his allegiance instead to Great Britain after accepting a massive 'loyalty bonus' deal. The RFL issues a list of 'loyal' players who will be staying in Britain, which includes Nigel Wright, Andrew Farrell and Martin Dermott (Wigan), and Bobby Goulding, Alan Hunte, Sonny Nickle, Chris Joynt and Steve Prescott (St Helens). Others who are destined for Australia include Gary Connolly, Jason Robinson, Martin Hall (Wigan), Jonathan Davies (Warrington) and John Devereux (Widnes).

Featherstone members vote against a merger with Wakefield. There are growing threats from the top clubs that they will go it alone if the present Second Division clubs continue to block the Super League plans. Eight clubs are seeking legal advice over 'an unconstitutional lack of consultation'.

26 APRIL More players sign British 'loyalty' contracts. They include the Wigan contingent of Va'aiga Tuigamala, Henry Paul, Scott Quinnell, Mick Cassidy, Terry O'Connor, Simon Haughton and Craig Murdock, and Scott

Gibbs (St Helens). A Super League debate in the House of Commons lasts 90 minutes. Sports Minister Iain Sproat appeals to a Commons committee to launch an investigation into Murdoch's plans.

27 APRIL The RFL's board of directors call a special general meeting in four days' time, increasing speculation that more clubs will be included in the Super League.

28 APRIL Wigan captain Shaun Edwards and I join forces in attacking the way in which the RFL has handed out 'loyalty bonuses'. As Challenge Cup final rivals we make our surprise attack during the traditional Wembley walkabout on the day before the big game. We both feel bitter at not receiving 'loyalty bonuses', despite our long Great Britain service.

29 APRIL I continue my 'loyalty' attack in the Wembley dressing-room immediately after the final, saying that I am prepared to lead a players' revolt.

30 APRIL All change – the Super League plans are restructured after a near six-hour meeting of clubs at the Hilton Hotel, near Huddersfield. The surprise decisions result in a return to three divisions, and a withdrawal of merger proposals. Widnes are the only club to vote against the proposals, while Keighley are absent as they consult their lawyers. The clubs are allocated places in the new divisions on the basis of where they finished in the 1994–95 season, with the exception of London, Paris and National Conference League club Chorley.

The 12-club Super League will be: Bradford Northern, Castleford, Halifax, Leeds, London Broncos, Oldham, Paris St Germain, St Helens, Sheffield Eagles, Warrington, Wigan and Workington Town.

First Division will comprise the following 11 clubs: Batley, Dewsbury, Featherstone Rovers, Huddersfield, Hull, Keighley Cougars, Rochdale Hornets, Salford, Wakefield Trinity, Whitehaven and Widnes.

The new Second Division will be made up of ten clubs: Barrow, Bramley, Carlisle, Chorley, Highfield, Hull KR, Hunslet, Leigh, Ryedale-York and Swinton.

National Conference League club Chorley are a surprise entry in the Second Division, but there is no place for Doncaster, who are in the hands of a receiver. And the idea of a new Welsh club being included has been dropped, at least for the time being. Promotion and relegation is likely to be on a one up/one down basis, and the first summer season will kick off on 28 March 1996 after an interim season played within the new league format. Murdoch has raised his cash injection from £77 million to £87 million, to be shared as follows: Super League clubs each to receive £900,000 per season for five years; First Division clubs to get between £200,000 and £700,000 in accordance with their performance each term, with £150,000 per season for Second Division clubs. It is also revealed that soccer giants Newcastle United have enquired about entering a club.

I MAY Keighley say they are continuing their legal action against the RFL and will seek £500,000 compensation for being left out of the Super League.

2 MAY Widnes start legal proceedings against the RFL after losing their Super League place when it was reduced to 12 clubs. The RFL hit back at my claim that Leeds players have not been offered 'loyalty bonuses': they say that Ellery Hanley, Craig Innes and Alan Tait have all been offered money following receipt of an application from Leeds for financial assistance, but Leeds did not put my name forward and therefore I am not on the 'loyalty' list. However, I find out that several other Leeds players have received loyalty payments – Nick Fozzard, Paul Cook, Graham Holroyd, Marcus Vassakopoulos and Kevin Iro. Ellery Hanley and Craig Innes subsequently leave to join the ARL.

17 MAY Tom Smith resigns as a Widnes director because of a conflict of interest in the Super League dispute with his role as a member of the RFL's board of directors.

26 MAY Widnes lose their legal battle against the RFL and face costs of around £50,000. A High Court judge in Manchester, Mr Justice Jonathan Parker, says that there is no serious issue to be tried, but accepted that the 30 April vote of 32–1 in favour of the Super League proposals represented the overwhelming wish of the game.

Rugby League (Europe) Ltd was launched on 19 September 1996 by the Super League clubs, who wished to have a greater say in the financial planning and marketing of the new competition. It was led by Bradford Bulls' chairman Chris Caisley, together with the chief executives of St Helens (David Howes as co-director) and Halifax Blue Sox (Nigel Wood as the company secretary). The shareholders were to be the 12 Super League clubs, with one special share allotted to the RFL. Colin Myler, a former *Daily*

Mirror and *Sunday Mirror* editor, was subsequently appointed the RFL's chief executive. Chris Caisley, who became chairman of the RLE, stressed that there was no desire among the clubs to break away from the RFL or to interfere with matters which were the preserve of the whole game, such as disciplinary proceedings and by-laws. In response to these moves, the First and Second Divisions also formed their own marketing organisation.

The second year's allocation of News Limited funding was also announced in September 1996, with £11.4 million being shared by the Super League clubs, £4.725 million by the First Division clubs, and £1.11 million going into the Second Division. The 12 Super League member clubs agreed on a basic £850,000 per club, plus an additional payment depending on final league position down to tenth place, as follows: first, £120,000; second, £80,000; third, £60,000; fourth, £40,000; fifth and sixth, £35,000; seventh and eighth, £20,000; ninth and tenth, £10,000. Earlier in 1996, the Rugby League Council had ratified a proposal from the RFL's board of directors that all payments from the News Limited Super League contract would be subject to a levy of 7.5 per cent. This would be used to fund a number of key areas, including appearance fees for home clubs featuring in televised matches, the marketing of the new competition, and the travelling costs of all clubs to and from Paris.

19.

LIFE AFTER LEEDS

WHEN I SIGNED for Huddersfield Giants in February 1996 for a club-record fee of £135,000 after nine fabulous years at Headingley, I reckoned that Leeds could have no complaints financially. I had originally cost the club £178,250, so they had at least covered a large part of this. I joined Huddersfield as their player–coach, and many Leeds supporters still ask me to this day the reasons why I left my home-town club.

I had one year left on my contract and was hoping to secure my future at Leeds. I had asked team manager Hugh McGahan for a two-year extension to my contract, anticipating that if I avoided injury I could compete for a first-team place until I was 33, and then offer my services to the club in a coaching capacity. Hugh asked for time to consider, and then arranged a couple of meetings between himself, myself and Dean Bell. In the end they advised me that they couldn't agree to my request. Their concern was to bring in new players to improve the squad, but they had a limited budget available. I could understand the position they were in, for my terms would have prevented them signing a couple of younger players who would have represented the future of Leeds. Still, I thought that I had one season left at the club at least.

The situation changed considerably after a game against Swinton in the fourth round of the 1996 Silk Cut Challenge Cup, when I suffered a serious injury, tearing a pectoral muscle which was to keep me out for two or three months. Dean Bell called me into his office with Hugh McGahan for a chat, and they told me that although I would be free to leave after the remaining 12 months of my contract had run out, the club had received an interesting offer from Huddersfield. I told them I wasn't interested, as Huddersfield were a First Division side; at the time I did not know of their ambitions. But I gave the matter more thought and decided I ought at least to meet with the chairman of Huddersfield, Ken Davy. The Leeds team at the time appeared to be breaking up: Craig Innes had just left for Manly in Australia, and the directors at Headingley were keen to reduce the weekly wage bill even further. The Huddersfield set-up and plans for the future appeared attractive, and I went back to Hugh McGahan and asked him whether Leeds would sell me if the right offer came in from Huddersfield. His answer straightaway was yes, which took me a little by surprise. I then told Dean Bell to ring the Huddersfield coach, Darryl Van de Velde, and ask him to ring me as soon as possible.

I arranged to meet Ken Davy and Darryl at the offices of Ken's company, DBS, in Huddersfield. I spoke with my advisers and with the Huddersfield club for over two weeks before finally agreeing to join them for a fee of £135,000. Huddersfield had offered me a four-year contract: in professional sport one never knows how long a career will last, and the financial security of a long-term contract is essential in a collision sport such as rugby league. Furthermore, Huddersfield were keen for me to sign, they had faith in me as a player, and they also wished to appoint me as assistant coach to Darryl Van de Velde, as they valued my experience as something that would help to bring the team on. I had the greatest regard for Darryl after closely observing his methods and the success he had achieved while he was with Castleford in the early 1990s. I saw this as an ideal opportunity to switch gradually from playing to coaching inside the security of a good contract at an ambitious club.

I agreed to sign for Huddersfield on the Friday prior to Leeds' Challenge Cup quarter-final against Halifax on the Sunday, and a big press conference was arranged to take place at the new McAlpine Stadium in Huddersfield on the Monday. As it transpired, Leeds lost stand-off half Tony Kemp with a broken arm in the quarter-final – a hurdle they successfully negotiated on their way to the semi-final. A number of Leeds supporters knew that I was moving on to start a new career with Huddersfield, and were concerned at the problem the club now had with Tony Kemp's injury.

After the game I called into the Town Hall Tavern in Leeds to meet up with some pals, as was usual for me after a Sunday match. There I received a telephone call from Alf Davies' wife, and she asked me if I could ring Alf as soon as possible. Alf must have contacted her and told her to try to reach me at the pub! Realising that there must be some urgency attached to the call, I rang him straightaway. Alf asked me if I could speak with Huddersfield to check out the possibility of my playing for Leeds in the semi-final of the Challenge Cup against Bradford Bulls at the McAlpine Stadium – even though I had technically left Leeds on the Friday afternoon! This came as a bolt out of the blue, and so I spoke with my adviser John Penistone about the phone call. John then spoke on my behalf with Alf Davies and asked, if Leeds wanted me to play in the semi-final of the cup, what would the position be if I helped them to win through to Wembley: would Leeds also wish to retain my services for the final? Alf confirmed that Leeds were only interested in me helping them through the semi-final stage, and they were quite happy for me then to join Huddersfield. John questioned Alf on the financial arrangements if Leeds won the semi-final with my help, but Alf had no proposal to make. John then suggested that the club should make a payment of £5,000 for my services, bearing in mind the rewards which the Leeds players would generally receive on reaching a final. Alf told him that I would only receive the same fee as the other players for playing in that one semi-final game.

The bottom line was, I had agreed with Huddersfield to join them. The Huddersfield club said they were not interested in allowing me to play for Leeds in the semi-final, and the matter was closed. The press conference went ahead on the Monday at the McAlpine Stadium as arranged, and I committed myself to the Huddersfield cause. It was 26 February 1996, and my Leeds career was behind me. I was looking forward to giving everything to Huddersfield as a player and as an assistant coach to Darryl Van de Velde. Huddersfield is the birthplace of rugby league, and it was a big challenge for me. The club was ambitious to finish top of the new First Division and gain promotion into Super League at the first time of asking. I was looking forward to bringing back the good times to a sleeping giant of the game.

Huddersfield – now called the Giants – had made some decent signings for the new season, with Greg Mackey and Alan Wilson from Australia and Phil Veivers from St Helens joining Dean Hanger, Greg Austin and New Zealander Darrall Shelford, who were already at the club. But the season as a whole was disappointing, and we finished fifth in the First Division despite the financial investment by the board of directors on new players. I pulled a hamstring in only my second match, and missed six weeks of my early career with the club. Darryl Van de Velde resigned at the end of the season as he had ambitions to continue coaching at the top level. He was an excellent coach but needed better players to take his club forward, and so he moved on.

Following Darryl's resignation Les Coulter, the chief executive of Huddersfield Giants, asked me if I could go along to his home on a Monday afternoon. As I had served as assistant coach under Darryl he felt that I might be more influential in attracting big-name players to the club, and Les wanted to propose that I should take over as player–coach at the board meeting that evening. I must emphasise that I didn't ask to take over the position of head coach when Darryl resigned: I was proposed by the chief executive for the position. I had two interviews for the job, one with Bob Scott, the Huddersfield vice-chairman at that time, and a second with Bob and Les Coulter. The second interview was held at Ken Davy's DBS offices in Huddersfield, and it was then that I found out for the first time that there were two other names in the hat, Steve Ferres and Neil Kelly.

In the end Steve Ferres was appointed after being highly recommended by Rugby League Headquarters, and he took up the job in the 1997 season. Steve had his own business and had taken the position as head coach on a part-time basis, with the assistance of Ian Fairhurst. We went back to being part-time players, as opposed to being virtually full-time professionals under Van de Velde. Training was on a Tuesday night with a weights session thrown in; on Wednesdays we trained ourselves at Deighton Sports Centre at Huddersfield; and there were further sessions on Thursdays and Saturdays.

My second season at Huddersfield started pretty well, but unfortunately as time went on the players found it more and more difficult to respect Steve Ferres as a top coach. By mid-July it was clear that there was serious unrest. One particular player called a meeting after training at the White Horse pub on Leeds Road in Huddersfield. We used to go there after games and training sessions – though we generally drank non-alcoholic beverages. A ballot was arranged among the players to find out how many wanted Steve to leave the club. Apparently two of the directors did not support Steve, and they may have encouraged this particular player to find out the strength of feeling among the squad. If the ballot had gone heavily against the coach, then the two directors concerned would have felt justified in persuading the board to sack him.

When I heard about this ballot I was not happy at all; I even spoke with chief executive Les Coulter to suggest to him that it shouldn't be allowed to happen. The season had been going pretty well, and the time for any action to be taken was surely not now, but the board should decide for themselves at the end of the year. I told the players in no uncertain terms that Steve should stay on till the end of the campaign, and that we should all concentrate on playing and battle for the good of the club. We owed it to ourselves as professionals and to the Huddersfield spectators to give everything for whoever was coaching us at the time. We should do our best to finish at the top of the league and go on and win the Premiership final at Old Trafford, and then it should be left to the board to decide the best way forward.

The players agreed, and we then went 13 games unbeaten to reach that Premiership final. It was a great occasion for the club, and especially the supporters who felt that the good times were finally coming back. I was most unfortunate to miss out on the great day, having pulled my hamstring again in the semi-final against Keighley. We had finished second in the league behind our close rivals Hull FC, and we met them again at Old Trafford, gaining a magnificent 18–0 victory.

When the season finished the board sacked Steve Ferres, rightly or wrongly and for whatever reasons. I must say this: Steve thinks to this day that I was personally behind his dismissal and finds it very hard to approach me and have a chat, but I can assure him that I was in no way involved – in fact I stuck up for him midway through the season. I hope one day he will understand and accept this to be the case.

On 10 November 1997 the club's chief executive Les Coulter once again approached me and offered me the job of head coach of the Huddersfield Giants. Huddersfield had finished second in the First Division but had still been promoted to Super League when Paris St Germain had folded after just two seasons in the new set-up. For our first season in the top flight, Les wished me to be in charge of the coaching, and Phil Veivers was invited to take over as my assistant – which pleased me, as Phil and I had had a good relationship during the time we had been at Huddersfield together. I was looking forward to the challenge. Les went to the chairman, and we all sat down together to dream about this fantastic opportunity for Huddersfield to get back into the big time. A three-year plan was put in place to run in line with my coaching contract, which recognised that the future was a learning curve, not only for myself as a coach but also for the club and its management. While there was to be no relegation at the end of the season, my main objective was to ensure that all my players knew that they had to compete for 80 minutes in every game.

Before the 1998 season started I asked every player to write down the position he felt we could finish in what would be our first season in Super League. The average placing was eighth, and I felt this was quite achievable. The pre-season preparations went well, and we entertained Bradford Bulls at the McAlpine Stadium in our first Super League game in front of over 12,500 fans, who provided a great atmosphere. The Bradford Bulls had been in Super League from its inception and had high fitness levels, so we knew it was going to be a pretty hard opening game – and this it proved to be. We were beaten 36–6 but not disgraced, and I felt it was a creditable performance. I can remember Denis Betts, who was summarising the game for Sky Sports, telling Eddie and Stevo that Huddersfield could surprise a few people this season.

Although my main objective was for the players to compete, we found it harder and harder to do so as the season went on, as our fitness levels fell well short of those of our competitors. However, we managed our first win after eight games when we beat Warrington at home 28–6, and two games later we followed this up with our first away win over Castleford at Wheldon Road. This 16–10 win gave me great satisfaction, and I felt we were now beginning to make our way in the top flight. It appeared that everybody was delighted, and the players seemed to be gaining in confidence, which was important.

I attended a board meeting with the directors of Huddersfield Giants on 8 July to discuss in some detail my proposals for the following year with regard to playing staff. I told them I was looking to sign a number of players, and I also suggested several whom I wished to offload. I had seen a centre at Salford, young Nathan McAvoy, who has since gone on and proved himself at the highest level with the Bradford Bulls. I also suggested that Bobby Goulding could be a vital signing if we could get him, as he would add experience and a great kicking game to the club. I rated Henry Paul highly and was keen to see if we had any chance of attracting him from Wigan, for I had heard that he was thinking of moving on when his contract expired. I also wanted to consider signing the Leeds winger Leroy Rivett, and to speak with New Zealand's Tony Iro. These were some of the names in the frame for

Huddersfield Giants' second Super League campaign for 1999. I felt that they represented the kind of skill and experience that would consolidate the club's standing, and that I had good prospects of attracting them to Huddersfield as I knew many of them well and felt that they trusted me.

I should point out at this time that I was not on the best of terms with one of the club's directors. Dr Paul Morgan was a sports psychologist, and our chairman Ken Davy valued his expertise in addition to the financial support which he provided for the club. Paul wanted to play a part in the dressing-room and sought to organise psychology sessions for the team. Throughout my career I had come across a number of people who were employed to motivate players, but at the end of the day I always thought it was more important for a player to believe in his own abilities and develop his own confidence, rather than have a psychologist do it for him! And certainly, the average rugby league player is not the ideal patient for this type of treatment. Dr Paul Morgan had some involvement with the Great Britain side, and when I checked with a couple of players who had experienced his sessions, they told me that a good number of the squad had ended up falling asleep. I did not stop Dr Morgan's sessions going ahead with the Huddersfield squad, but they did not prove too helpful. I had a couple of run-ins with Dr Morgan as a result, as I felt there was no place for a director in the dressing-room, particularly before a game.

The week following the board meeting that discussed player acquisitions for the following season, I received a phone call from chief executive Les Coulter after our regular Friday training session. Les asked me for my British Rugby League Coaching Scheme qualifications, and particularly if I had achieved the Level 3. I told him that I hadn't, and asked him why he was asking me. All he would say in reply was that it was a technical problem, but I should not worry about it because 'we'll work it out'. I immediately smelt a rat.

We had won only two out of 13 games, but I believe we had turned the corner. We were approaching a mid-season break in Super League and I had arranged with Phil Veivers and the other members of the coaching staff to take the senior squad away for five days to Bangor in North Wales from 13 July. This was to improve team spirit and to provide a change in routine, and the timing seemed ideal following our recent couple of wins. Yet the phone call remained at the back of my mind for some time – it just did not seem right. The trip to Wales went very well, and the team spirit was tremendous: I was looking forward to the second half of the season and to finishing on a high note.

When we returned to the McAlpine Stadium the following Monday, Les Coulter called me into his office and once more asked me about my qualifications and the Level 3 coaching certificate. I again asked him: 'What's going on? Are they thinking of making a change of coach?' We were due to play Hull at Gateshead a week on Friday, and this question of my coaching qualifications was beginning to worry me. Again Les told me not to worry about it – it was a technical problem, and they would work around it. The following Friday morning I received another phone call from Les on Harold Box's mobile phone. Les asked me if I could attend a board meeting that evening at 7 p.m. I told him this was not possible, as I had already made arrangements to support a good friend of mine, George Davies, at a sportsmen's dinner at Castleford. I was then asked if I could attend on the Saturday morning at 11 a.m., which I could. I now knew that there was something serious in the pipeline, and the following morning I arrived at the club offices and met briefly with Margaret Caldwell, one of the board members. I was then called into the boardroom to meet with Les, Ken Davy and Dr Paul Morgan.

The table in the boardroom was quite large, and you can imagine the scene: I was sitting opposite Dr Morgan with Ken Davy at one end and Les Coulter at the other. They asked me if I knew the reason for the meeting, and I replied that I believed it was something to do with my coaching qualifications. I was then told that I couldn't be head coach of the Giants any longer as I did not have the requisite qualifications, and they asked me instead to come to an agreement with them to return to being a player. When I had been appointed head coach, the board of directors had insisted that I stand down as a player to concentrate fully on the coaching position! They were now asking me to put matters into reverse and suggesting that the club had missed my playing abilities during the season! My experience and vision at stand-off would be a vital asset to the club if I came back as a player and relinquished the position of head coach!

Needless to say, I was stunned and refused to agree to the changes they proposed. I asked them if Phil Veivers had the requisite coaching qualifications and they said they had checked that: Phil had his Level 3 coaching certificate, and would take over as head coach in my place. The meeting went on until 12.30 in the afternoon, when Ken Davy and Dr Paul Morgan left Les Coulter and me to try to come to some agreement before a statement was prepared and released to the press. As soon as the two directors walked out of the room, I said to Les that I believed Dr Morgan was behind my sacking as head coach. I also asked for a copy of the 'Framing of the Future' policy document.

'Framing the Future' was a report published by the RFL on 30 August 1994. A survey of the professional game had been carried out by the sports marketing firm GSM, and following its report, heated debate and controversy had arisen, especially when the RFL's board of directors proposed revolutionary changes for the clubs on the back of it. In response to the survey's findings – which, among other things, demonstrated that there were only four clubs in Division One showing a profit – the directors made sweeping recommendations, including a reduction in the number of professional clubs through amalgamations, the adjustment of voting rights, the institution of a salary cap and the imposition of a minimum standards charter. This charter demanded that all clubs' grounds should be of a certain standard, that they should make a certain number of management or administrative appointments, and that their coaching staff should be qualified to a certain level. While the minimum standards charter was accepted by the clubs as long ago as 1996, I am not aware of any firm timetable against which clubs are required to satisfy it, even to this day.

Les passed me a copy of 'Framing the Future' as we sat together in the boardroom, and as I had a brief look through it I saw underneath a piece of paper with two items written on it. The first was worded 'Garry Schofield to resign', and the second was 'Paul Morgan to contact Andy Goodway regarding the position of head coach or team manager'. 'Les, what's all this about?' I enquired. Les replied, 'Listen, you've not seen that piece of paper. If Ken or anybody else finds out that you have, this could cost me my job.' After Huddersfield sacked me, Les Coulter and I stopped communicating with one another. Although Huddersfield Giants have now also sacked Les, we both appreciate each other's position at that meeting.

As soon as I got home I called up a good friend of mine who is a barrister, Gerald Lumley, and outlined all that had happened in the meeting that day. Gerald suggested that this may be a case of unfair dismissal, and he kindly contacted a local solicitor on my behalf. The solicitor considered all that had transpired on the Saturday, and agreed that a case of unfair dismissal had to be answered. He advised me to attend training on the Monday morning, which I did, for our first session since our return from Bangor. I told the players that I was no longer their head coach, according to the Huddersfield board. This came as a total surprise to them all, particularly after the excellent relationship we had developed over our five days away in Wales. Les Coulter called a meeting at the McAlpine Stadium with the players after the training session that morning to outline the reason why the club could no longer entertain me as their head coach, and to explain what would happen for the rest of the season.

The players were told that the club wanted me to return to playing at stand-off half, but they knew that my lack of coaching qualifications had been the real reason, for they knew that Les had been repeatedly asking me for my levels of coaching accreditation in recent weeks. The players felt that the club had been looking for an excuse to sack me for poor results, even though we had won two of our last three games and were really fired up for the challenge to the end of the season. The solicitor then advised me to terminate my employment with the Huddersfield Giants, and legal proceedings would be commenced.

I was then told by Phil Thomas, the rugby correspondent of *The Sun*, that the minimum standard requirements for the qualifications of Super League coaches did not need to be fulfilled until October 1999. Phil confirmed therefore that Huddersfield were implementing something that did not yet have to be in force! It was clearly just an excuse to change coaches, and it would seem to have stemmed from my disagreements with Dr Paul Morgan. It appeared that he wanted his own nominee, Andy Goodway, at the club – but when they approached Andy following my sacking, the Huddersfield Giants were turned down. At the time, Andy had ambitions to be the next Wigan coach.

Phil Veivers finished the season as Huddersfield's head coach, Level 3 qualifications and all, but unfortunately the Giants did not win another game in Super League in 1998. For the following season the club appointed Malcolm Reilly as their head coach, and as I followed their results closely, it was interesting to see that Malcolm's record at Huddersfield Giants was no better than mine. Malcolm is a fantastic coach, the best British coach I've worked under, and he has had tremendous success with both Great Britain and Newcastle Knights – but after 13 matches at Huddersfield, he too had just two victories to show for his efforts. The Giants again finished bottom that season, and Malcolm gave in his notice before the club merged with Sheffield Eagles, and the incumbent Eagles coach John Kear took over the position of head coach. John is also the England coach at the time of writing – and in Super League 2000, Huddersfield/Sheffield won one of their first 13 games.

To my mind, this simply shows that it doesn't matter how many coaching qualifications you have or haven't got, at the end of the day it is the ability of the players that counts, and the ability of the coach to get the best out of them. I was confident that I could have taken Huddersfield forward, and if the players I was hoping to sign had come on board, then I am sure that the 1999 campaign would have been more successful than the 1998 campaign. There are many examples of top coaches suffering with struggling sides – at the time of writing, for example, John Monie is having great difficulty down at London Broncos after a wonderful number of years as coach of Wigan. It is all down to the quality of players you've got – to a great extent, anyway.

My court case with Huddersfield Giants will be concluded one way or the other by the time this book is published, and I will look forward to going back to McAlpine Stadium as a summariser for BBC Radio Leeds with a big smile on my face. Ken Davy is still chairman of Huddersfield Giants, and I must say that I got on very well with him: the difficulty was created with Dr Paul Morgan. I feel that the Huddersfield board let both me and the club's fans down, and looking back I would say it was the worst career move I ever made. I wish I had stayed at Leeds to see out my final year's contract, and then taken my time before deciding the next move.

After leaving Huddersfield I was unoccupied in rugby for a while, although I kept in touch with Phil Veivers and I was grateful to him for putting me in contact with an agent. Phil had connections with Bangor rugby union club, and it was their facilities we had used when we had our five-day break in the middle of the 1998 season. I spoke with the agent, and he asked if I would be interested in playing for Aberavon, one of the leading Welsh rugby union sides. I agreed, and I played there for six weeks before receiving a phone call early in 1999 from my good friend Colin Maskill, who was coaching the Doncaster Dragons rugby league club at the time. I had enjoyed playing in Wales, but the travelling became quite tiring – I was covering 260 miles there and back by car – and the time away from home eventually got to me. The players and officials of the Welsh club were fantastic, and they made me feel a valuable part of their game, but when I received Colin's call to come and talk with Doncaster I was naturally interested.

Chairman Peter Smith told me that he had recently taken over at the club and was engaged in sorting out their financial affairs. When we met it was clear he was very ambitious, and I liked the ideas he had to take Doncaster Dragons out of the First Division. This looked an interesting challenge for me, and with Colin Maskill there as coach it seemed right for me to join them. Aberavon had agreed that they would not stand in my way if a rugby league opportunity came along, and I reluctantly asked to be released.

I played for Doncaster over a six-week period, during which time we enjoyed a couple of good wins and put up some decent performances. I then received a memo from the chairman, Peter Smith, asking me to take a 50 per cent pay cut! Once more I was amazed at the carryings-on of a director of a professional rugby league club. Not six weeks earlier we had negotiated a 12-month contract, and he had confirmed to me that he was turning the club round financially, and yet here he was now, looking to halve my salary. He was not even prepared to discuss this with me at a meeting or over the telephone – he had simply sent me a memo! I'm afraid that nothing was surprising me any more: I left training that night in Doncaster and wanted nothing more to do with the club.

Towards the end of March 1999 I received a phone call from Bill Clift, who was the chief executive of Bramley rugby league club. He suggested I might like to sign for Bramley for the rest of the season, as he was fully aware of the way I had been messed about by Doncaster. I spoke with both Bill and his head coach, Mike Ford, and they were very fair to me. Bramley played their home games at Headingley, and this may well have influenced me to join them. And so on 1 April 1999 I ran out once again on to the hallowed turf for my début. I was already of the opinion that this might very well be the place where I would finish my professional rugby league career.

Mike Ford had under his wing a number of players at Bramley with whom I was familiar. Leeds Rhinos had a policy of releasing good youngsters to Bramley for the experience, and the Gibbons twins, Dan Potter, Andy

Poynter and Ryan McDonald, together with the altogether more experienced Richard Russell, all impressed me. The season went well, although I was finding it very hard to motivate myself to go to training, and the enjoyment simply wasn't there. I had always promised myself that if I wasn't enjoying the hard work, then it would be time to call it a day. As it happened, the third last game of the season was against Doncaster away, and it was that particular match which made up my mind that I was coming to the end of my playing career. We were hammered by Doncaster 34–12, and as I walked off the pitch to the dressing-room I was showered with foul-mouthed abuse from some of the spectators – one in particular who was over retirement age. I thought to myself that I didn't need this any more, and looking back on the career I had been fortunate to enjoy, this was no way to finish it. My children Danielle and Jonathan would often come and watch me play both at home and away, and the events of this Sunday afternoon were certainly not what I wanted my children to endure as I left the field.

I decided there and then that I would ask Bramley if they would allow me to end my contract the following week, when we were due to play York at home. The last game of the season was against Dewsbury away, and I was keen to finish at Headingley. This would be a fitting end for me, playing my last game at the ground of my home-town club. The only sad part about it was there would only be around 350 people there that afternoon to watch me bow out. At the Monday training session, I went up and spoke with Mike Ford and asked if it was okay. I thanked Mike for giving me the opportunity of playing for Bramley, and he was happy enough to allow me to call it a day against York.

I must say that I found Mike an excellent coach, very switched on and very ambitious, and one day in the future, when a number of the Australian coaches have returned home, I hope that he will be among the local lads who are promoted to take on a coaching position at a Super League club. He is now at Oldham doing a good job there, and I follow his career with interest.

If somebody had said to me way back in 1983 that I would retire after almost 18 years in the game, having played over 500 games, travelled round the world and made many, many friends, not just in Great Britain but in Australia and New Zealand, then I would have thought them a little crazy.

20.

THE FUTURE OF RUGBY LEAGUE

I DO NOT PROFESS to be an expert when it comes to understanding the way our game is run today. Most of my dealings with Rugby League Headquarters and the Rugby League Council have been as a player, and latterly to a much lesser extent as a coach. My views on the current state of the game and its future are not radical, but they are forthright as I am passionate in my desire to see rugby league move forward.

To begin with, the game cannot operate effectively with so many different bodies managing its different aspects. The RFL and its headquarters at Red Hall in Leeds does not seem to me to hold any real power these days – although control of the game at the highest level in this country is vested very clearly in the Rugby League Council, a body which is made up of chairmen and representatives of all professional clubs, not just those in Super League but also the Northern Ford Premiership (formerly First and Second Division) clubs. Currently, organisations such as Super League (Europe) Limited, the RFL, BARLA and the Association of Premiership Clubs operate to keep everyone happy, and many of the decisions taken by these groups and by the Council are simply to protect the interests of the clubs which the delegates represent. The sport needs a single governing authority made up of no more than four individuals who have the ability to grab rugby league by the scruff of its neck and move it forward into the twenty-first century. The game needs a revamp from top to bottom if we are ever going to have any chance of matching the Australians again. The governing body I propose, just four individuals, should have no club ties whatsoever and should be prepared to run the game for its own good, rather than for the benefit of their own egos.

Super League (Europe) Limited, led by Chris Caisley who is also the Bradford Bulls chairman, no longer really has any interests outside of

Yorkshire and Lancashire, London Broncos apart. The sport at the top level is operating almost exculsively within the M62 corridor. Even Cumbria is no longer considered to be an important part of the northern game, even though its amateur scene is very strong and always has been. But the county's three professional clubs, Workington Town, Whitehaven and Barrow, all now operate in the Northern Ford Premiership, and if Cumbria had ever seriously wanted to be represented in the top flight of Super League then their one chance might well have been to create a merger when the idea was first mooted in 1995. Workington Town were one of the original 12 Super League clubs, but they lasted just one season, as without the combined resources of the county they were not strong enough to survive. After being relegated and going bankrupt, they never recovered their position as a Super League club. Since then the chairmen of those clubs have lacked the courage and ambition to do something about Cumbrian rugby league for the good of the game in their part of the country.

Other Super League clubs soon dropped off the pace for similar financial reasons: early casualties Paris St Germain and Oldham Bears have been followed more recently by Gateshead Thunder and Sheffield Eagles. Indeed there are now two clubs, one in Super League and one in the Northern Ford Premiership, which retain the name Sheffield in their title. The future of the top Super League clubs outside the top five or six looks bleak, as Halifax, Salford, Huddersfield/Sheffield Giants, Hull Sharks, Wakefield Trinity and London Broncos are all struggling under the financial strain of competing at the top level.

London especially are a case in point. The RFL has financially supported a London club for the last 20 years, and the Broncos currently receive the backing of Richard Branson and his Virgin empire. They change grounds on a regular basis in the capital, have no real foundation or tradition, and have constantly been allowed to field a team made up mostly of Australians. Although development officers have been appointed from time to time, there are still precious few schools playing rugby league in London. How can they compete with football and rugby union?

The game has been funding this club for two decades, but in that time London Broncos have showed little sign of developing beyond their original circumstances. The Broncos' stars are almost entirely Australian. In Yorkshire and Lancashire over the last 20 years young fans have always had role models to support, with Offiah, Hanley, Farrell and Robinson at Wigan, Iestyn Harris and Adrian Morley at Leeds, the Paul brothers at Bradford Bulls, Kevin Iro, Paul Newlove and Sean Long at St Helens – I could go on. These are players who are heroes to the youngsters who follow the game in our part of the world. But in London nobody has heard of Steele Retchless, the Australian second-row forward with the Broncos who is one of the club's best players.

This, too, is where our game is really failing. Back in 1982, when the 'Invincibles' came over from Australia and washed aside our international and club sides, we set about restructuring our game in order to try to recover the lost ground. But now, in the year 2000, we are even further behind the Australians than we were in 1982. One of the main reasons is that there are too many Australians, and possibly also New Zealanders, playing in this country for a break and a decent pay. British rugby league is suffering badly as a result. If you try selecting a Great Britain side, it is a struggle to find competition for either half-back berth, scrum-half or stand-off half, and for the loose forward role: indeed, Great Britain have been forced to play Andy Farrell, Wigan's outstanding loose forward, at stand-off in recent international fixtures. This is surely because the majority of clubs in Super League, and indeed in the Northern Ford Premiership, have overseas players occupying these positions. I have nothing against Australians playing over here, but I believe that rugby league's situation is going the same way as other sports in this country. Too much overseas involvement is preventing the home-grown talent coming through.

Then just move on and look at the coaching situations in Super League. Until recently there was just one English coach in Super League, John Kear, and he failed to survive the 2000 season with Huddersfield. It does seem that the British game is being used by coaches who can't gain employment back home in Australia, so they come over here to further their careers. The directors of Super League clubs seem to accept that everything the Australian coaches say is gospel – and we now have Northern Ford Premiership clubs going the same way. That is not to say that we do not have a number of top-class overseas coaches in our game, such as Frank Endacott at Wigan and Stuart Raper at Castleford. Interesting though, isn't it, to reflect that the highly successful Bradford Bulls coach Matthew Elliott was merely a skills coach and fitness conditioner when he came over from

Australia, while Hull's Shaun McRae was a conditioner with Canberra Raiders and had never been a head coach at senior level before he took up the position at St Helens!

The overseas coaches in Great Britain are generally looking to succeed over here purely so that they can prove themselves in order to win coaching positions back home. Graham Murray was a prime example: he did a tremendous job for Leeds Rhinos in 1998 and 1999, but as he said all along, home is home, and when the first opportunity came along he was off.

I firmly believe that the refereeing standards in our great game have gone down since I first started playing in 1983. In those days it seemed that the referees were characters in their own right; they went about their job irrespective of the crowd, and they gave their decisions as they saw them. There was a mutual respect on the field of play between the players and most of the referees, most of the time. This was helped considerably by the fact that the officials would chat with the players after the game in the bar.

The referees today seem to want to be part of the Super League hype, and in a way it must be difficult for them not to be drawn into the limelight. It was always the sign of a good ref during a game that the fans never really noticed him, and the game flowed. The top Australian referees still seem to have this ability to fade into the background. There does seem to have been a breakdown in communications between the officials and the players, an unwillingness to discuss certain incidents and decisions that took place during a match. These days more ill-discipline and backchatting seem to be creeping into the game – something that the referees would not stand for in the old days. Certainly the Super League referees are much fitter, and with the advent of new technology and the faster pace of the game they could not survive if they were not. They also have to give their decisions much more promptly, which adds to the pressure on them, and with so many camera angles available for televised matches they are probably under more scrutiny than they have ever been. But I just feel that they would perhaps benefit from more direct communication with the players after games.

The lower division games I have seen concern me, for the refereeing has not been of the highest standard, and there appear to be no young officials coming through. Again, if the game is to compete in the new millennium, it must give the referees every chance to develop their technique and communication.

THE FUTURE OF RUGBY LEAGUE

With hindsight, the financial support and effort that was invested in Super League in London, Paris and Gateshead would surely have been better utilised at schools, junior and amateur club level. Part of the Murdoch monies were originally earmarked for development purposes, and both the junior end of the game and professional clubs' grounds could have benefited more if greater discipline had been applied to ensure expenditure in those areas. You only have to witness a Super League fixture at Headingley and see at half-time the Under-7s and Under-8s entertaining the fans. They are all from the junior sections of amateur clubs – not from schools. The amateur game has always been strong up north, and its administration and development should be integrated more in the whole rugby league set-up. Schools rugby league appears to be dying, even though a number of clubs, towns and cities have rugby league development officers. This is to me perhaps the most serious point of the current decline in rugby league. It is the amateur clubs by and large who are strong, and they are the ones who should be encouraged to take the lead in the development of junior rugby league. School sport in general has waned, and will only improve with greater political commitment – or should that be non-political – and with sound support from the teaching fraternity. But that seems to be a long way off.

In the 'Framing the Future' minimum standards document there was a section covering grounds, and part of the News Corporation monies were supposed to go to develop better facilities for spectators. But at the beginning of the Super League era the professional game moved from winter to summer, and clubs had a great deal to organise in that first season. Longer-term planning was put on hold, and with better weather for the fans, few clubs made the development of their grounds an urgent priority. It may be that the various boards of directors wanted to see how season ticket income and match attendances would pan out in summer before setting out too many ambitious proposals.

Now, though, five years on, too many Super League grounds show little signs of major investment. The 'Framing the Future' document called for all Super League clubs to have seating for at least 6,000 spectators: it seems to me that there are as many as nine clubs who fail to qualify in this respect. Even Leeds might be hard pushed to provide this seated capacity. The three clubs that do satisfy the requirement all happen to share their grounds with professional football clubs. Have the remaining Super League clubs got plans to develop their grounds? Leeds seem to be moving forward with Yorkshire County Cricket Club by means of a joint development and a Lottery application, although they are still awaiting approval. Bradford Bulls have been proposing to redevelop Odsal for many years now I believe plans were approved last year, although it seems to have gone rather quiet again in this direction. St Helens are seeking a new home for the year 2002, with a brand-new 20,000-seater stadium – but what of the rest? What plans do they have?

What hope is there for the Northern Ford Premiership clubs? None of these meet the 'Framing the Future' criteria. We had the farce last year of Hunslet Hawks, who won the Northern Ford Premiership Championship and were seeking automatic promotion to Super League. They had approval from Leeds City Council to upgrade their stadium to 5,000 seats by means of the erection of a second stand to accompany the single main stand that already existed, together with an athletics track. Then there appeared to be some problem with the Council concerning a promise made many years ago, when the club had to leave the Elland Road stadium: Hunslet claimed to have been told at the time that money for a new rugby league stadium had been put on one side – although nothing was subsequently confirmed or denied by the local authority. The delays caused as the RFL waited for Hunslet to demonstrate that they could develop a Super League-standard stadium – when three-quarters of the Super League clubs could not themselves fulfil these standards – did our game no credit at all.

Both London Broncos and Huddersfield/Sheffield Giants are currently averaging around 3,000 spectators for every home game, and I am sure that Hunslet Hawks could have accommodated such an attendance comfortably within what are good standard facilities at the South Leeds Stadium. Was it reasonable, then, to expect them to develop a 10,000-capacity stadium in order to qualify for promotion? Had Hunslet's application for promotion been successful, Huddersfield/Sheffield would have been relegated – even though they play at the new 25,000-capacity McAlpine Stadium, sharing facilities with Huddersfield Town football club. Perhaps this experience would have made the Giants all the stronger for coming back to Super League a year or so later.

The next hurdle ahead for the Northern Ford Premiership clubs will come in a couple of years' time. The Premiership sides currently receive £150,000 from the News Corporation funds; in 2001 they will receive £100,000 and in 2002 their final payment will be £50,000. Thereafter there will be no more money available from central broadcast contracts to any Northern Ford Premiership club. It seems to me that the clubs at this level will then revert fully back to winter rugby and employ part-time players who are paid match terms only, with little future for their rugby careers. Standards are certain to fall rapidly in the lower division after 2002, and I believe that the Premiership will eventually become like the National Conference League is now. The Premiership clubs will become feeder clubs for the bigger Super League outfits, and I can even see the number of those competing in the élite competition being reduced to eight or nine. Huddersfield, London and Salford could well drop down or out, as there has been no sign in recent years of them attaining the standards of the top six or seven clubs in Super League. The quality players will be engaged by those few clubs with the financial ability to reward them; I am afraid that there are too many average players earning a living at the moment in Super League.

In 2002 the Super League contract with News Corporation is up for renegotiation, and it is not inconceivable that Rupert Murdoch's organisation might pull out altogether. This could happen, as Murdoch ostensibly set out in 1995 with the intention of spreading the game of rugby league for his own purposes throughout the nation, so that Super League was contested in every major British city every summer. In 1995 rugby league should have made it clear during the negotiations that such an expansion was never a realistic possibility. Now the clubs may regret jumping into bed so quickly with News Corporation. If Murdoch does pull out because of lack of national exposure, then the game would really be in a state.

I can see only one outcome to that eventuality: Super League would revert to winter rugby, and the top players would move where the money was – and those better financial opportunities might well lie within rugby union. No doubt the game's administrators will already be concerned as 2002 approaches. Even now the financial pressures are being felt at the top level in rugby league, with Jason Robinson seemingly on the way to English rugby union from Wigan, and Leeds Rhinos trying desperately to hold on to Iestyn Harris in competition with the Welsh Rugby Union.

Much of the finance invested by News Corporation when Super League began was used by clubs to settle their historic debts, such as paying off VAT and PAYE arrears. Management generally has been lacking at some clubs over many years, and surely the RFL must have been aware of this. But they made no great effort to turn the clubs round financially, and to me that is the key. It is the reason why I fear for this great game in the next few years.

21.

THE GREATEST COACHES AND PLAYERS

COACHES I PLAYED UNDER

ARTHUR BUNTING, HULL FC 1983–85 Arthur gave me my chance in the first team at the start of my first season. His man-management was first class, and he had the knack of keeping all the players happy, from the seasoned internationals to the rookie youngsters. Team spirit was a key part of his philosophy, combined with excellent individual coaching and game plans.

FRANK MYLER, GREAT BRITAIN 1984 Frank worked hard as an international coach, although I feel his tactics were questionable in 1984. His team selection to face the Kangaroos was based on damage-limitation, in response to the performance of the 1982 Australian 'Invincibles' touring side.

FRANK STANTON, BALMAIN 1985–86 Frank was undoubtedly the best coach I played under, with first-class coaching methods. Also the Australian team coach, he never wanted to take away any player's individual flair. He let us know quite clearly what he thought in the dressing-room, and what he expected from us in public.

PETER FOX, YORKSHIRE 1984–87 Although Peter was unbeaten as Yorkshire's coach, he was mainly renowned as a motivator who did not tolerate prima donnas. My first training session with him at Post Office Road in Featherstone proved to be typical of the pattern he adopted. The forwards were closely put through their paces, and as for the backs, we were left to our own devices!

LEN CASEY, HULL FC 1986–87 Unfortunately for Hull, Len's coaching was simply outdated. He coached as he played, very physically. His style was to send us out to bash the other guys – which was not the way to play, believe me.

BILL ANDERSON, BALMAIN 1987 Bill was a schoolteacher who seemed to be theoretically competent only to reveal, in practice, that not all Australians were good coaches. You can't successfully do the business on the blackboard, as Balmain found out to their cost.

MAURICE BAMFORD, LEEDS 1987–88 AND GREAT BRITAIN 1985–86 Maurice was very passionate about rugby league and held all the top coaching positions in the course of his career – Leeds, Wigan and Great Britain. Yet he proved that being a poet was no way to win games. He seemed to struggle when the pressure was really on, taking it out on any crockery that happened to be around the dressing-room.

MAL REILLY, LEEDS 1988–89 AND GREAT BRITAIN 1987–94 Mal was the best English coach I worked with. His will to win was phenomenal and rubbed off on all who played for him. He was not overtly tactical, but was a true winner and master motivator, immensely proud of his own fitness and achievements.

JOHN BAILEY, WESTERN SUBURBS 1989 John was not the greatest Aussie coach, though I only played eight games under him at a time when, apart from Ellery Hanley and me, the Western Suburbs team was young and inexperienced.

DAVID WARD, LEEDS 1989–91 David was a very good coach, and if Leeds had made available to him the same funds that Dougie Laughton was to spend, then David would have certainly been a great success. He was not given enough time, and in hindsight proved a big loss both to Leeds and to my ambitions. More a motivator than a tactical planner, he was ably backed up by Norman Smith. Between them they helped to create the best team spirit during my time in the Leeds dressing-room, and as a result we ran Wigan a close second in the Championship.

THE GREATEST COACHES AND PLAYERS

DOUGIE LAUGHTON, LEEDS 1991–95 Dougie was my worst nightmare. He proved to be the poorest coach, bereft of tactical ideas and unable to motivate the team. After training on a Saturday morning, Dougie's idea of a video session on the strengths and weaknesses of our opposition was to put the tape on and go back to his office. He had no time for a game plan and we simply drifted off home after lunch. Dougie set out to sign up the best players he could, and then leave it up to us to go out and play. His man-management was appalling, and the day he resigned was a day I will always remember fondly.

DEAN BELL, LEEDS 1995–96 For Dean the post may have come too soon but I found him to be a very good coach. He thought deeply about the game and prepared us well. He made a deep impression on us after the previous incumbent. One day Dean will be a great coach, perhaps guiding the Kiwis.

DARRYL VAN DE VELDE, HUDDERSFIELD 1996–97 Darryl was an excellent coach with good ideas and a deep knowledge of the game, who was meticulous in his preparations. Regrettably, the players he had were just not up to the task of matching his talent.

STEVE FERRES, HUDDERSFIELD 1997–98 Steve was highly regarded within the game, failing only to gain the respect of the most important group – his own players. I managed to stop the team seeking his dismissal in mid-season, and while we finished the season as Premiership Trophy winners at Old Trafford, the board still sacked him shortly after.

THE GREATEST WORLD TEAM OF MY TIME

Full-back	Gary Kemble – Hull FC and New Zealand
Right Wing	Eric Grothe – Leeds, Parramatta and Australia
Right Centre	Mal Meninga – St Helens, Canberra and Australia
Left Centre	Gene Miles – Wigan, Brisbane and Australia
Left Wing	Martin Offiah – Widnes, Wigan and Great Britain
Stand-off	Wally Lewis – Wakefield, Brisbane and Australia
Scrum-half	Peter Sterling – Hull FC, Parramatta and Australia

Prop-Forward	Lee Crooks – Hull FC, Leeds, Castleford and Great Britain
Hooker	Benny Elias – Balmain and Australia
Prop-Forward	Kevin Ward – Castleford, St Helens and Great Britain
Second Row	Wayne Pearce – Balmain and Australia
Second Row	Paul Sironen – Balmain and Australia
Loose-Forward	Ellery Hanley – Bradford Northern, Wigan, Leeds and Great Britain
Substitutes:	Dean Bell – Leeds, Wigan and New Zealand
	Steve Norton – Castleford, Hull FC and Great Britain

THE BEST GREAT BRITAIN TEAM OF MY TIME

Full-back	Joe Lydon – Widnes and Wigan
Right Wing	Jonathan Davies – Widnes and Warrington
Right Centre	Gary Connolly – St Helens and Wigan
Left Centre	Paul Newlove – Featherstone, Bradford Northern and St Helens
Left Wing	Martin Offiah – Widnes and Wigan
Stand-off	Garry Schofield – Hull FC and Leeds
Scrum-half	Andy Gregory – Widnes and Wigan
Prop-Forward	Lee Crooks – Hull FC, Leeds and Castleford
Hooker	Martin McDermott – Wigan
Prop-Forward	Kevin Ward – Castleford and St Helens
Second Row	Denis Betts – Wigan
Second Row	Phil Clarke – Wigan
Loose-Forward	Ellery Hanley – Bradford Northern, Wigan and Leeds
Substitutes:	Shaun Edwards – Wigan
	Steve Norton – Castleford and Hull FC
	Mike Gregory – Warrington

MY TOP TEN GAMES

- ✦ Scoring my first hat-trick as a professional for Hull against Leeds in 1983.
- ✦ Scoring two tries in the Yorkshire Cup final for Leeds against Castleford at Elland Road in 1988.

- ✦ Playing against the Aussies in the first Test in Sydney in 1984 and scoring a try.
- ✦ Playing against the Aussies in the second Test at Brisbane in 1984 and scoring another try which was voted the best try of the decade in the 1980s.
- ✦ Scoring four tries for Great Britain against the Kiwis at Central Park in the second Test of 1985.
- ✦ Scoring four tries against the mighty Wigan at Headingley in 1989.
- ✦ The whole Test series against New Zealand – the first, second and third Tests of 1990.
- ✦ The second Test against the Aussies in Melbourne in 1992 when I was the captain – which has to go down as my best game ever.
- ✦ The World Cup final in 1992 at Wembley.

MY TOP TEN REFEREES

1. Billy Thompson
2. Ronnie Campbell
3. Dave Campbell
4. John Holdsworth
5. Fred Lindop
6. Robin Whitfield
7. Russell Smith
8. Bill Harrigan
9. Greg McCallum
10. Kevin Roberts

22.

STATISTICS

MY GREAT BRITAIN TEST MATCHES

17.2.84	France	won 10–0 Headingley, Leeds
9.6.84	Australia	lost 8–25 Sydney
26.6.84	Australia	lost 8–18 Brisbane
7.7.84	Australia	lost 7–20 Sydney
14.7.84	New Zealand	lost 0–12 Auckland
19.10.85	New Zealan	lost 22–24 Headingley, Leeds
2.11.85	New Zealand	won 25–8 Central Park, Wigan
9.11.85	New Zealand	drew 6–6 Elland Road, Leeds
16.2.86	France	drew 10–10 Avignon
1.3.86	France	won 24–10 Central Park, Wigan
25.10.86	Australia	lost 16–38 Old Trafford, Manchester
8.11.86	Australia	lost 4–34 Elland Road, Leeds
22.11.86	Australia	lost 15–24 Central Park Wigan
24.1.87	France	won 52–4 Headingley, Leeds
8.2.87	France	won 20–10 Carcassonne
24.1.88	France	won 28–14 Avignon
6.2.88	France	won 30–12 Headingley, Leeds
22.5.88	Papua New Guinea	won 42–22 Port Moresby
11.6.88	Australia	lost 6–17 Sydney
18.3.90	France	won 8–4 Perpignan
7.4.90	France	lost 18–24 Headingley, Leeds
27.5.90	Papua New Guinea	lost 18–20 Goroka
2.6.90	Papua New Guinea	won 40–8 Port Moresby

24.6.90	New Zealand	won 11–10 Palmerston North
8.7.90	New Zealand	won 16–14 Auckland
15.7.90	New Zealand	lost 18–21 Christchurch
27.10.90	Australia	won 19–12 Wembley
10.11.90	Australia	lost 10–14 Old Trafford, Manchester
24.11.90	Australia	lost 0–14 Elland Road, Leeds
27.1.91	France	won 54–10 Perpignan
16.2.91	France	won 60–4 Headingley, Leeds
9.11.91	Papua New Guinea	won 56–4 Central Park, Wigan
31.5.92	Papua New Guinea	won 20–14 Port Moresby
12.6.92	Australia	lost 6–22 Sydney
26.6.92	Australia	won 33–10 Melbourne
3.7.92	Australia	lost 10–16 Brisbane
12.7.92	New Zealand	lost 14–15 Palmerston North
19.7.92	New Zealand	won 19–16 Auckland
24.10.92	Australia	lost 6–10 Wembley
7.3.93	France	won 48–6 Carcassonne
16.10.93	New Zealand	won 17–0 Wembley
30.10.93	New Zealand	won 29–12 Central Park, Wigan
6.11.93	New Zealand	won 29–10 Elland Road, Leeds
20.3.94	France	won 12–4 Carcassonne
16.11.94	Australia	lost 8–38 Old Trafford, Manchester
30.11.94	Australia	lost 4–23 Elland Road, Leeds

SCORING RECORD

1983–84 Season

Hull FC

DATE	COMP.	H/A	OPPONENTS	RES.	SCORE	TRIES	GOALS	DROP-GOALS
14.9.83	IC	A	Keighley	W	30–8	1		
9.10.83	SLC	A	Leeds	W	40–13	3		
23.10.83	SLC	A	Leeds	L	12–18	1	1	
30.10.83	SLC	H	Salford	W	58–6	2		
20.11.83	JPS	A	Featherstone	L	14–20	1		
11.12.83	SLC	8	Fulham	W	36–11	2		
18.12.83	SLC	A	Wigan	L	12–14	2		
27.12.83	SLC	H	Featherstone	W	37–4	1		
2.1.84	SLC	A	Featherstone	W	22–12	1		
8.1.84	SLC	H	Bradford N	W	16–8	2		
11.1.84	SLC	H	St Helens	W	30–24	2		
5.2.84	SLC	H	Oldham	W	20–8	1		
12.2.84	CC	A	Cardiff City	W	34–6	2	2	
25.2.84	CC	A	St Helens	L	14–24	2		
3.4.84	CC	A	Widnes	W	30–12	3	3	
7.3.84	SLC	A	Salford	W	42–6	1	5	
16.3.84	SLC	A	St Helens	L	10–22	1	3	
21.3.84	SLC	H	Leeds	W	23–10	1	3	
25.3.84	SLC	H	Wakefield Trinity	W	66–12	1	9	
1.4.84	SLC	A	Whitehaven	W	28–10		4	
8.4.84	SLC	H	Castleford	W	40–10	2	4	
15.4.84	SLC	A	Bradford N	W	29–10	1	4	
20.4.84	SLC	A	Hull KR	W	36–16		8	
23.4.84	SLC		Whitehaven	W	54–0	1	7	
29.4.84	PT	H	Bradford N	W	42–12	2	2	
7.5.84	PT	H	Castleford	L	12–22	1	2	
TOTAL						37	57	0

Great Britain

DATE	COMP.	H/A	OPPONENTS	RES.	SCORE	TRIES	GOALS	DGS
17.2.84		H	France	W	10–0			

Great Britain Under-24s

DATE	COMP.	H/A	OPPONENTS	RES.	SCORE	TRIES	GOALS	DGS
11.11.83		A	France	W	28–23			
4.12.83		H	France	W	48–1	1		

Great Britain Colts

DATE	COMP.	H/A	OPPONENTS	RES.	SCORE	TRIES	GOALS	DGS
18.1.84		A	France	W	24–10	2		

Yorkshire Colts

DATE	COMP.	H/A	OPPONENTS	RES.	SCORE	TRIES	GOALS	DGS
26.11.83		H	Lancashire	L	14–28	1		

1984–85 Season

Hull FC

DATE	COMP.	H/A	OPPONENTS	RES.	SCORE	TRIES	GOALS	DGS
2.9.84	SLC	H	Workington T	W	46–2	2	1	
9.9.84	SLC	A	Widnes	L	10–11	1	1	
16.9.84	YC	H	Halifax	W	30–10		5	
23.9.84	SLC	A	Warrington	L	14–21	1	3	
26.9.84	YC	A	York	W	38–8	2	7	
30.9.84	SLC	H	Barrow	W	44–14	2	8	
7.10.84	SLC	A	Hull KR	L	17–26		4	
16.10.84	YC	H	Leeds	W	24–1	3	3	
21.10.84	SLC	A	Leigh	L	30–33		5	
27.10.84	YC	Hull City	Hull KR	W	29–12		4	1
4.11.84	SLC	A	Hunslet	W	26–10	1	3	
11.11.84	SLC	H	Warrington	W	34–12		5	
18.11.84	JPS	A	Fulham	W	36–14	2	3	
2.12.84	JPS	H	Oldham	W	26–14		3	
5.12.84	SLC	H	Leeds	L	6–10	1	1	
9.12.84	SLC	H	Halifax	W	32–4		6	
21.1.85	SLC	H	Widnes	W	21–16		1	
3.2.85	SLC	A	Oldham	W	22–10		3	
14.2.85	CC	H	Carlisle	W	52–6		6	
24.2.85	CC	A	Halifax	W	22–6		2	
27.2.85	SLC	H	St Helens	W	46–24	1	5	
3.3.85	SLC	H	Leigh	W	40–14	2	4	
13.3.85	CC	A	Widnes	W	19–12	1	3	
17.3.85	SLC	H	Oldham	W	30–8	1	5	
22.3.85	SLC	A	St Helens	L	18–47		3	
26.3.85	SLC	A	Castleford	L	18–26	1	3	
12.4.85	SLC	H	Hull KR	L	12–36		1	
17.4.85	SLC	H	Bradford N	W	24–18		4	
20.4.85	SLC	A	Workington T	W	64–18	2	2	
TOTAL						23	101	1

Great Britain – British Lions Tour of Australia and New Zealand

DATE	COMP.	H/A	OPPONENTS	RES.	SCORE	TRIES	GOALS	DGS
2.6.84		A	Newcastle	W	28–18	1		
9.6.84		A	Australia (1st Test)	L	8–25	1		
15.6.84		A	Central Queensland	W	44–12	4	5	
26.6.84		A	Australia (2nd Test)	L	8–18	1		
7.7.84		A	Australia (3rd Test)	L	7–20			
10.7.84		A	Northern Districts	W	42–8		1	
14.7.84		A	New Zealand (1st Test)	L	0–12			
TOTAL						6	7	

England

DATE	COMP.	H/A	OPPONENTS	RES.	SCORE	TRIES	GOALS	DGS
14.10.84		A	Wales	W	28–9			

STATISTICS

Great Britain Under-21s

DATE	COMP.	H/A	OPPONENTS	RES.	SCORE	TRIES	GOALS	DGS
25.11.84		H	France	W	24–8			
16.12.84		A	France	W	8–2			

1985–86 Season

Hull FC

DATE	COMP.	H/A	OPPONENTS	RES.	SCORE	TRIES	GOALS	DGS
29.9.85	SLC	A	St Helens	W	25–22	1		
6.10.85	SLC	H	Hull KR	W	28–6	2	2	
27.10.85	SLC	H	Bradford N	W	28–16		1	
3.11.85	SLC	H	Swinton	W	16–10		1	
17.11.85	Tour	H	New Zealand	L	10–33	1	1	
29.1.86	CC	H	Dudley Hill	W	38–10	2	4	
2.3.86	SLC	A	Wigan	L	6–44		1	
5.3.86	SLC	A	Salford	L	12–15	1	2	
9.3.86	SLC	A	Dewsbury	W	30–12	2	3	
12.3.86	SLC	H	Wigan	L	10–26		1	
31.3.86	SLC	H	York	W	16–12		1	
6.4.86	SLC	A	Leeds	W	35–18	2	2	1
9.4.86	SLC	H	Leeds	W	10–4	1	1	
13.4.86	SLC	A	Widnes	L	20–26		4	
16.4.86	SLC	A	Oldham	L	14–15	1	3	
20.4.86	SLC	H	Warrington	L	20–33		4	
22.4.86	SLC	A	Hull KR	W	28–2	1	2	
26.4.86	PT	A	Halifax	L	20–32	1	2	
TOTAL						15	35	1

Great Britain

DATE	VENUE	H/A	OPPONENTS	RES.	SCORE	TRIES	GOALS	DGS
19.10.85	Leeds		New Zealand	L	22–24			
2.11.85	Wigan		New Zealand	W	25–8	4		
9.11.85	Elland Rd		New Zealand	D	6–6			
16.2.86		A	France	D	10–10			
1.3.86		H	France	W	24–10	1	2	
TOTAL						5	2	

1986–87 Season

Hull FC

DATE	COMP.	H/A	OPPONENTS	RES.	SCORE	TRIES	GOALS	DGS
5.10.86	SBC	A	Hull KR	L	6–29	1		
14.10.86	SBC	H	Bradford N	W	27–22	1		
19.10.86	SBC	H	Halifax	W	28–23	1		
2.11.86	SBC	H	Leeds	L	10–32	1		
30.11.86	JPS	A	Salford	W	27–12	2		
7.12.86	JPS	H	Blackpool B	W	48–22	2		
13.12.86	JPS	A	Bradford N	W	20–8	3		
26.12.86	SBC	H	Featherstone	W	26–6	1		
28.12.86	SBC	A	Featherstone	L	12–18	1		
4.1.87	SBC	H	Oldham	W	20–16	2		
4.2.87	CC	A	Bramley	W	10–2			1
15.2.87	CC	A	Mansfield M	W	38–7	2		
22.2.87	SBC	A	Oldham	L	18–24	1		
11.3.87	SBC	A	Bradford N	D	20–20	1		
15.3.87	SBC	A	Leeds	L	22–28	2		

17.3.87	SBC	H	St Helens	W	36–22	1		
25.3.87	SBC	H	Salford	L	8–14	1		
29.3.87	SBC	H	Warrington	L	12–46	1		
3.4.87	SBC	A	Widnes	W	18–10	2		
7.4.87	SBC	H	Castleford	W	18–6	1		
12.4.87	SBC	H	Wigan	L	12–18	1		
20.4.87	SBC	A	Wakefield T	W	38–4	4		
TOTAL						32	I	

Great Britain

DATE	VENUE	H/A	OPPONENTS	RES.	SCORE	TRIES	GOALS	DGS
25.10.86	Old Trafford	H	Australia	L	16–38	2		
8.11.86	Elland Road	H	Australia	L	4–34	1		
22.11.86	Wigan	H	Australia	L	15–24	2		1
24.1.87	Leeds	H	France	W	52–4			
8.2.87		A	France	W	20–10			
TOTAL						5		I

1987–88 Season

Leeds

DATE	COMP.	H/A	OPPONENTS	RES.	SCORE	TRIES	GOALS	DGS
25.10.87	Tour	H	Auckland	L	25–29	2		
1.11.87	SBC	H	Wigan	D	18–18	1		
8.11.87	SBC	H	St Helens	W	24–21	1		
22.11.87	JPS	H	Halifax	W	20–10	1		
6.12.87	SBC	H	Castleford		44–0	2		
12.12.87	JPS	A	Wigan	W	19–6	1		
13.1.88	CC	A	Kells	W	28–0	1		
17.1.88	SBC	H	Widnes	W	26–21	2		
31.1.88	CC	H	Castleford	W	22–14	1		
7.2.88	SBC	A	Leigh	L	6–18	1		
14.2.88	CC	A	Wigan	L	14–30	1		
2.3.88	SBC	A	Widnes	L	6–32		1	
1.4.88	SBC	H	Bradford N	L	18–32	1	1	
4.4.88	SBC	A	Halifax	W	28–20	2		
6.4.88	SBC	A	Hull	L	16–28		2	
13.4.88	SBC	A	Swinton	W	24–22	4		
20.4.88	PT	A	Bradford N	W	22–14	1		
7.2.88	SBC	A	Leigh	L	6–18	1		
14.2.88	CC	A	Wigan	L	14–30	1		
2.3.88	SBC	A	Widnes	L	6–32			1
1.4.88	SBC	H	Bradford N	L	18–32	1	1	
4.4.88	SBC	A	Halifax	W	28–20	2		
6.4.88	SBC	A	Hull	L	16–28		2	
13.4.88	SBC	A	Swinton	W	24–22	4		
20.4.88	PT	A	Bradford N	L	18–32	1		
TOTAL						32	7	I

Great Britain

DATE	COMP.	H/A	OPPONENTS	RES.	SCORE	TRIES	GOALS	DGS
24.1.88		A	France	W	28–14	2		
6.2.88		H	France	W	30–12	1	5	
TOTAL						3	5	

STATISTICS

1988–89 Season

Leeds

DATE	COMP.	H/A	OPPONENTS	RES.	SCORE	TRIES	GOALS	DGS
28.8.88	SBC	A	Featherstone	W	32–18	1		
4.9.88	SBC	A	Oldham	W	28–22	2		
11.9.88	SBC	H	Widnes	L	14–30	1		
25.9.88	SBC	H	St Helens	W	32–0	1	6	
28.9.88	YC	H	Wakefield T	W	15–10		3	
2.10.88	SBC	A	Hull	L	12–14		2	
5.10.88	YC	H	Hull	L	12–8	1		
9.10.88	SBC	H	Wigan	W	22–14	4		
16.10.88	YC Final	A	Castleford	W	33–12	2		1
23.10.88	SBC		Hull KR	W	21–8	1		
27.11.88	SBC	A	Salford	W	24–6	1		
5.3.89	SBC	H	Wakefield T	W	28–16	1	1	
15.3.89	SBC	A	Hull KR	W	18–13	2		
19.3.89	SBC	H	Castleford	W	32–18	1		
24.3.89	SBC	H	Bradford N	W	10–7	1		
27.3.89	SBC	A	Halifax	W	22–20	1		
TOTAL						20	12	1

Great Britain – British Lions Tour

DATE	VENUE	H/A	OPPONENTS	RES.	SCORE	TRIES	GOALS	DGS
22.5.88		A	Papua New Guinea	W	42–22	2		
24.5.88		A	Northern/ Highland Zones	W	36–18	1	1	
5.6.88		A	Northern Division	L	12–36	1		
11.6.88	Sydney	A	Australia (1st Test)	L	6–17			
15.6.88		A	Combined Brisbane XIII	W	28–14	1		
TOTAL						5		1

Great Britain

DATE	VENUE	H/A	OPPONENTS	RES.	SCORE	TRIES	GOALS	DGS
29.10.88	Leeds	H	Rest of the World XIII	W	30–28	1		

Yorkshire

DATE	VENUE	H/A	OPPONENTS	RES.	SCORE	TRIES	GOALS	DGS
21.9.88	Leeds	H	Lancashire	W	24–14	1		

1989–90 Season

Leeds

DATE	COMP.	H/A	OPPONENTS	RES.	SCORE	TRIES	GOALS	DGS
3.9.89	SBC	H	Wakefield T	L	14–22	1		
8.11.89	RT	H	Ryedale-York	W	32–2	4		
12.11.89	SBC	A	Salford	W	38–18	1		
19.11.89	SBC	H	Widnes	W	26–12	1		
26.11.89	SBC	A	Bradford N	L	13–14			1
10.12.89	RT	H	Bradford N	W	27–8			1
7.1.90	SBC	A	Widnes	W	20–8	1		
21.1.90	SBC	H	Bradford N	W	13–8			1
4.2.90	SBC	A	St Helens	L	26–32	1		

11.2.90	SBC	H	Barrow	W	90–0	2		
18.2.90	SBC	H	Sheffield E	W	44–2	2		
25.2.90	SBC	A	Leigh	W	26–14	2		
11.3.90	SBC	A	Warrington	L	6–9			1
25.3.90	SBC	A	Wakefield T	W	36–17	1		
1.4.90	SBC	H	St Helens	W	50–14	1	2	
13.4.90	SBC	H	Featherstone R	W	25–14	1		
22.4.90	PT	H	Castleford	W	24–18	2		
6.5.90	PT	H	Widnes	L	7–27			1
TOTAL						20	2	5

Great Britain

DATE	VENUE	H/A	OPPONENTS	RES.	SCORE	TRIES	GOALS	DGS
18.3.90		A	France	W	8–4		2	
7.4.90	Leeds	H	France	W	8–4			
TOTAL							2	

Great Britain – British Lions Tour

DATE	VENUE	H/A	OPPONENTS	RES.	SCORE	TRIES	GOALS	DGS
27.5.90		A	Papua New Guinea	L	18–20			
2.6.90		A	Papua New Guinea	W	40–8	1		
24.6.90		A	New Zealand	W	11–10			1
8.7.90		A	New Zealand	W	16–14	1		
15.7.90		A	New Zealand	L	18–21	1		
TOTAL						3		1

Yorkshire

DATE	VENUE	H/A	OPPONENTS	RES.	SCORE	TRIES	GOALS	DGS
20.9.89	Wigan	A	Lancashire	W	56–12	1		

1990–91 Season

Leeds

DATE	COMP.	H/A	OPPONENTS	RES.	SCORE	TRIES	GOALS	DGS
26.8.90	YC	H	Bradford N	L	16–24	1		
30.9.90	SBC	H	St Helens	W	23–4	1	1	
7.10.90	SBC	A	Bradford N	W	21–12			1
11.11.90	SBC	H	Rochdale H	W	64–4	2		
18.11.90	RT	H	Halifax	W	58–6	2		
27.11.90	SBC	H	Castleford	W	41–16	1	1	
2.12.90	RT	H	Hull KR	W	26–22	2		
16.12.90	SBC	A	Sheffield E	W	24–6	1	2	
23.12.90	SBC	A	Wigan	L	16–22		2	
26.12.90	SBC	H	Bradford N	W	26–8		5	
3.2.91	SBC	A	Castleford	L	14–16	1		
10.2.91	CC	H	Dewsbury	W	40–20	2	4	
3.3.91	SBC	H	Hull KR	W	24–18	2	2	
17.3.91	SBC	A	Hull KR	W	28–16	1	4	
29.3.91	SBC	H	Wakefield T	W	7–0	1	1	
1.4.91	SBC	A	Wakefield T	D	14–14	2		
21.4.91	PT	A	Castleford	W	24–20	1		2
5.5.91	PT	A	Hull	L	7–10		1	1
TOTAL						20	23	4

STATISTICS

Great Britain

DATE	VENUE	H/A	OPPONENTS	RES.	SCORE	TRIES	GOALS	DGS
27.10.90		H	Australia	W	19–12			1
10.11.90		H	Australia	L	10–14			
24.11.90		H	Australia	L	0–14			
27.1.91		A	France	W	45–10	2		1
16.2.91		H	France	W	60–4	3		
TOTAL						5		2

1991–92 Season

Leeds

DATE	COMP.	H/A	OPPONENTS	RES.	SCORE	TRIES	GOALS	DGS
15.9.91	YC	A	Hull	L	11–16	1		
22.9.91	SBC	A	Castleford	W	13–8	1		1
29.9.91	SBC	H	Swinton	W	46–8	1	1	
13.10.91	SBC	H	Warrington	L	13–22	1		1
3.11.91	SBC	A	Wigan	W	19–0			1
16.11.91	RT	A	Warrington	W	17–8			1
23.11.91	RT	A	Hull	W	12–4	1		
1.12.91	RT	H	Castleford	W	24–4			2
7.12.91	RT	Bfd City	Salford	W	22–15	1		
18.12.91	SBC	H	Bradford N	W	22–12	1		
1.1.92	SBC	H	Salford	W	36–10	1		
21.1.92	CC	A	Bramley	W	36–12	1		
8.3.92	SBC	H	Widnes	W	40–28	1		
22.3.92	SBC	A	Hull	L	14–22	1		
5.4.92	SBC	A	Hull KR	W	13–4			1
26.4.92	TP	A	Warrington	D	18–18		1	1
29.4.92	TP	H	Warrington	W	22–8	2		
TOTAL						13	2	8

Great Britain

DATE	VENUE	H/A	OPPONENTS	RES.	SCORE	TRIES	GOALS	DGS
9.11.91	Wigan	H	Papua New	W	56–4	1		

Yorkshire

DATE	VENUE	H/A	OPPONENTS	RES.	SCORE	TRIES	GOALS	DGS
18.9.91	Leeds	H	Lancashire	W	17–12			

1992–93 Season

Leeds

DATE	COMP.	H/A	OPPONENTS	RES.	SCORE	TRIES	GOALS	DGS
30.8.92	SBC	H	St Helens	L	14–27	1		
13.9.92	YC	H	Hunslet	W	28–20	1	2	
20.9.92	SBC	H	Hull KR	W	34–6	1		
23.9.92	YC	A	Hull	L	16–26	1		
2.10.92	SBC	H	Warrington	W	13–4	1		1
11.10.92	SBC	A	Wigan	L	6–24	1	1	
1.11.92	SBC	H	Widnes	W	48–16		8	
18.12.92	SBC	H	Halifax	W	42–14		5	
26.12.92	SBC	H	Castleford	W	40–12	1	1	
8.1.93	SBC	A	Warrington	W	31–24	2	1	1
31.1.93	CC	H	Barrow	W	54–18	1		
14.2.93	CC	H	Rochdale H	W	68–6	3		

| 25.4.93 | PT | A | Widnes | W | 22–10 | 1 | | |
| TOTAL | | | | | | 14 | 18 | 2 |

Great Britain – British Lions Tour

DATE	VENUE	H/A	OPPONENTS	RES.	SCORE	TRIES	GOALS	DGS
24.5.92		A	Highland Zones	W	24–15	2		
31.5.92		A	Papua New Guinea	W	20–14			
12.6.92	Sydney	A	Australia (1st Test)	L	6–22			
26.6.92	Melbourne	A	Australia (2nd Test)	W	33–10	1		1
3.7.92	Brisbane	A	Australia (3rd Test)	L	10–16			
12.7.92	Palmerston Nth	A	New Zealand	L	14–15			
19.7.92	Auckland	A	New Zealand	W	19–16			1
TOTAL						3		2

Great Britain – World Cup Final

DATE	VENUE	H/A	OPPONENTS	RES.	SCORE	TRIES	GOALS	DGS
24.10.92	Wembley	H	Australia	L	6–10			

Great Britain

DATE	VENUE	H/A	OPPONENTS	RES.	SCORE	TRIES	GOALS	DGS
7.3.93		A	France	W	48–6	3		

England

DATE	VENUE	H/A	OPPONENTS	RES.	SCORE	TRIES	GOALS	DGS
27.11.92	Swansea		Wales	W	36–11	1		

1993–94 Season

Leeds

DATE	COMP.	H/A	OPPONENTS	RES.	SCORE	TRIES	GOALS	DGS
5.9.93	SBC	H	Warrington	W	21–19	2		1
19.9.93	SBC	H	Hull KR	W	42–6	1		
3.10.93	SBC	H	Hull	D	22–22	1		
26.12.93	SBC	H	Wakefield T	W	20–16	1		
12.2.94	CC	H	Warrington	W	38–4	1		
1.4.94	SBC	A	Wakefield T	W	29–20		2	1
20.4.94	SBC	H	Widnes	W	58–16	1		
30.4.94	CC	Wembley	Wigan	L	16–26	1		
8.5.94	PT	A	Bradford N	L	16–42	1		
TOTAL						9	2	2

Great Britain

DATE	VENUE	H/A	OPPONENTS	RES.	SCORE	TRIES	GOALS	DGS
16.10.93	Wembley	H	New Zealand	W	17–0			
30.10.93	Wigan	H	New Zealand	W	29–12	1		1
6.11.93	Leeds	H	New Zealand	W	29–10			
20.3.94		A	France	W	12–4			
TOTAL						1		1

STATISTICS

1994–95 Season

Leeds

DATE	VENUE	H/A	OPPONENTS	RES.	SCORE	TRIES	GOALS	DGS
19.8.94	SBC	A	Workington T	W	W22–16	1		
28.8.94	SBC	H	Featherston R	W	36–14	1		
25.9.94	SBC	A	Widnes	W	48–10	1		
16.10.94	SBC	H	Sheffield E	W	30–18	1		
30.10.94	SBC	H	Wakefield T	W	38–10	1		
6.11.94	SBC	H	Workington T	W	42–16	2		
27.11.94	SBC	H	Doncaster	W	30–18	2		
4.12.94	RT	H	Swinton	W	54–24	2		
11.12.94	SBC	H	Wigan	W	33–28			1
18.12.94	RT	A	Workington T	W	18–14	1		
1.1.95	SBC	H	Halifax	W	42–14	1		
11.1.95	SBC	A	Oldham	W	21–14			1
15.1.95	SBC	H	Bradford N	W	46–30	2		
12.2.95	CC	H	Bradford N	W	31–14			1
12.3.95	CC	H	Workington T	W	50–16	1		
1.4.95	CC	Elland Road	Featherstone R	W	39–22	1		1
14.4.95	SBC	H	Hull	W	44–19	1		
3.5.95	PT	H	Bradford N	W	50–30	1		
TOTAL						19		4

Great Britain

DATE	VENUE	H/A	OPPONENTS	RES.	SCORE	TRIES	GOALS	DGS
16.11.94	Old Traff	H	Australia	L	8–38			
20.11.94	Leeds	H	Australia	L	4–23			

1995–96 Season

Leeds

DATE	COMP.	H/A	OPPONENTS	RES.	SCORE	TRIES	GOALS	DGS
30.8.95	SBC	H	Warrington	W	40–6	2		
3.9.95	SBC	H	St Helens	W	36–24	1		
10.9.95	SBC	H	Halifax	W	60–27	1		2
1.10.95	SBC	A	Oldham B	W	43–14	1		1
3.11.95	SBC	H	Wigan	W	23–11	1		1
12.11.95	RT	H	Salford	W	46–22	2		
1.1.96	SBC	A	St Helens	W	20 014	1		
10.1.96	SBC	H	Oldham B	W	28–26	1	2	
TOTAL						10	2	4

Huddersfield Giants

DATE	COMP	H/A	OPPONENTS	RES.	SCORE	TRIES	GOALS	DGS
31.3.96	FD	H	Salford R	L	21–26		2	
5.4.96	FD	A	Whitehaven	W	37–4	1	5	
8.4.96	FD	H	Rochdale H	W	28–16		2	
14.4.96	FD	H	Keighley C	L	10–12		1	
26.5.96	FD	A	Featherstone R	L	22–23	2		
30.6.96	FD	A	Rochdale H	W	36–10	2		
7.7.96	FD	A	Keighley C	W	37–10		5	1
14.7.96	FB	H	Batley B	W	56–6	1		
TOTAL						6	15	1

TRIES THE LIMIT

1997–8 Season
Huddersfield Giants

DATE	COMP.	H/A	OPPONENTS	RES.	SCORE	TRIES	GOALS	DGS
2.3.97	FD	H	Whitehaven	W	46–16	1		
31.3.97	FD	A	Wakefield T	W	40–10	1		
6.4.97	FD	H	Featherstone R	W	18–12	1		
8.4.97	FD	A	Hull KR	W	21–0			1
27.4.97	FD	H	Workington T	W	50–34	3		
26.5.97	FD	A	Warrington W	W	26–18			1
1.6.97	FD	H	Hull KR	W	56–10	1		
6.6.97	FD	A	Dewsbury R	W	23–4			1
5.7.97	FD	H	Hull S	L	18–31	1		
20.7.97	FD	H	Widnes V	W	58–18	1		
3.8.97	DP	A	Dewsbury R	W	34–12			1
10.8.97	DP	H	Hunslet H	W	46–26	2		
14.8.97	DP	A	Bramley	W	34–28	1		
17.8.97	DP	A	Batley B	W	26–4	1		
25.8.97	DP	H	Dewsbury R	W	22–0	3		
14.9.97	DP	H	Featherstone R	W	37–12	2		1
TOTAL						18	0	5

1999 Season

Doncaster Dragons

DATE	COMP.	H/A	OPPONENTS	RES.	SCORE	TRIES	GOALS	DGS
31.1.99	CC	H	Oldham B	W	35–21	1		

Bramley

DATE	VENUE	H/A	OPPONENTS	RES.	SCORE	TRIES	GOALS	DGS
11.7.99	NFP	H	Workington T	W	28–12	1		
25.7.99	NFP	H	Hull KR	W	23–14			1